The Economics of Affordable Housing

The economic system of competitive capitalism has proven to be both resilient and flexible over time and has contributed to the economic welfare of citizens in liberal and coordinated market economies in diverse regions and countries. At the same time, over the entire post-World War II period, there has been a notable endemic shortage of affordable housing in many advanced economies.

This book points at both the causes and the consequences of this circumstance and provides an integrated economic and legal view of how housing production is dependent on housing finance, which, in turn, means that legal conditions and the sovereign state play an active role. Further, the book contributes to the literature from two otherwise partially separated disciplines—housing and urban development studies on the one hand and the institutional centrality of the finance industry in the contemporary economic system on the other. The author asserts that although somewhat assimilated due to the ambitions of policy makers to optimize social and economic welfare for their constituencies, the combining of these two realms of expertise generates many favorable outcomes, but also some costs derived from finance industry instabilities. The book connects theoretical perspectives and provides an empirical explanation for how affordable housing is generated in an actual real world economy context.

The book will be relevant to the work of a number of academic disciplines including economics, government studies, housing policy and urban planning, social geography, and law and society.

Alexander Styhre is chair of organization theory and management, Department of Business Administration, School of Business, Economics and Law, University of Gothenburg, Sweden.

Routledge Advances in Regional Economics, Science and Policy

Designing Smart and Resilient Cities for a Post-Pandemic World
Metropandemic Revolution
Anthony Larsson and Andreas Hatzigeorgiou

Political Geography of Cities and Regions
Changing Legitimacy and Identity
Kees Terlouw

The Economic Geography of the Car Market
The Automobile Revolution in an Emerging Economy
Edited by Bartłomiej Kołsut and Tadeusz Stryjakiewicz

Worker Mobility and Urban Policy in Latin America
Policy Interactions and Urban Outcomes in Mexico City
David López-García

Cities Learning from a Pandemic
Towards Preparedness
Edited by Simonetta Armondi, Alessandro Balducci, Martina Bovo and Beatrice Galimberti

Urban Change in Central Europe
The Case of Kraków
Jacek Purchla

Clusters and Sustainable Regional Development
A Meta-Organisational Approach
Evgeniya Lupova-Henry and Nicola Francesco Dotti

The Economics of Affordable Housing
Alexander Styhre

For more information about this series, please visit: www.routledge.com/series/RAIRESP

The Economics of Affordable Housing

Alexander Styhre

Routledge
Taylor & Francis Group
LONDON AND NEW YORK

First published 2023
by Routledge
4 Park Square, Milton Park, Abingdon, Oxon OX14 4RN

and by Routledge
605 Third Avenue, New York, NY 10158

Routledge is an imprint of the Taylor & Francis Group, an informa business

British Library Cataloguing-in-Publication Data
A catalogue record for this book is available from the British Library

Library of Congress Cataloging-in-Publication Data
Names: Styhre, Alexander, author.
Title: The economics of affordable housing / Alexander Styhre.
Description: 1 Edition. | New York, NY : Routledge, 2023. | Series: Routledge advances in regional economics, science and policy | Includes bibliographical references and index.
Identifiers: LCCN 2022025289 (print) | LCCN 2022025290 (ebook) | ISBN 9781032155111 (hardback) | ISBN 9781032155128 (paperback) | ISBN 9781003244417 (ebook)
Subjects: LCSH: Housing. | Housing policy. | City planning.
Classification: LCC HD7287 .S89 2023 (print) | LCC HD7287 (ebook) | DDC 363.5--dc23/eng/20220815
LC record available at https://lccn.loc.gov/2022025289
LC ebook record available at https://lccn.loc.gov/2022025290

ISBN: 978-1-032-15511-1 (hbk)
ISBN: 978-1-032-15512-8 (pbk)
ISBN: 978-1-003-24441-7 (ebk)

DOI: 10.4324/9781003244417

Typeset in Bembo
by SPi Technologies India Pvt Ltd (Straive)

Contents

Preface

In the period May 10 to May 21, 2021, yet another Israeli-Palestinian armed conflict unfolded, but this time very much being unexpected by the Israeli military establishment, *The New York Times* reported on May 15, 2021 (Kingsley, 2021). In May 2021, it had been seven years since the last significant conflict with Hamas occurred, and 16 years since the last major Palestinian uprising. One significant event that preceded the skirmishes was the eviction of six Palestine families in the Sheikh Jarrah neighborhood in Eastern Jerusalem. The event followed a court decision that ruled to the advantage of Israeli families, who according to Israeli law have the right to make claims to land in East Jerusalem that was owned by Jewish families before 1948. A similar legal protection of Palestinians' right to land owned prior to 1948 does not exist, and as every single Palestinian can relate to the experience of being evicted from one's homestead (as one Palestinian commentator argued), the court decision and the eviction of the six families added to the inflammatory situation. While this event is a set in a particularly difficult context and include historical, political, and economic conditions that are complicated to fully oversee and assess for any layperson, it is no wonder that conflicts over land and housing preceded this crisis. It is of course difficult to extract any meaningful general learnings regarding housing policies or related issues on basis of this specific event, but the sense of humiliation when losing one's home and homestead is something most people can intuitively relate to and understand, also people living in communities with more harmonious relations than many Israelis and Palestinians tend to do. Housing not only provides elementary protection from nature's force and climatological conditions, it is also indicative of the individual's or the family's legal standing and social recognition, and a failure to protect what is regarded to be both an elementary human right, and what is treated as constitutive of the dignity of a human being—their right to proper housing—incurs a sense of being subject to a violation of elementary rights.

This volume has little to say about the political relations between Israelis and Palestinians, but the episode is nonetheless exemplary of how the sovereign state and its judiciary can execute its monopolized power whenever it has (or claims to have) the right to do so, i.e., when it is prescribed by its legislation. Housing is commonly understood to be an elementary human right, comparable to the right to access proper schooling and education, or qualified health care, but it is oftentimes understood as being a market based resource, only indirectly provided by the sovereign state. The endemic shortage of affordable housing, also in highly sophisticated welfare states, equipped with very a fine-grained tax collection apparatus, is a global phenomenon, which, similar to the distribution of finance asset holdings, is highly uneven. Some wealthy households access spatial apartments or freestanding villas, whereas others are occupied in dwellings that provide only minimal living space per inhabitant. This condition was attended to during the many lockdown episodes during the *annus horribilis* of 2020, making it evident that, e.g., many schoolchildren were suffering from sub-standard housing facilities, and therefore had more difficulties keeping up with the teaching curriculum. In, e.g., Sweden, the higher incidence of Covid-19 infections among immigrant groups was partially explained in the media on basis of their access to more small-sized housing facilities, which allegedly made the pandemic more difficult to ward off. At the same time, policy makers did not call for any comprehensive reforms on the basis of such reports, but a few left-leaning politicians underlined this explanation as being plausible and indicative of underlying economic inequalities. However, as this volume hopes to make clear, the shortage of affordable housing is not only a matter of what may be referred to as housing assets supply; affordable housing is, as the name indicates, a matter of what is affordable for the person or household renting or buying a home. Unfortunately, based on limitations in human cognitive capacities and the uncertainties in the shadow of the future, it is difficult to know ex ante what is in fact affordable: the prospective homebuyer may ask what will I earn a year from now, or a decade into the future, and what would my retirement compensation look like decades into the future? In fact, none can tell with precision. In addition, affordability is also a matter of making reasonably accurate predictions regarding the value of the housing asset in the near future and in a medium-term perspective. Also in that respect, both homebuyers and their mortgage lenders are in a difficult position to assess what affordability may mean in substantive terms: All the money that can be allocated to housing expenses? A certain proportion of the projected income stream?, or some other way to calculate degrees of affordability under various plausible scenarios? Taken together, this predicament means that homebuyers are in a difficult position to not only assess their own private economic situation but also to estimate the *overall economic conditions* over the coming years: are there any signs of a long-term recession on the horizon or can one assume that current economic conditions will prevail? The concern is that not even professional communities with significant experience and track records are able to make accurate predictions regarding economic conditions in the near future. In fact, because of the sheer number of candidates, there is always someone making a successful prediction, thus being praised for their prescient capacities, but as the pool of professionals making such predictions or prophesies is sizeable, it is statistically insignificant that at least someone makes an adequate prediction every now and then, it is also unreasonable to expect laypersons to have this capacity.

The uncertainty regarding economic affairs, increasingly complex in an interconnected and globalized world, means that the sovereign state acts to protect its citizens from the worst case scenarios regarding housing welfare and economic welfare more generally. However, when the state acts in this role during a crisis, it means that it cannot act in the same role all the time, e.g., during the upward movement of the economic cycle. By implication, housing policy and housing welfare is only indirectly supported by the state and the municipalities, or else there are risks of housing market disruptions, or unnecessary cost incurred by the state apparatus overreaching its constitutional rights and competencies. This political model wherein the state and housing market participants are collaborating to jointly optimize housing supply and to ensure adequate housing welfare for the highest possible number of constituencies does in many ways provide possibilities for households with a regular income, derived from salaried work. For households in the low-end housing market, such as immigrants, unemployed, disabled persons, students, or even lowly compensated freelance workers, housing welfare is more difficult to achieve as their household budgets are slimmer, and as they are not always eligible for housing finance services, the situation is more problematic.

This volume seeks to address "the economics of affordable housing programs," a scholarly project that seeks to move beyond only construing the question of affordable housing as a matter of political will and ambition, or alternatively, as primarily being a singular finance market concern. Most politicians wish they could orchestrate alliances of housing market actors to once and for all solve this perennial issue, but from the history we learn that, in fact, they cannot. This is not because housing assets are more materially complex or difficult to produce than any other product or service but because housing assets are closely bound up with the global finance industry and its work to manage long-term assets holdings (say, a mortgage loan stock) and short-term debt on the money market. Much housing studies scholarship simply ignore the housing-finance nexus, partially because this perspective is excluded from their inherited or preferred scholarly domain of jurisdiction or discipline, or more simply because the housing finance industry is very complicated to fully overview, and to monitor on both the more structural level and in its details. The point being made here is that in order to understand housing markets, the supply of affordable housing, and the housing welfare generated (or the absence of such provision), it is impossible to turn a blind eye to the fact that the finance industry operates on basis of safe assets, i.e., tradable financial assets backed by high-quality collateral, to effectively generate the credit that provides finance capital for a variety of services, themselves in many cases being unrelated to housing markets. The finance industry may be top-heavy inasmuch as it includes considerable systemic risks, that it is premised on the sovereign state or transnational governance organizations (say, the World Bank, IMF, etc.) acting to insure the industry against default, and so forth, but it is nonetheless the industry that acts as the circulatory blood system of the economic system of competitive capitalism. This means that the housing market plays an oftentimes underappreciated but still central role in providing tangible collateral, i.e., physical built structures that have a specific user-value for its owners, tenants, or users. As, e.g., the quick growth of cryptocurrencies reveals, part of the economic system may run entirely on the basis of relational capital and the faith in the robustness of abstract digital media systems (the sustainability and robustness of such credit systems is to be determined), but the whole economic system is unlikely to reveal such capacities, at least under periods of turbulence. In the end, there needs to be a few things that are real, material, and tangible to back the credit being issued and circulating in the global economy, by the day and by the hour. Housing production and housing markets are thus not only something that is implicated in the finance industry's services; it is constitutive of its credit formation work on the basis of its capacity to provide safe assets—assets insured against default by the sovereign state and its defined agencies.

As indicated by several commentators and scholars, housing markets are commonly highly segmented, which leads to the situation wherein "little trading of houses between rich and poor agents, lenders, and borrowers" is observed (Justiniano, Primiceri, and Tambalotti, 2019: 2328). This in turn results in specific market niche conditions, e.g., housing prices "at the lower end of the market" are more volatile than homes with higher prices, Goodman and Mayer (2018: 53) notice. One specific concern for policy makers is that in the modern welfare state, the low-end housing market does not really operate as finance industry actors, which include the lion's share of the mortgage lenders, would wish. The low-end market participants do not of necessity have household budgets that qualify them for mortgage lending, and their inclusion in the labor market may be limited, or there are other conditions that exclude them from the regular housing market. Under such conditions, there is a need for state agencies or municipality-based agencies to act to provide at least a minimal level of housing welfare for also these groups. For medium to high net-worth households, the municipality-owned real estate company may be considered as an option for how to handle housing issues; for low net-worth households, this is not a matter of choice but a question of necessity. In the latter section of this volume, an empirical material shows how a Swedish municipality-owned real estate company actively works to provide qualitative affordable housing for its tenants, and it suggests that considerable results can be accomplished by such hybrid organizations. In this model, the municipality-owned real estate company is a fully owned corporate entity that is run on the basis of sound business principles regarding return-on-investment and equity, at the same time as the City Hall and the municipality assembly provides guidelines for how to serve the city in the interests of tenants, tax payers, and also other local housing market actors. Furthermore, to balance these goals and to do so within the horizon of possible business opportunities and investments is a non-trivial issue. Still, this is what it takes to construct a welfare state model wherein housing welfare is promoted for all, or at least most, citizens, not only those eligible for mortgage lending and home ownership. In the end, the volume is intended to provide some theoretical inspiration and some empirical support for the thesis that affordable housing and housing welfare is not an unattainable goal, but that it is in fact possible to provide, but also to point out that it is takes both business expertise and political *savoir-faire* to assist the low-end housing market segment properly, and as stipulated by housing welfare policies.

The German playwright Berthold Brecht (2003: 143) remarks regarding the ambition to speak the truth to power and to one's fellow human beings, that "First of all it is not even easy to find out which truth is worth saying." When working with this volume, this *bon mot* has been a form of guiding principle: there are many things that deserves to be said, and many things that despite such qualifications are likely to be ignored, so it may be a good idea to try to say something that appears to be of particular importance for the issue at hand. In my view, these are the two things ("truths" to Brecht) worth saying: (1) housing assets are not only material objects or artifacts; legally and financially speaking they are more—substantially more—than that; (2) housing welfare is a political objective worth pursuing, not least because qualitative housing facilities hold the promise of being supportive of a variety of other human liberties and capacities. Unfortunately, to provide housing welfare for not only *some* but for *all* citizens and benefactors is not as easy as the critics of current housing policies are prone to recognize.

Acknowledgements

I would like to recognize the support and assistance I have received from the various co-workers in the companies that have been studied as part of this project. A special thanks to Lars Bankvall, research director, Framtiden AB, for paving the way for a full-scale study of affordable housing activities. In the domain of academia, I want to thank Sara Brorström, Pernilla Gluch, and Fredrik Lavén, my colleagues with whom I have collaborated over the last few years to examine these business activities. I would also like to thank Kristina Abbotts, commissioning editor, Business and Management at Routledge/Taylor & Francis, Christiana Mandizha, editorial assistant, Routledge/Taylor & Francis, and Terry Clague, commissioning editor at Routledge/Taylor & Francis, for granting me the contract to publish this book. Finally, my family, Sara, Simon, and Max, are worthy of all the praise they can get as they help me understand that there is not only a beginning of the working day but also an end to it, and when that point in time comes, work should be laid down for a while.

Introduction

Affordable housing for all and other political ambitions

The question concerning affordable housing

Ian Dury's album *New boots and panties* (1977), a minor classic of the punk rock era includes the song "Plaistow Patricia," a disheartening story of a female adolescent drug addict. Plaistow, a residential area in North-East London, was heavily bombed during the blitz and, by the 1970s, the city district was largely made up of a local authority housing estate constructed in the 1960s. Dury's lyrics capture the mid-1970s despair, cynicism, and lack of prospect in the British society at the trough of a global recession, following two oil crises, soaring inflation, growing unemployment, and ongoing and seemingly ceaseless class-based conflicts, leading up the Thatcherism era beginning in 1979. Dury indicates that council flats are not a place that nourishes refinement and sophistication; they are too often the home of the poor, the unfortunate, and the destitute. "Plaistow Patricia" is a piece of popular music in the Dickensian documentary tradition of English literature and popular culture. Since the mid-1990s, the area has undergone a major redevelopment program. Perhaps Patricia, if she was still around, had to move elsewhere after these renovations were completed?

"Those who gets the most are *elites*; the rest are *mass*," Lasswell ([1936] 1958: 13) writes in his classic political science treatise. In few other areas this fairly crass statement appears more accurate and relevant than in the domain of housing. Some people live in spacious, well-kept homes, and can easily and at low costs access a variety of amenities such as natural reserves, shopping facilities, restaurants and cafes, and culture institutions. Other people live in crammed, overpopulated dwellings under severe conditions, exposed to both health hazards and a variety of annoying conditions such as noisy neighbors and local street crime that restrains everyday life and affect the life chances of the individual. Why is that? There are many answers to this question. A few will be discussed in this volume.

*****

John Boughton's (2018) *Municipal dreams* accounts for the history of council homes in the UK, a political response to the housing crisis that followed the nineteenth century urbanization, and that has remained a perennial issue ever since. As Boughton (2018: 3) remarks, council homes—homes provided by the municipality to support the most vulnerable groups in society, the handicapped, families on

DOI: 10.4324/9781003244417-1

welfare, single mothers, etc.—have always been a form of "aspirational housing": "the mark of an upward mobile working class and the visible manifestation of a state which took seriously its duty to house its people decently" (Boughton, 2018: 3).[1] In the era of free market policies, wherein the housing stock plays a decisive role in stabilizing the financial system in the role of collateral, i.e., to serve as durable and predictably valuable assets, the "duty to house people decently" may be at once taken seriously, and be an ambition that is counteracted by a variety of conditions and policies. In Boughton's (2018) account, the Thatcher era marked an end to the conventional wisdom that had prevailed over both Labour and Tory governments, that the state and the municipalities carried the duty to house its citizens properly and at a certain cost. "Housing—in new forms, in greater numbers, and crucially, state-built—was central to the post-war rebuilding," Boughton (2018: 90) proposes. Margaret Thatcher was determined to fulfill her ambition to roll back "the frontiers of the state" (Boughton, 2018: 169), and one of the prioritized issues was the institution of the council home that was comparably less popular than, for example, the National Health Service (NHS). A survey from the mid-1980s showed that while 74 percent of the population thought the NHS "was good value for money," only 42 percent felt the same of council housing (Boughton, 2018: 173). That is, council housing was an "easy target" and served as "'the perfect symbol of the failing public sector' for its ideological opponents" (Boughton (2018: 173). The Thatcher government sold off more than 40 state-owned businesses, employing 600,000 workers in total. During the Thatcher years, the economic support to council construction and maintenance fell by 43 percent, which undermined the capacity to provide qualitative housing for its beneficiaries (Boughton, 2018: 175). To counterweight these changes, Thatcher introduced the Right to Buy campaign, wherein council housing tenants were given the chance to buy the apartments where they lived. By 1997, the privatization of public goods (i.e., council homes) was worth an estimated £22 billion (Boughton, 2018: 169). To sugarcoat the deal and make the campaign successful, there were generous discounts applied to the purchase price, starting at 33 percent of the market value for those with three years of tenancy, and rising to the maximum of 50 percent for long-term residents. The underlying ideological rationale was to turn people into asset-owners, more receptive to market pricing mechanisms; the ulterior goal was to "radically diminish the role of council housing" and, by consequence, the state, Boughton (2018: 171) proposes. While the Right to Buy campaign benefitted certain households and played a key role in making the households more tuned to the mechanisms of the free market that Thatcher and her allies held in esteem and regarded as a primary device when reforming the state apparatus, it made the situation worse for remaining council home tenants. Rather than stabilizing communities by blending forms of ownership, the Right to Buy campaign contributed to an increased social polarization and "the concentration of poorer residents on poorer estates" (Boughton, 2018: 175). While some households could strengthen their economic welfare, not least on the basis of the discounts that made their housing deal more attractive, households who could not afford to buy their homes were stigmatized, and now rented from housing associations with smaller budgets and with a more unpredictable clientele. Furthermore, critical commentators such as Harvey (2005) pay attention to the unintended and unanticipated consequences of the Right to Buy campaign:

> Thatcher's programme for the privatization of social housing in Britain appeared as a gift to the lower classes which could now convert from rental to ownership at a relatively low cost, gain control over valuable asset and augment their wealth. But once the transfer was accomplished, housing speculations took over, particularly in prime central locations, eventually bribing or forcing low-income populations out to the periphery in cities such as London, and turning erstwhile working-class housing estates into centres of intense gentrification.
>
> (Harvey, 2005: 155)

Such criticism is consistent with Walter and Wansleben's (2020: 640) proposition, contrasting against the conventional wisdom that Thatcherism was propelled by ideological beliefs and commitments, that Thatcherism (at least in terms of its "macroeconomic management") was not characterized by "carefully planned, effective reforms," but rather resulted in "disruptive interventions" that aggravated "existing contradictions" between programs, rationalities and technologies. The Right to Buy campaign was thus subject to what Funk and Hirschman (2014: 672) refer to as "policy drift"—its stipulated goals did not materialize as negative unanticipated consequences overshadowed the estimated policy reform benefits. Under all conditions, the decline in the council housing units was significant: "The number of British dwellings owned by and rented from local authorities peaked at 6.6 million in 1979" (Christophers, 2018: 246); by 2015, this number had fallen to "just over 2 million."

Critics may regard the Thatcher era policy as being overoptimistic regarding the benefits of deregulating the market housing, but it is important to also recognize the difficulties related to the council housing model. Darren McGarvey's *Poverty Safari* (2017) gives an account of his upbringing in poor neighborhoods in Glasgow, and McGarvey addresses how urban planners and politicians fail, despite their best intentions, to recognize that housing is only one part of the more complex problem of how to make the residents develop a sense of community even if they are unemployed or otherwise feel cut off from the rest of society. In the 1950s, McGarvey (2017: 40) writes, the idea of high-rise social housing was imported from Continental Europe and was generally promoted as the solution for inner city urban area housing challenges. Quite soon, however, many of the tower blocks that were built in Glasgow and elsewhere in Britain and the rest of Europe came to be regarded as "dirty, dangerous and undesirable places to live" (McGarvey, 2017: 41). When the traditional industries like steel and coal lost their foothold, in many cases as a direct effect of political decisions and new industry policies, unemployment rose and "many people became idle and demoralized" (McGarvey, 2017: 41). Speaking on the basis of his own first-hand account and family history, McGarvey (2017: 48) argues that in poorer communities, there is a "pervasive belief" that things will never change, and that people with power and authority are primarily self-serving and are not to be trusted. The long-term consequence is an apathy and perceived lack of ambition that people raised outside of such communities have a hard time decoding and understanding:

> The high-rise building program and housing schemes were the solution to what was regarded as mainly a housing problem. What planners later realized was that people also required a sense of ownership, a stake and connectedness in their communities, as well as adequate living standards. And we all learned the hard way that highly populated areas, where people are deprived of connection, stake and ownership, can quickly fall into dereliction.
>
> (McGarvey, 2017: 133)

Decent housing is a good starting point, but it needs to be complemented by other initiatives to overcome the crippling passivity caused by unemployment.

Beginning in the 1990s, gentrification became a buzzword in the urbanism discourse (Hwang and Ding, 2020; Stein, 2019), but rather than being a movement or economic program that benefitted low-income residents in neighborhoods and city districts being gentrified, it further pushed them to the margin. Former working class neighborhoods with their own specific communities were frequently overtaken by more "market-friendly" activities and with new residents moving in. "Gentrification is cool when you're watching it from safe distance, but when it is your cultural history that is being dismantled, it leaves a sour taste in the mouth," McGarvey (2017: 59) reflects. Paying attention to the political activism of the city district of Pollok in Glasgow in the 1990s, McGarvey (2017) shows that the local community had difficulties counteracting urban development programs that were determined by financial and political interests. To win the battle over the question "Who has the right and the power to make decision over what happens to public spaces?" economic, political, and social arguments needs to be combined in thoughtful and media-friendly ways, or Big Money will always triumph.

Boughton's (2018) historical account of council housing (today widely addressed as "social housing" to underline the vulnerability of the residents), and McGarvey's (2017) personal story of a life in suburban poverty, wherein family and friends share the predicament of being unemployed, having low self-esteem and low self-confidence, abusing drugs and alcohol, and facing dietary challenges inasmuch as overconsuming fast-food and snacks results in health issues at a comparably low age (see, e.g., Case and Deaton, 2020; Deaton, 2013), may say something distinctively specific about the UK and its history and local conditions. At the same time, their stories are of relevance for most advanced and democratic economies wherein especially urban centers are plagued by the lack of affordable housing and the decline of housing welfare and even homelessness that follow. For instance, Anna Wiener's (2020) memoir on working in start-ups in the San Francisco Bay Area carefully sketches the hyper-competitive start-up culture and all its ambition, hopes for the future, and blatant ignorance for everything that stands between self-made tech-industry entrepreneurs and their projected private fortunes, and the "homelessness epidemic" that Wiener observed in her own, much-fabled Haight-Ashbury neighborhood. Even at the epicenter of the high-tech and biomedicine industries, the start-up Jerusalem to which thousands of entrepreneurs, engineers, and software developers make their pilgrimage, there is an inability to cope with the question of how to house the residents decently. What Boughton (2018) refers to as a "municipality dream" of providing such housing to all its citizens has to be more than a dream: it needs to be part of the political agenda in every single community that deals with the question of how to provide affordable housing.

A house as an institutional fact: housing as financial asset

As remarked time and again, housing units are both physical artifacts with specific material qualities at a particular location, *and* they play a key role in the household economy and in the global finance industry as a financial asset. In this latter role, the housing unit is inscribed into a legal-administrative framework in ways that render it as an "institutional fact" (Searle, 1995), that is, at the same time a piece of property, an asset of legal inscription (i.e., the ownership of or the right to access a housing unit is stipulated by contracts, which means that such rights are legally inscribed within the legal system of the sovereign state; Pistor, 2019, 2020), and has considerable social consequences. In order to map all these relations, the elementary components need to be defined. To define the sovereign state is a good starting point. King and Le Galès (2017: S14) formally define the state on the basis of three parameters: (1) as "[a] permanent and complex set of interdependent, differentiated, legitimate institutions"; (2) as an entity that is "fragmented," but with "representations and institutions of unity based in a defined territory"; and (3) as being self-referentially defined as "what is recognized as a state by other states." More importantly—definitions are basically, as Quine ([1966] 1976: 78) puts it, "a convention of notational abbreviation" that provide shared terms but do not solve anything themselves—the state is "characterized by its administrative capacity to govern a society" (King and Le Galès, 2017: S14). By developing and using "tools of government, metrics and policy instruments," the state establishes "constraining rules" that serve to solve conflict, exercise authority, protect citizens, define and protect rights, allocate resources, create categories of classification, etc. (King and Le Galès, 2017: S14). What ultimately justifies the state in a democratic society (historical societies have in many cases justified the state and the rule of the sovereign, say the monarch, on the basis of theological and mythological descriptions) is its capacity to protect the population from "the foreign enemy, from thieves and gangsters, from poverty, from predatory corporate firms and monopolies, and from pollution, exploitation, diseases, various risks, terrorist attacks or climate change" (King and Le Galès, 2017: S16). Housing policy and housing supply can thus be seen as being part of the responsibility of the protective state.

On the next level of analysis, i.e., the institutional fashioning of the state apparatus, Barker and Schulte (2016: 59), who study accounting standards and accounting standards negotiations and adjustments, propose that an institution is "a system of constitutive rules," and that such rules creates the possibilities for institutional facts. Furthermore, as in, e.g., the case of accounting, institutional facts are characterized by being "ontologically subjective" (i.e., social actors can individually decide to what extent they believe in institutional conditions as being "real" in the conventional semantic meaning of the term in everyday language) at the same time as they are "epistemologically objective." For instance, an individual may have private beliefs regarding whether the monetary system actually mirrors underlying factual economic conditions, but regardless of these private beliefs, the individual is participating in an economy wherein the day-to-day circulation of currency and references to stipulated monetary value generate social effects that that can be determined in terms of truth or falsity, i.e., the monetary system is epistemologically objective. For instance, an individual may question the accuracy of the exchange rate between the US dollar and the euro, but this institutional fact, derived from a variety of uncoordinated activities and decisions among policy makers and market actors, has certain material effects regardless of such private beliefs.

Consistent with Barker and Schulte's (2016) analytical model, Power (2021: 13) argues that accounting practices such as audits are premised on their capacity to generate "facticity"—the "quality of taken-for-grantedness or 'givenness' of experience." Similar to Barker and Schulte (2016), Power (2021: 8) proposes that accounting "does not just 'represent' the pregiven facts of organizational performance," but is "agentic in its own right." That is, accounting practices do not "mirror" actual economic conditions but are rather per se constitutive of institutional facts, generated on the basis of a variety of tools and devices developed within the accounting discipline and its practices: "[A]ccounting is able to be 'practical' precisely because it is also theoretical in the sense of abstracting, reducing, and commensurating complex economic and other phenomena into organizing typologies, such as the balance sheet" (Power, 2021: 8). The practical value of accounting practices derives from the capacity to make claims appear to be legitimate and justifiable, i.e., the "facticity" of the accounting routines is protecting them from critical reflection and evaluations. However, "[f]acticity is an institutional rather than a transcendental accomplishment," Power (2021: 13) writes, echoing Barker and Schulte's (2016) distinction between social facts as simultaneously being ontologically subjective and epistemologically objective. Consequently, Power (2021: 13) continues, "accounting facticity has little to do with truth or accurate representation"; instead, accounting numbers "[c]ome to be seen, and made sense of, by actors as referring to an organizational reality of performance" (Power, 2021: 13). In, e.g., auditing, the data and alleged facts generated never simply trace "what happened," but such data and facts are more accurately understood as "a redescription of an action according to an institutional purpose—accounting for performance in a specific way—that is more or less widely accepted by organizational actors" (Power, 2021: 13). In this way, accounting generates data and information, and second-order interpretations and aggregations thereof, which contributes to an institutional system that can generate a variety of effects, whereof many are highly beneficial for constituencies (e.g., the fiscal system, the transferring of economic resources between social actors, etc.). Institutional facts may not be truths in an ontological sense, but they nonetheless generate facticity that hopefully results in benevolent social consequences.

To introduce the concept of institutional facts is helpful as it underlines the importance of shared beliefs and the value of trust in institutional relations. Institutional facts also denote how practical accomplishments, including, e.g., how housing ownership is stipulated by contracts and (oftentimes) associated with mortgage lending contracts that define the rights and liabilities of borrower and lender, matter in day-to-day life. One of the difficulties involved from a governance perspective is that policy makers need to monitor, e.g., market conditions (say, housing market price changes or the nominal rate of interest) on the basis of the same institutional apparatus (including, e.g., agencies and routine practices) that generated such institutional facts in the first place. This may generate a blindness towards inconsistencies or sheer fallacies being part of the policy making model (as happened during the period preceding 2008 financial crisis where the build-up of considerable levels of systemic risk in the finance industry was ignored by regulatory agencies, including the Federal Reserve, as soaring housing prices on the American market were interpreted in favorable terms as being indicative of the current policies being effective), which may result in substantial resolution costs if indications of undesirable market conditions are trivialized or ignored. Under all conditions, to regard housing unit ownership contract as an institutional fact is supportive of understanding the wider politico-economic significance of households' commitment to housing ownership.

Housing ownership as institutional fact and financial asset

At the same time as a house serves as the residential home for a family or an individual, it is also a financial asset, both in the eyes of owners and for the wider housing finance industry that provides, e.g., mortgage lending. This means that any housing unit that is included in the housing finance system contributes to the maintenance and reproduction of the credit formation process that is vital for the real world economy. Needless to say, the practices and routines for turning a house into a financial asset are quite intricate and combine various calculative practices and assessment methods. A house "becomes a liquid asset only when there are agreed-upon conventions for evaluating it in comparison with other houses," Lakoff (2006: 21) remarks. As will be detailed in Chapter 2 of this volume, housing finance is premised on the condition that the mortgages of households are long-term contracts, in many cases with a duration of 30 years or even longer, whereas the finance industry operates on the basis of balancing long-terms lending and short-term borrowing on the money market. This means that households are exposed to market risks and market turbulence as the finance industry is incentivized to increase their housing finance activities (e.g., the mortgage loan stock), and to inflate their balance sheets to maximize the return on equity invested. One of the foremost consequences of this tension between long-term holdings and short-term liquidity demands is that the finance industry is prone to overlend, which results in inflated housing prices. For instance, a sizeable scholarly literature documents a remarkable growth in household debt in the 1997–2006 period in the US (and especially in the 2003–2006 period), following soaring housing prices. In the period, the so-called S&P/Case-Shiller Index of home prices rose by approximately 125 percent, whereas the US Consumer Price Index only increased by 28 percent (White, 2013: 104). This marked shift in housing prices was interpreted in sanguine terms by regulatory agencies such as the Federal Reserve, being indicative of a combination of effective economic policy and the household's faith in the economy in near the future (Golub, Kaya, and Reay, 2015), and by the early 2000s, "there was a widespread belief that housing prices could only go up" (White, 2013: 104). This optimism or, alternatively, lack of a more precautious attitude towards mortgage lending, propelled by an unprecedented willingness to lend money to homebuyers, resulted in a more risk-tolerant behavior among several categories of market actors. A 2006 survey published by the National Association of Realtors reported that 46 percent of first-time homebuyers had made "no down payment at all," and that the median down payment for first-time buyers "was only 2 percent of the purchase price" (Calomiris and Haber, 2014: 19). When credit supply is abundant, both households and mortgage lending institutions were conspicuously risk-tolerant, an attitude that resulted in the largest systemic crisis of competitive capitalism to date.

Regardless of this episode, this tendency to increase housing asset ownership is a long-term trend in the American economy. In 1945, 54 percent of American families owned a car, and 44 percent owned their home (potentially with a strong racial bias in favor of white families); by 1970, 63 percent of American families owned their homes, and now "there were as many cars as families" (Stein, 2010: 1). In the period, the proportion of poor families shrank significantly, from more than 40 percent of the families in 1945 to circa 10 percent in 1970. This growth in wealth and welfare translated into larger homes, and additional homes such as cabins and beach-houses for many middle-class American families. Despite a shrinking average household size in the period between 1973 and the mid-2000s (at the brink of the finance industry collapse)—from 2.9 persons in 1973 to 2.5 persons in 2003—the average home size almost doubled from 1,400 square feet in 1970 to 2,700 square feet in 2007 (Wisman, 2013: 930). This increase in housing welfare also came with an increased marginal cost. In 1973, the average homeowner paid roughly twice their annual income for a home; in 2007, they were paying five times their annual income (Wisman, 2013: 930).

Whether it has been a rational choice of American households to invest in more spacious homes, given the unprecedented growth in housing prices, or whether this housing price bubble is an effect of what economists call a credit supply shock, brought by a substantial inflow of overseas savings into the American economy, and an expansion of the finance industry per se, is discussed in more detail in Chapter 2 of this volume. The question of the culpability of all housing market actors are arguably secondary to the fact that the housing price bubble of the 2003–2006 period left many households in a most precarious situation. Davis (2010: 350) says that in the period, no less than one-quarter of all new jobs created in the American economy were in "real estate-related industries." Furthermore, one-in-four houses sold in 2005, at the peak of the bubble, were purchased as an investment and not as a primary dwelling, being a robust indication of the level of speculation at this stage of the market expansion episode. When the housing bubble eventually busted, home values dropped by one-third on average from the peak of the housing boom in 2006 through the end of 2011. Already by mid-2008, the "composition of home sales had shifted dramatically," with nearly 40 percent of all sales classified as "distressed or foreclosure sales," Berger, Turner, and Zwick (2020: 277) write. The net loss of the housing boom and its ensuing bust is calculated to be in the range of about $7 trillion in household wealth (Wilmarth, 2013: 1315).[2] Many homeowners (circa 15 percent) found themselves in the situation where they "were below the waterline" i.e., mortgage holders owned more than their homes was worth on the market (McCoy, Pavlov, and Wachter, 2009: 1332). Contrary to the conventional wisdom that home ownership served as a primary insurance against, e.g., labor market turbulence, the once so benevolent housing asset ownership was now more of a liability for many American households. "[F]or many home owning debtors, the home is a 'cement life raft.'" Sullivan, Warren, and Westbrook (2006: 227), who examine the growing number of household bankruptcies in the US, write: "That is, the debtors' financial troubles may be related in significant part to their efforts to cling to homes that are weighted down with debt." What households had learned as a rule of thumb, that you can never lose a home once you have bought it, proved to be factually wrong as overlending and many documented cases of predatory lending, in a not negligible proportion of cases revealing racial bias, overturned the home as financial asset model, and instead created a destruction of household wealth on an industrial scale.

There are many things to be learned from the 2008 financial crisis, not least that even the officials at the apex of the regulatory system may fail to detect and neutralize discordant information, data that are ignored, or dismissed as anomalies or outliers as they are inconsistent with the dominant analytical model or credo. As the finance industry is incentivized and geared towards maximizing the credit supply and finance capital lending, weak or inconsistent policy making and regulatory control may result in disastrous outcomes for the households. The risk of financial losses are less pronounced in the finance industry as the instrumental and systemic power of the industry result in de facto ex post resolution activities (most notably bailouts) that arguably undermine the incentives to lend money prudently, and to calculate and anticipate credit risks with precision. However, it may be that finance industry actors and decision makers, despite such insurances and protection, are cognizant of the short-term costs and long-term consequences of recurrent systemic failures, and therefore have implemented mechanisms and devices that reduce the systemic risks. Whether this is the case, or if such managerial initiatives are effective, remains to be seen. Under all conditions, in order to fully understand the political ambition to provide affordable housing, the housing as financial asset perspective needs to be recognized and understood. Rather than being some peripheral or complementary condition, it is the very basis for national housing markets, and not least in the low-end of the housing market, where the possibilities for borrowing money to buy a home are more limited.

Housing policy: to reconcile the housing as utility and financial asset perspectives

Affordable housing is commonly defined in terms of a threshold, wherein households commit a maximum of 30 percent of their after-tax income to housing expenses (Lee, 2016: 231). At the same time as this fairly straightforward definition is commonly used in the scholarly literature and in policy documents, affordable housing is "[o]ne of the most versatile social labels in the urban milieu," Friedman and Rosen (2020: 960) write: "Comprising an array of housing options intended to cater to the more disadvantaged population segments, the housing arena is rife with opinion and dissension regarding the most viable and efficacious manner in which to produce affordable housing." Given the conditions of historical and current regional and national housing markets, policy makers need to balance the welfare state ambition to provide affordable housing but without creating excessive costs elsewhere in the housing market or the housing finance industry, or to overtax its citizens to the point where the value of fiscal discipline is questioned. Furthermore, housing policy needs to carefully detect consequences for marginal non-subsidized households, i.e., low-income households not being eligible for housing subsidies as they find themselves just above some calculated income level, as such transfers to even poorer households may violate social norms regarding justice and fairness, which may translate into grievances and discontent regarding political decision making in other spheres and more generally. By and large, housing policy is a difficult domain that needs to consider a variety of conditions. In the US, Diamond and McQuade (2019: 1064) write, federal, state, and local governments "spend over $97 billion a year on different forms of housing assistance." Despite these efforts, there is an overwhelming demand that cannot be saturated in basis of these expenses, which locates policy makers in a situation wherein they have to make difficult decisions regarding how to allocate resources and who should benefit. As Apgar (1990) notices, this is a far from trivial question to handle:

> [H]ousing policy must balance the often competing goals of expanding the ability of participating low-income households to pay for decent housing while at the same time working to limit the adverse effects that rent increases and the loss of low-cost nonsubsidized stock have on households falling outside of the housing assistance 'safety net.'
>
> (Apgar, 1990: 28)

At the same time, housing policy initiatives do in many cases provide lasting advantages for the beneficiaries, which is both rewarding and assuring, but also underline the problem of how to select beneficiaries, and on what grounds such selection criteria are consistent with social norms regarding justice and fairness. Chetty, Hendren, and Katz (2016: 855–856) examine the Moving to Opportunity (MTO) experiment, organized by the US Department of Housing and Urban Development, and which "[o]ffered a randomly selected subset of families living in high-poverty housing projects subsidized lower-poverty neighborhoods in the mid-1990s." The MTO project was in operation between 1994 and 1998 in five large American cities, and the sample included 4,604 families, in turn divided into three groups: (1) one "experimental voucher group" that was offered a subsidized housing voucher that "came with a requirement to move to a census tract with a poverty rate below 10 percent"; (2) one voucher group that was offered "a standard subsidized housing voucher" but with no additional contingencies; and (3) one control group that was not offered a voucher but retained access to public housing

(Chetty, Hendren, and Katz, 2016: 856). The results were substantial and positive for the first group after checking for a variety of conditions, including the gender of children and family race or ethnicity (Chetty, Hendren, and Katz, 2016: 859). More specifically, Chetty, Hendren, and Katz (2016: 859–860) calculate that "moving a child out of public housing to a low-poverty area when young (at age eight on average)" in an MTO-type experiment will increase the child's "total lifetime earnings by about $302,000." This means that children being lucky in the MTO lottery could benefit substantially.

The lingering concern is whether such experimental activities are consistent with democratic principles and the ethos of the contemporary welfare state, making social prospects a matter of being fortunate in a discrete lottery event, designed and sponsored by the state or the local municipality. Many commentators would claim that the adverse effects of a large-scale implementation of such policies would do more harm than good as it would undermine the legitimacy of the democratic welfare state as it surrenders its ambition to support *any* child or family in need of, e.g., qualitative housing or schooling. At the same time, the MTO experiment is indicative of the effectiveness of carefully designed and implemented housing policies. At the same time, as the cost for such policies are potentially considerable, MTO-type policies are presumably an exception from more conventional initiatives, and several commentators have been highly critical of the ineffective housing policies used over the last decades in many jurisdictions.

The prestigious British economic affairs magazine *The Economist* (2020) addressed dysfunctional housing market policy as a major obstacle for economic growth in many cities and metropolitan areas:

> A trillion dollars of dud mortgages blew up the financial system in 2007–08. But just as pernicious is the creeping dysfunction that housing has created over decades: vibrant cities without space to grow; ageing homeowners sitting in half-empty homes who are keen to protect their view; and a generation of young people who cannot easily afford to rent or buy and think capitalism has let them down.
>
> (*Economist*, 2020: 1)

In fact, *The Economist* (2020: 1) portrays the housing market as "[t]he rich world's most serious and longest-running economic failures." Not least, ineffective housing policy creates conflicts between generations, wherein the younger generation are excluded from housing markets, which creates hurdles for younger people to pass to have families of their own, and which therefore dampens the prospect of future economic growth. "In 1990 a generation of baby-boomers, with a median age of 35, owned a third of America's real estate value. In 2019, a similar sized cohort of millennials aged 31, owned just 4%" (*The Economist*, 2020: 2). On balance, housing market policy should be supportive of economic and social welfare, and serve as a reliable indication of the superiority of the economic system of competitive capitalism, but in fact, the current policy fails on such measures: "Far from shoring up capitalism, housing policies have made the system unsafe, inefficient, and unfair" (*Economist*, 2016: 3).

The Economist is particularly concerned with the long-term commitment to promote home ownership for *all* households, wherein low net-worth households have been exposed to finance industry practices that have leveraged their default risk rather than provided them with a mortgage contract that anchor their household economy in robust and predictable financial and economic relations. The current housing policy is premised on an "infatuation with home ownership" (*Economist*, 2020: 1) and itself generates "property pathologies" (*Economist*, 2020: 2) that can no longer be ignored, nor explained on the basis of exogenous conditions and/or current market conditions. *The Economist* is no primary proponent of expanding welfare state provision but often defends the economic system of competitive capitalism against its detractors; however, the skepticism regarding the home ownership policy is shared by several scholars. Dickerson (2009), a legal scholar, is fairly straightforward in her account of the current policy:

> [A]s long as this country continues to tell consumers that 'owning a home remains the best long-term investment a family can make' [as stated in a White House policy document from 2007], and continues to encourage people to do whatever it takes to achieve the home ownership dream, renters and existing homeowners will continue to make unwise housing investment decisions.
>
> (Dickerson, 2009: 223)

More generally, Atkinson (2019) suggests that policies that regard credit as a social provision (e.g., in the form of home mortgage loans) are mistaken inasmuch as declining real wage growth in combination with the current price stability policy of central banks (see, e.g., Hockett, 2015; Borio, 2011) preclude home ownership for the younger generation or low-income households as they cannot take on sizeable mortgage loans. That is, the "persistently grim economic prognosis" (Atkinson, 2019: 1104) for the middle class in the US means that "credit is not for everyone" (Atkinson, 2019: 1157). In other words, policies that promote credit supply as a means to promote home ownership and similar welfare-inducing campaigns "either fall prey to their own optimism or else indirectly endorse continued regressive redistribution," Atkinson (2019: 1105) argues.

Goodman and Mayer (2018) call attention to policy initiatives in the US over the last three decades and the meagre outcomes they have generated. In May 1995, President Bill Clinton released the National Homeownership Strategy, issued by the US Department of Housing and Urban Development, "an 87-page, 100-point plan" with the goal that it would "boost homeownership in America to an all-time high by the end of the century." The next presidential administration framed home ownership as "as a way to reduce racial inequality," and in 2003, President George W. Bush signed the American Dream Downpayment Initiative to assist "first-time homebuyers" with obtaining a down payment (Goodman and Mayer, 2018: 31). In the 1995–2005 period, the homeownership rate increased in the US, but following the Great Recession austerity policies, the homeownership rate of 2015 fell more than what can be explained by demographics," Goodman and Mayer (2018: 32) write: "[I]n the aftermath of the Great Recession, homeownership fell with tight credit conditions, problematic student loan debt, stagnant real incomes, and perhaps a subtle change in attitudes toward homeownership" (Goodman and Mayer, 2018: 32). Currently, the US homeownership is back at the same level as in 1990, at the same time as its "increased substantially in most other developed countries" (Goodman and Mayer, 2018: 32). In fact, over the 1990–2015 period, 13 of 18 countries examined increased their homeownership rates, and the United States shares this decreasing ownership rate with Bulgaria, Ireland, Mexico, and the United Kingdom, whereof at least Ireland experiences a considerable housing market boom in the period prior to the 2008 finance industry crisis.

In fact, Atkinson (2019) argues, credit is not the social provision it is assumed to be by policy makers who advocate subsidies and insurances that benefit the finance industry, based on the belief that such benefits will trickle down to the household level. On the contrary, such subsidies and insurances are ineffective in promoting, e.g., affordable housing (Richardson, Van Nieuwerburgh, and White, 2017; Bubb and Prasad, 2014). In this view, both a pro-market institution, such as the economists, and legal and urban studies scholars such as Dickerson (2009) and Atkinson (2019) address their concerns regarding the inclusion of virtually all households in the housing finance industry, regardless of their ability to repay the mortgage loans that they can be expected to hold, being a particularly difficult challenge in cities with substantial per-square-meter housing costs. In the end, it is important to notice that thoughtful and carefully designed housing policies can contribute with net economic and social welfare, but housing policies can also bias and distort housing markets so that they incur additional costs for all actors, and/or unduly benefit certain groups, such as middle-class households, or (in the US) white families at the expense of other households. Chapter 1 of this volume provide a more detailed review of the literature pertaining to housing policy.

Outline of the volume

This volume addresses the question of why affordable housing is so complicated to provide despite the stated ambition to do so. The volume is divided into a theoretical section that examines how real estate and housing are tangible assets with a distinct user-value that also serves as collateral in the finance industry. That is, the question of housing is not simply a matter of urban planning and political deliberations regarding the use of public (i.e., municipality-owned) space, but housing as financial asset is also part of the credit formation system that upholds and propels advanced capitalist economies, grounded in the finance industry maintenance of credit relations. The academic discipline of urban studies, a loosely knit network of theories, methods, doctrines, and conventional wisdom and practices, oftentimes ignores or downplays the role of finance industry in shaping urban space, and not least how the question of "affordability" is being addressed. This negligence is unfortunate as it turns a blind eye to the role of housing assets in the credit formation process, and consequently much of the failure to provide affordable housing becomes obscured.

The second section of the volume reports empirical data from a study of an urban renewal project in Gothenburg, Sweden's second city and with roughly one million inhabitants. Like many other Swedish cities, Gothenburg has a number of suburbs that are populated by primarily low-income households, and in many cases a variety of immigrant groups are overrepresented in the suburbs. Over the period of two decades, 2000–2019, Sweden more than doubled the population born outside of Sweden, from 10 to 20 percent of the population, and primarily on the basis of generous migration policies. Sweden has today, together with France, the highest proportion Muslim population for any European non-Muslim country, and as opposed to France, Sweden has no colonial past that may explain this growth. The Swedish welfare state has committed considerable resources to provide housing and schooling facilities to immigrants, but soaring gang-based criminality in the 2015–2020 period has again made the metropolitan suburbs a key political issues. In some cities, such as Malmö, together with the comparably smaller town of Södertälje having the highest proportion of inhabitants born outside of Sweden, or with parents born in some other country, the police authority has organized specific campaigns to reduce street-crime and gang-related violence, including the Operation Rimfrost (Operation Hoarfrost) during the winter of 2019–2020. To date, the campaign to fight organized crime has been only modestly successful. The specific case reported is located in one of the five urban districts in Gothenburg that the police label as being "particularly socially vulnerable" in terms of its exposure to poverty, low labor market inclusion, and the presence of organized crime and gang-related violence. Being widely regarded as a failure of the Swedish welfare state model, cities that hosts urban districts labelled as particularly socially vulnerable increase the investment and governance activities in these neighborhoods. The second part of the volume report results and outcome from these initiatives. While the willingness to renovate, refurbish, and rehabilitate the suburban space is a measure to reduce social and economic vulnerability—a fertile soil for organized crime and gang-related activities—there are many issues that need to be considered, not only the built space itself. Ambition and visionary thinking are certainly political virtues, but also the wider socio-economic conditions need to be considered when embarking on a campaign to, e.g., block unlawful and opportunistic behavior. That is, the urban space is merely one—albeit arguably a central—component in making society durable.

The final chapter of the volume summarizes some of the key argument and points at the centrality of the housing-finance nexus, a relation that essentially determine the supply of affordable housing in an economy. Without recognizing the role of housing assets in the global credit formation process, much valuable empirical research is dead in the water as it merely makes housing production a matter of political ambition, and not as a financially determined business.

Summary and conclusion

Housing affairs concern most citizens in any given society, either directly or indirectly. At the same time, housing policy and the consequences of housing and housing financing policy decisions are traditionally separated into a number of adjacent but fairly compartmentalized scholarly fields of inquiry, say, in housing markets economics, urban studies, economic sociology, social work studies.

The purpose of this volume is to provide an integrated overview of relevant literature and, in the second part of the volume, provide some empirical illustration of how affordable housing policies are practically handled in "on the ground" organizations such as municipality-owned real estate companies. The field of affordable housing policy making and the production of affordable housing and the management of such a highly valued stock of housing units demands cross-sectional and transdisciplinary research work, now and in the future, and this volume attempts to provide a shared ground for the understanding of how housing assets are both of immediate user-value for its residents, and how it plays a more indirect role in the capital formation process. These two issues are covered in some detail in the two chapters of the first part of the book.

Notes

1 The question here is why policy makers have signaled that affordable housing is a legitimate welfare state provision, despite considerable evidence that the sovereign state is unable to live up to such promises made to voters and constituencies. In order to shed light on this condition, Pierre Bourdieu's (2020: 8) view of the state as being constituted on the basis of "the principles of public order" is applicable. In Bourdieu's (2020) view, the state cannot be examined as "a bloc," but is better understood as a "field"—"a space structured according to oppositions linked to specific forms of capital with differing interests" (Bourdieu, 2020: 20). More specifically, Bourdieu (2020: 27) distinguishes between the state as an "bureaucratic apparatus," i.e., a specific form of social organization determined by enforceable legislation, administrative and regulatory rules, etc. (the State 1 model), and "the territory on which the authority of this apparatus is exercised" (the State 2 model). The state is thus both a form of practice, or bureaucratic organization monitoring a variety of activities, and as a legally constituted territory, wherein certain geographical areas are part of a specific sovereign state (e.g., Helgoland in the North Sea is part of the German *Bundesrepublik*).

In order for this state apparatus to remain legitimate in the eyes of constituencies, the state apparatus needs to consider the question of equality. As equality is a most difficult philosophical and political term, the ability to support reasonable levels of equality (e.g., in terms of housing welfare) is a thorny issue for policy makers. That is, proponents of equality, Dworkin (1981: 187) writes, "must decide whether the equality they seek is equality of resource or welfare, or some combination or something very different, in order plausibly to argue that equality is worth having at all." A key political question is whether individual differences in skills, talent, scholarly aptitude, etc., should be permitted to be reflected in the resources each individual can acquire on the basis of their work, or if the sovereign state should compensate, e.g., less fortunate, ambitious, or talented individuals for their disadvantages. In many cases, e.g., progressive fiscal schemes are introduced to re-distribute income so that more fortunate, ambitious, and talented individuals remain incentivized to optimize their performance and revenues at the same time as the welfare of disadvantaged groups can be financed. Furthermore, how to draw the line of demarcation between "too little" and "too much" equality given these natural differences is a central political issue. Acting under such conditions, policy makers oftentimes argue that certain forms of equality, including, e.g., housing, education, and health care should be provided at a basic and elementary levels accessible for all citizens, whereas other resources can be permitted to be distributed more unevenly to preserve the legitimacy of redistribution policies. It is noteworthy that countries with a lower level of economic inequality, such as the Scandinavian countries including Sweden, still have significant differences in housing welfare despite the best intentions to treat affordable housing as welfare state provision. Few Swedish citizens or residents (e.g., immigrant groups not granted permanent residency) live under miserable conditions, but the difference in housing welfare between the top decile and the lowest decile is still significant, measured in terms of square meters per resident in the housing unit, the access to amenities, and the economic wealth generated and the subsidies provided. Apparently, housing welfare remains an unfinished business within the organization of the welfare state, currently mixing market activities and market regulation with a variety of direct subsidies, and by transferring of finance capital to households and other relevant actors.

2 It is important to recognize that the housing market bubble also generated indirect effects that add to the total costs in addition to the loss of housing welfare and the Federal State's resolution activities. Charles, Hurst, and Notowidigdo (2016) notice that the employment rate for prime-aged, non-college men, widely regarded as an index of the health of the US economy, tended to stay around 85 percent in the 1980 to 2000 period, but in 2014, six years into the Great Recession, the same figure stood at only 79 percent, no less than 6 percentage points below the 1980–2000 average level. Charles, Hurst, and Notowidigdo (2016: 181) argue that the housing boom served to "mask" the labor market effects of the manufacturing job decline that followed after 2000, when US Congress granted China a Permanent Normal Trade Relations (PNTR) agreement (Pierce and Schott, 2016: 1632). What Covarrubias, Gutiérrez, and Philippon (2020: 15) refer to as "The China shock" primarily reduced the pool of jobs growth and labor compensation for less-educated workers, but the housing boom served to postpone these effects until its busted. In fact, what Charles, Hurst, and Notowidigdo (2016: 185) refer to as "the national housing boom," which was characterized by "massive increases in housing prices, new construction and renovations, and real estate transactions," began in the late 1990s, and "completely collapsed over a short time period beginning in 2007." In the 1980 to the mid-1990s period, the total number of construction jobs in the US "fluctuated between four and five million," but from the mid-1990s, the total construction job stock "surged by three million," and peaked at "nearly eight million jobs in 2006" (Charles, Hurst, and Notowidigdo, 2016: 185). After 2007, the share of all prime-aged noncollege men, employed in either construction or manufacturing, has "fallen sharply," going from "roughly 30 percent in 2008 to 23 percent in 2014," Charles, Hurst, and Notowidigdo (2016: 187) report. The effect was that the structural shift in the US economy, supported by policy making in Washington DC, became visible in a comparably short period of time, Charles, Hurst, and Notowidigdo (2016: 181) propose:

> When the housing market collapsed in 2007, there was a large, immediate decline in employment among these workers, who faced not only the sudden disappearance of jobs related to the housing boom, but also the fact that manufacturing's steady decline during the early 2000s left them with many fewer opportunities in that sector than had existed at the start of the decade.
>
> (Charles, Hurst, and Notowidigdo (2016))

The housing bubble was thus, in hindsight, a comparably ineffective and costly response to the structural change in the US economy that US Congress anticipated. For instance, the abundant but temporary employment opportunities provided in the housing market and its various industries may have convinced young noncollege individuals to delay going to college, "presumably because they erroneously believed that housing-related job opportunities would exist in the longer-term," Charles, Hurst, and Notowidigdo (2016: 197) speculate. For these groups, several labor market opportunities vanished as they delayed their chance to obtain skills demanded in high-growth sectors like high-tech manufacturing and tradeable services. To make a fair assessment of the entire housing bubble cycle, these indirect costs also need to be included.

Part I

Institutional conditions

1 Affordable housing policies

Introduction

As stated in the introduction, a house plays a dual role in the advanced financialized economy inasmuch as it is simultaneously a residential home for a person or a family, i.e., a commodity that generates what Fernandez and Aalbers (2016: 73) refer to as "housing asset-based welfare," and serves as collateral in the credit formation process that occurs on the local and global scale.[1] This chapter and the next will outline the institutional framework and the underlying theoretical model that maintain and reproduce this dual role of housing, which has considerable economic, financial, and political implications. This chapter discusses the political aspects of housing production and subsidizing, being a policy domain that includes a variety of economic ideas, doctrines, and objectives, in many cases resulting in policies that cannot fully apprehend all stipulated goals.

"[T]he United States has long encouraged, supported, and subsidized home ownership," Dickerson (2009: 193) writes. At the same time as affordable housing has been understood as a welfare state provision, indeed a component of the citizens' rights upon which the welfare state model is constructed, in the US and elsewhere, housing policy has been contingent on social norms and perceived threats. For instance, Levitin and Wachter (2020: 35–37) argue that policies promoting homeownership was treated as a device that counteracted labor radicalization and the "red menace"—Soviet-style communism—in the interwar period. Homeownership was widely treated as the most effective way to transform working and middle-class families into a pacified bourgeoisie that favored a quiet life over political radicalism. It is noteworthy that the advocacy of home ownership policies has been less pronounced after 1990 in a variety of jurisdictions. Kohl's (2019: 924) study of housing policy documents from 19 countries in the 1945–2018 period, which included the sudden and unexpected collapse of the Soviet Union in 1989–1990, shows that "manifestos" published between 1956 and 1975 were "2.6 times more likely to mention housing than those from 1990 to 2006." The key idea formulated in such manifestos was that "[d]emocratized homeownership is beneficial for modern societies" insofar as it creates "more stable democracies, fosters individual virtues and counteracts revolutionary pressures through a broader distribution of wealth and better housing supply" (Kohl, 2019: 914).

DOI: 10.4324/9781003244417-3

Somewhat ironically, while the New Deal generation of policy makers were worried about left-leaning radicalism on the American soil, their promotion of homeownership in metropolitan suburban areas rather resulted in a contrapunctual tendency, to create a fertile soil for a conservatism that per se proved to be radical in its claims regarding the call to roll back the welfare state from the middle of the 1970s. The raise of the suburbs was supportive of "a homeowner's philosophy of individual rights, meritocracy, and property ownership" (Philips-Fein, 2011: 731). Philips-Fein (2011: 731) continues: "Ironically, postwar federal government support for highways and mass homeownership helped create communities that would ultimately prove deeply hostile to New Deal liberalism." Recent studies have demonstrated that the New Deal policies were far away from being politically neutral inasmuch as it primarily supported an already privileged white working or lower middle class, whereas various ethnic groups including black, Latino, and Asian communities were disfavored (Taylor, 2018, 2019). "Homeownership became a particularly important engine of racial inequality in the United States," Quinn (2017: 58) writes: "Owning a home was a boost up the social ladder given disproportionally to veterans over nonveterans, men over women, and whites over nonwhites."

Regardless of failure to provide welfare state provision for all communities, home ownership has remained a highly prioritized political and economic goal in most welfare states. Homeownership serves as an insurance against labor market turbulence and economic downturns (Conley and Gifford, 2006), and empirical data indicates that homeowners endorse a self-sufficiency ethos that reduces the pressure on the state and the government to provide benefits and subsidies (Ansell, 2019). "Our overall conclusion: homeownership is a valuable institution. On average, it allows families to build wealth and serves as a measure of financial security," Goodman and Mayer (2018: 32) write. In addition to such immediate political benefits, the household lending channel, which generates credit on the basis of mortgage debt, generates so-called safe assets that are vital for the global credit formation process. In other words, to own a home on the basis of mortgage lending means to play an active (albeit small) role in the global financial market. These mechanisms and their legal and regulatory frameworks are discussed in Chapter 2 of this volume. In this chapter, the political support of home ownership will be examined, being a long-term commitment made by sovereign states in the post-World War II period. As the scholarly literature reveals, it is increasingly difficult to maintain the model that has dominated over the last half a century, as the level of household debt is soaring to unprecedented levels at the same time as real wage growth been reduced (in many parts of Europe) or eliminated (in the US), which leaves prospect home buyers with limited budgets with few alternatives. Younger people, unemployed, and households with only one wage earner are to a higher degree excluded from the housing market, and must rely either on patrons and co-financiers (e.g., parents or wealthy relatives) to access housing facilities (see, e.g., Moor and Friedman, 2021; Manzo, Druta, and Ronald, 2019). That is, affordable housing is increasingly becoming more of a political slogan or stated ambition than a factual conditions in many jurisdictions.

Elementary components of housing policy

Affordable housing as social provision and welfare device

As has been observed by numerous commentators, as a matter of fact, the supply of affordable housing is shrinking in advanced economies, which has important implications for social and economic welfare. "The shortage of adequate affordable housing has been described as a public health crisis," Travis (2019: 142) remarks. In the US, by 2014, 14 million Americans lived in "concentrated poverty in extremely poor neighborhoods"—the highest figure ever recorded, and "twice as many as in 2000" (Florida, 2017: 98). "Struggles over housing have become one of the most pressing social, economic and political issues of our time," Alexander, Bruun, and Koch (2018: 122) add. The concern is that housing (and preferably affordable housing) suffers the tension from simultaneously being a "commodity" and "right" (Pattillo, 2013); on the one hand, housing production, housing sales and resales, and the financing of such business activities is "perhaps the most important engine of the US economy," Pattillo (2013: 512) writes. "Housing is an essential component of global financial circuits. It is traded, swapped, hedged, and liquidated through various instruments," Akers and Seymour (2018: 130) add. On the other hand, the access to qualitative housing is part of the welfare state provision in most advanced economies. As affordable housing is either an explicit or implicit responsibility of the state, and ultimately the government, the failure to provide affordable housing easily translates into a more general skepticism towards political elites as the housing situation is immediately experienced on a day-by-day, hour-by-hour basis. Alexander, Bruun, and Koch (2018: 123) emphasize the centrality of housing policy in statecraft:

> Housing has often been seen as an expression of a social contract between citizens and the state, one which entitles citizens to material resources—namely housing—in return for certain obligations rendered to the state. The parameters of this social contract have changed significantly from the post-war decades to the present. While in the post-war decades, housing was often presented as a right gained through criteria of citizenship and labour, the advent of neoliberalism, financialisation and austerity have redrawn the lines between those who are included and those who are not.
>
> (Alexander, Bruun, and Koch, 2018: 123)

Furthermore, in this new housing policy making regime, "housing policies are at the same time part of a country's political economy and dislocated from it," Rolnik (2019: 6) argues. This means that local political climate and democratic traditions shape how housing assets are generated, priced, and allocated, yet making the global finance industry the primus motor of housing supply. By implication, housing policy becomes the zone wherein local residents experience what Fields (2017: 2, original emphasis omitted) refers to as "real-world financialization," the place wherein "everyday life is enmeshed with finance via mortgages, rental contracts, and other mechanisms," and within which the distance between "financial techniques that abstract from local places and the concrete impacts of such practices in the everyday lives of urban residents" are collapsed. No matter how separated low-income households' economic affairs are from global finance industry activities under regular conditions, housing policy making tend to connect household and the finance industry interests. In this housing policy framework, the home becomes "[a]t once a conduit through which broader political and economic relations are enforced and acted out," a place of "domestic retreat," and not least "a means through which people engage with kin, community and other local actors," Alexander, Bruun, and Koch (2018: 129) summarize. Expressed differently, housing policy becomes "[a]n essentially contested domain where competing understandings of citizenship are constructed, fought over and acted out" (Alexander, Bruun, and Koch, 2018: 122).

In Los Angeles, a high-growth metropolitan area, the median renting household today spends 47 percent of the average income on housing (Lee, 2016: 231), a figure that is explained on the basis of stagnant real wages, population growth, and "zoning policies that favor single-family and luxury housing" (Lee, 2016: 231). In the US, the majority of poor renting families spend over half of their income on housing, and almost a quarter spend more than 70 percent (Desmond and Bell, 2015: 16). A closer look at the historical and political conditions that shaped housing policy in, e.g., the US indicates that such outcomes are no coincidence (Taylor, 2018, 2019). Faber (2020) examines how New Deal agencies established in the 1930s, including The Home Owners Loan Corporation (HOLC), Federal Housing Administration (FHA), and the GI Bill actively created the "contemporary US homeownership society." In this model, "people and communities of color" were largely excluded from affordable mortgage credit on the basis of a combination of explicit and implicit means, which generated racialized neighborhood boundaries that largely have remained to this day. If agencies unintendedly (or on purpose, some critics suggest) introduce policies and mechanisms that result in neighborhoods with mixed racial and ethnic groups suffering property value declines, such policies de facto incentivized white communities to "segregate themselves" (Faber, 2020: 740). In this account, racial relations in the American society were translated into policy objectives and practices in economic and financial terms so that primarily white communities benefitted from federal mortgage lending subsidies. The agencies implemented an A to D grading system to geographically discriminate between different areas and city districts, and this model strongly contributed to a segregationist distribution of families and households. In the model, neighborhoods dominated by low-income immigrants, or—most importantly—black families, "effectively guaranteed a D grade" (Faber, 2020: 742). For instance, in 1930, not even one single black person in St. Louis, a city that was the home of 94,030 African Americans, resided outside of D areas (Faber, 2020: 742). After World War II, when veterans returned home, FHA and the GI Bill served to provide credit supportive of privately owned housing. Between 1950 and 1960, one-third of all privately owned housing units were financed by FHA and the GI Bill (Faber, 2020: 742). In summary, Faber (2020: 764) writes, "New Deal housing policies had enormous effects on racial geography in the United States by encouraging segregation through the drawing and grading of neighborhoods."

It is also noteworthy that there has to date been only modest scholarly research regarding the relationship between federal subsidized mortgage-lending policies and long-term trends in segregation despite this being an important explanatory factor regarding disparities in total household asset ownership on an aggregated level. In 2013, "the median white US household had $13 in asset wealth for each $1 held by the median black US household" (Faber, 2020: 744). This 13-to-1 differential can be postulated to not be explained strictly on the basis of human capital investment, scholarly aptitude, ambition, and other personal qualities and aspirations but needs to be explained on the basis of institutional and historical conditions, and social norms and other structural conditions pertaining to household wealth. In Faber's (2020) account, history matters, and it matters in a long-term view and with a significant magnitude; policy decisions provide mechanisms and incentives that determine social action on the household levels that would put their mark on both economic and social welfare metrics and in terms of a racialized spatial geography, neatly segregating racial and ethnic groups in ways that violate the legal and democratic principle of equality before the law.

Housing as communitarian asset

As Levitin and Wachter (2020: xvii) remark, speaking primarily of housing as an asset class being tied to the credit formation process of the finance market, housing is "a communitarian asset." Legally speaking, the homeowners (say, a married couple) access a house as their private property, and yet the mortgage loan they have contracted for, stipulating a variety of conditions including duration, interest rates, re-negotiation clauses, and so forth, is at the same time a commitment to work hard and diligently to honor the contractual relation, per se being a contribution to civil society. Levitin and Wachter (2020: 26) notice that these close legal and financial ties between households and global financial markets, with the state acting as the intermediary and the principal of the finance industry, yet responding to the political will (in democratic states), are of relatively recent origin. Before the New Deal, there was no financialized home mortgage market in the US, and housing was not yet a tradable asset in the contemporary sense of the term (Levitin and Wachter, 2020: 26). The development of Government Sponsored Enterprises, large mortgage lending institutes such as Ginnie Mae, Freddie Mac and Fannie Mae, established in the post-World War II period in the US, served to establish lasting and robust bonds between households, finance industry, and the Federal State. This model has operated reasonably well until the liberalization of financial markets legislation by the end of the Clinton Presidency (1993–2001), when a broader variety of market actors were invited to participate in housing financing activities. In Levitin and Wachter's (2020) account, the political ambition to provide affordable housing, oftentimes on the basis of a combination of ex ante and ex post regulatory rules in combination with subsidies to both building societies and households, is co-produced with the welfare state model, whereas the financialized home mortgage industry is of considerably more recent origin. Nevertheless, under all conditions, the closer ties between households, financial markets, and the state and transnational governance agencies further pronounce rather than diminish the incentives in policy making quarters to support home ownership. The concern is that home mortgage lending is a lucrative business if the mortgage lender is in the position to hold the mortgage loan contract until maturation (i.e., the lender is included in the labor market, holds other assets, etc.), whereas it is considerably more difficult to lend money to households with smaller budgets. As can be learned from the subprime mortgage lending debacle, including a considerable degree of fraud and cases of predatory lending (Agarwal et al., 2014; Bond, Musto, and Yilmaz, 2008), i.e., market activities that violate the norms of prudent lending practices and robust risk management assessments, lending at the fringe of the economy is either difficult or riddled by undesirable activities that generate systemic risks elsewhere in the financial and economic system. This means that mortgage lending in low-risk segments of the housing market can be effectively serviced by private finance industry actors, whereas mortgage lending to households with smaller budgets and/or a more limited understanding of the legal implications from entering mortgage lending relations may demand subsidies or support from the state or state-governed agencies. These policy issues are particularly pronounced if there is a shortage of housing facilities—as is quite often the case, and in many cases being an endemic condition—in urban areas such as major cities. Hansson (2017: 477), for instance, calls for urban planning reform as being part of a larger restructuring of the Swedish housing market given the "severe housing shortage in Swedish growth regions." Swedish governments have traditionally relied on an idiosyncratic combination of a regulated market model and subsidies to both building societies and construction industry and households residing in rental units (so-called *bostadsbidrag*) or tax exemptions for households residing in privately owned units (30 percent of the annual interest rate on mortgage loans are subject to tax reductions). Unsurprisingly, the effectiveness of this policy is disputed, and one of its primary effect is market inertia as, e.g., selling and buying private units is associated with both fees and a taxation of the financial surplus generated (currently at 30 per cent of the profit from sales generated). Hansson's (2017) call for policy reforms is particularly relevant for the larger cities as the degree of urbanization is a prominent trend, and not least for low-income households that tend to settle in suburban city districts.

Taken together, studies of housing policy reveal a variety of conditions that solve certain imminent concerns but also generate unintended consequences, a widely observed phenomenon in policy studies (see, e.g., Funk and Hirschman, 2014). It is important to recognize that even though the current financialized mortgage lending model can be criticized on the basis of a number of conditions and form a variety of political perspectives, the contemporary housing industry model has also generated considerable levels of what Fernandez and Aalbers (2016: 73) call housing-based wealth, an issue that needs to be examined in more detail as it is part of the justification of the theoretical model that propels the current housing policy.

Housing supply and policy making: affordable housing production in nested policy milieus

The production of affordable housing can be approached through a number of policy devices, including legislation, increased regulatory oversight, subsidies to either real estate or construction companies and/or households, and other forms of "stimulations" that are supportive of an increased appetite to invest in affordable housing services. Furthermore, as Metcalf (2018) remarks, all these activities within the housing market are still dependent on local and regional labor markets, and labor market inclusion to make any substantial difference in terms of what is regarded as affordable housing. As housing markets are local whereas people oftentimes commute to work, there is a social dilemma involved in regional housing policy making as one municipality, county, etc. can freeride on investment in housing facilities in another municipality in the region. Such free-rider problems are widely recognized in policy making in market settings (Olson, 1965), and are not supportive of affordable housing policy objectives. These concerns are particularly pronounced in high housing cost cities. In fact, Metcalf (2018: 61) takes a rather pessimistic view of the effects of formal affordable housing policies in expensive cities as they are likely to be "quite small in their impact when compared to the size of the problem." Nevertheless, in terms of practically promoting the supply of affordable housing, which seems to be vital for long-term economic growth, policy makers can use four principal tools: (1) direct provision of social housing; (2) vouchers to increase the purchasing power of households; (3) price controls on rents; and (4) regulations on development of new housing supply (Metcalf, 2018: 61). As indicated, these tools use and combine a variety of mechanisms including direct finance capital transfers, legal reforms, and tighter regulatory control of housing markets, but in Metcalf's account, none of these tools are sufficient to "fix the housing market," especially not in expensive cities.

First, social housing was part of the post-World War II welfare state model, and the 1950s and 1960s were the heyday of social housing policies, but by the end of the period, public housing fell into disrepute based on a combination of conditions. Social housing areas had been the laboratory for architectural experiments and novel building design, oftentimes shaped by a modernist beliefs in the house or the home as some kind of rational machine as suggested by the Swiss architect Le Corbusier. Public sector inefficiencies resulting in poor management of local housing authorities added to the situation, and perhaps also the economic idea that it was effective to concentrate a significant number of poor people in one location was a questionable premise in the first place. Also the economic decline that followed from the two oil crises in the 1970s served to further deprive many social housing areas. While social housing is today an integrated component in many jurisdictions, including, e.g., the Netherlands, Metcalf (2018: 64) writes off social housing as a practically feasible housing policy model in the US on the basis of the estimated cost to saturate the demand. Furthermore, as Apgar (1990: 2) notices, this policy creates demarcation problems inasmuch as the state or the municipality may in effect aid "some of poor at the expense of the non-subsidized poor," which may violate social norms regarding fairness and equality before the law, which creates a skeptical attitude towards state interventions in other areas.

Second, direct subsidies to low-income households in the form of vouchers that reduce the rent the paid by the tenant is another housing market regulation tool. In 1974, new federal legislation established the so-called Section 8 program, wherein households pay 30 percent of their income in rent, and with the local housing authority stepping in to cover the rest of the monthly rent to the landlord (Metcalf, 2018: 64). As affordable housing is formally designed as the ability to pay no more than 30 percent of the nominal income in housing expenses, the voucher system is consistent with overarching housing policy declarations, but the current system is severely underfinanced, Metcalf (2018: 64) remarks: one study estimated that only 25 percent of the households that are eligible for the subsidy according to the income standards of the US Department of Housing and Urban Development receive "federal assistance." Furthermore, in expensive local housing markets, such as the Los Angeles metropolitan area, a perennial problem is that the voucher dollar amount is insufficient to cover the rent asked by landlords, which means that many landlords are not willing to rent to voucher holders anyway, which undermines the stipulated policy outcomes (Metcalf, 2018: 64). Third, rent control is a policy tool that is comparably rare in American cities as it is incompatible with the faith in market efficiency that many American policy makers maintain. It is primarily in the states of New York, New Jersey, and California that rent control is playing a factual role in keeping housing costs at a reasonable level. As Metcalf (2018: 66) remarks, many card-carrying economists are skeptical regarding rent control as policy device, a stance that Metcalf refers to as "something like an oath of office for the profession." However, empirical evidence indicates that the "real-world rent control" in the three states listed above do not generally have any substantial negative impact on local and regional housing markets (Metcalf, 2018: 66). This means that economic doctrines regarding the distorting effects of rent control and other federal or state-based monitoring of housing market activities tend to be overstated. One adverse effect of rent control is what has been referred to as "renoviction" in the housing studies literature (Thörn and Thörn, 2017: 294), that is, landlords may raise the rent only if they renovate their facilities, which means that landlords have an incentive to create a positive (from their view) differential between the full renovation cost and the increased marginal projected income stream derived from the higher rent. For some low-income families, the renovation de facto results in unbearable rents, which means that they need to seek new accommodation, i.e., they are "renovicted." In the stricter jurisdictions, landlords can act in such ways if, and only if, there are vacancies in the housing units, but the mechanism applies just the same in this case. In comparison to social housing and the voucher system, Metcalf (2018: 66) takes a more sanguine view of rent control and argues that when rent control has been established in housing markets, it does not typically suppress the supply of housing or affordable housing, more specifically. Furthermore, in practical and hands-on terms. It should be recognized that for individual households, there are "significant upsides" as they can now enjoy "lower housing rents than they otherwise would, with the attendant benefits of greater community stability" (Metcalf, 2018: 66). This means that rent control appears to partially protect cities from predatory housing practices, which generates economic and social welfare in significant proportions.

Fourth and finally, Metcalf (2018: 66) examines housing market regulation, which Metcalf regards as the primary cause of several major housing market inefficiencies. This umbrella term includes four different categories: (1) zoning;

(2) building standards; (3) permits to add supply; and (4) fees (Metcalf, 2018: 66). Zoning codes regulate "what land uses are allowed on a site—housing, office, retail, and so on" (Metcalf, 2018: 66), thus being the principal housing and land planning device for cities, municipalities, and counties when planning the local and regional built environment. In contrast, the building standards or the building code regulate not *what* is to be built, but *how* it is to be built, including the size of the windows of the building, how large the rooms must be, how much heat can be lost through the walls (insulation), etc. The combination of zoning and building codes embodies the professional idea and the conventional wisdom regarding what constitutes "decent housing." Such codes also implicitly include subjective criteria regarding aesthetics and livability. In many, perhaps most cases, such professionals ideas are consistent with popular beliefs and the interest of the wider public, but Metcalf underlines that such beliefs may also "effectively outlaw single room occupant apartments, rooming houses, and other shared housing models that once provided cheap housing to the working class" (Metcalf, 2018: 67). This means that city planners and urban developers reveal a tendency to underestimate the demand for cheap and affordable housing as they gravitate towards supporting some generalized nuclear middle-class family needs and way of life in their professional roles and service, and when planning urban spaces and residential areas. In addition to these complications, Metcalf (2018: 67) emphasizes that city and municipality administrations are themselves concerned with covering their costs and financing future development activities, which means that real estate companies and construction companies need to both acquire permits to build and to pay significant fees for these services. The underlying policy idea is that land owned by the city or municipality is a public good that should not be transferred to a private corporation without economic and social benefits for the taxpayers being secured. This democratic principle and credo is worth honoring, but the question is how much of these fees and additional costs that are transferred to the end-users, the buyers of the new homes being produced? Metcalf (2018) argues that this risk should not be ignored in policy making quarters, not least in cities with a limited stock of affordable housing units:

> Cities collect fees and exactions to support affordable housing production, transit expansion, parks, and general municipal budgets. The total costs of fees and exactions in a city like San Francisco range between $60,000 and $150,000 for each market-rate unit.
>
> (Metcalf, 2018: 68)

In summary, policy making conducive to an increased affordable housing supply is a far from trivial practice, which includes many factors to consider and to effectively balance. In the end, Metcalf (2018) argues that intendedly rational policies that comply with principles of efficiency and fairness tend to generate unintended and potentially irrational consequences:

> In the long run, we can expect fees, exactions, and other financial requirements to reduce the quantity of land that is developed. Said differently,

> the market price for housing has to remain high enough to cover the cost of the fees and exactions, so these function as a price floor that keeps housing more expensive than it otherwise would be.
>
> (Metcalf, 2018: 69)

On the basis of these consequences, it is important to ask hard questions regarding the efficiency of the current housing market policy, wherein "unnecessarily high housing costs due to local barriers" tend to "outweigh the gains in housing access provided from the other programs," Metcalf (2018: 69) contends. That is, the policy trade-off concern is whether the tax money committed to support one category of lower-income households by providing subsidized housing is justifiable if such activities comes at the cost of raising the average housing unit price in the market, thus being detrimental for all other households (Metcalf, 2018: 69)?

The policy makers' predicament is what Metcalf (2018: 69) refers to as "the collective action problem of local housing policy." There are many conditions that cities and municipalities cannot control but that still affect the households' capacity to pay their rent or to buy a home, and the sheer volume of low net-worth households in, e.g., expensive cities undermines the possibilities for any market-based reform as they would not be able to pay market prices in any plausible scenario of housing supply increases (Metcalf, 2018: 71). Furthermore, policy makers need to be cognizant of the activism of specific groups, including elected and hired officials who run campaigns to preserve city districts to protect their privileges. So-called NIMBY (not-in-my-backyard) activists initiating neighborhood preservation campaigns have successfully built political coalitions to block urban development projects (Metcalf, 2018: 72). That is, activists that otherwise would commend policy making supportive of an increased affordable housing policy are actively pushing back such policies in their own residential areas. Another economic condition that serves to inflate production costs in the real estate and construction industries is the cyclical movement of these industries. The historical boom–bust cycle trajectory of the real estate industry results in chronic labor shortages as workers must exit the industry during recessions, and higher wages are necessary to attract construction workers back to industry (Metcalf, 2018: 74, footnote 6). Higher wages in turn increase the market prices of new housing, which then justify that trade unions negotiate even more generous compensation for its members, which results in a self-reinforcing upward movement of both housing production costs and housing prices. Through these self-amplifying industry dynamics, production costs are set at a plateau level that in turn inflates market prices.

In the end, despite all the conditions that serve to suppress the supply of affordable housing, Metcalf (2018) singles out political and policy-related issues as the key to housing market reforms. In the current political system, in the US and elsewhere, in, e.g., European welfare states, the undersupply of housing is a "logical outcome" from the combination of "jurisdictional fragmentation, competition between cities, local control over land use, and control of the city politics by incumbent homeowners" (Metcalf, 2018: 72). Furthermore, as will be discusses in Chapter 2 of this volume, the intricacies of the housing finance industry, being part of an expansive transnational finance market, further complicates the planning horizon of policy makers. Nevertheless, Metcalf (2018: 74) advises city and municipality policy makers to "look for ways to eliminate some of the regulations that are less essential," but without compromising on issues related to health and safety. Such reforms would preferably include a greater supply of single-room occupancy apartments, more relaxed rules regarding the supply of parking facilities, and to look for ways to actively incentivize market actors to innovate in the domain of housing production, say, by using prefabricated units to reduce cost, while maintaining quality criteria. This may be no easy reform to orchestrate, but the current policy is ineffective in providing affordable housing and (in the US) only subsidizes a minority of the households eligible for federal support.

Housing policy and the generation of housing equity inequality: the institutional perspective

The conventional view is that housing policy is part of the welfare state program, and that housing policy has two principal objectives: (1) to provide affordable and qualitative housing for all citizens and residents, (2) to act to reduce market-generated forms of economic inequality. There are good reasons to believe that housing policy fails to accomplish such stated goals, not least the second goals regarding what Pfeffer and Waitkus (2021) refer to as wealth inequality. Generally speaking, individual and household wealth is associated with a number of conditions, including "[i]ndividuals' labor market trajectories, demographic outcomes, and, perhaps most importantly, the socioeconomic attainment of following generations" (Pfeffer and Waitkus (2021: 568) . In, for example, social democratic welfare states such as Sweden and Norway, income inequality is handled on the basis of progressive fiscal policies, transferring economic resources from medium to high-income households to low-income households, not least through the financing of welfare state services such as health care and schooling, provided at a limited cost. However, when considering wealth inequality in Sweden and Norway, there is a notable divergence between income inequality and wealth inequality. Sweden has the lowest Gini coefficient—a standard measure of economic equality—(.264) of the 15 countries examined by Pfeffer and Waitkus (2021: 577–578), i.e., it is the most income-egalitarian country, but when wealth inequality is included in the overall assessment of economic equality, Sweden (and Norway) are "[t]he next most unequal countries in terms of wealth, behind the United States (net worth Gini of .868 and .813, respectively)" (Pfeffer and Waitkus, 2021: 579). In comparison, a number of Southern European countries show comparably high levels of income inequality, but score lower on the wealth inequality measure (Pfeffer and Waitkus, 2021: 569). Such empirical data suggests that inequality in net worth is "[s]urprisingly high in contexts that are typically considered more egalitarian based on their level of income inequality" (Pfeffer and Waitkus, 2021: 569).

To explain the divergence between income inequality and wealth inequality, Pfeffer and Waitkus (2021: 570) emphasize the role of national and regional housing markets, and accompanying mortgage lending markets and mortgage financing. To better understand the connections between wealth inequality, housing markets, and housing finance, Pfeffer and Waitkus (2021: 572) stress two conditions: (1) the role of "financialized mortgage markets," and (2) the spread of a "finance culture" among households." As has been noticed in the housing studies literature, the modern welfare state maintains an ambiguous relationship to housing welfare, i.e., in capitalist societies hosting a highly differentiated finance industry, "the universal right for shelter is typically not met by public provision but instead supported by subsidized private ownership" (Pfeffer and Waitkus, 2021: 571). This means that finance industry characteristics play a key explanatory role for the differentials in wealth equality on the household level, also in welfare states and sovereign states based on a political culture valuing economic equality and egalitarianism. "Housing equity is jointly and interactively determined by the structures and dynamics of housing markets and mortgage markets," Pfeffer and Waitkus (2021: 589) propose. More specifically, the level of finance industry market penetration in national mortgage markets can be operationalized and measured in terms of the magnitude of the trade of certain mortgage-backed instruments: "On average," Pfeffer and Waitkus (2021: 581) write, "countries with more widely spread debt obligations also have higher levels of wealth inequality and concentration, although the relationship is somewhat less pronounced than the associations with homeownership rates." Peffer and Waitkus (2021) summarize their results:

> Cross-national differences in income inequality do not predict cross-national differences in wealth inequality, because the latter are most centrally driven by housing equity. In turn, the distribution of housing equity, we argue, is crucially determined by financialization and housing market dynamics, that is, in institutional spheres outside the labor market and the classical realms of the welfare state.
>
> (Pfeffer and Waitkus, 2021: 590)

Even Scandinavian welfare states, embedded in a social democratic political culture (also largely embraced, albeit adhered to under other political declarations, by center-right governments in Sweden, Norway, and Denmark), fail to generate economic equality despite implementing progressive fiscal policies (which results in taxation being a substantial part of the national GDP in these countries) to reduce the effects of income inequality. When households make investment in housing facilities, they are included in the national and global finance industry mortgage lending circuit, which results in a marked—and arguably unexpected, at least at this level—growth in wealth inequality. In the case of Sweden, households that invest in housing are subsidized through both interest payment deductions in annual income tax declaration and through "repair and refurbishment" tax reduction policies (so-called *Reparation, Ombyggnad, Tillbyggnad-avdrag*, widely referred to as ROT tax deductions). Furthermore, the major Swedish banks and the finance industry are subsidized by and receive tax exemptions and other insurances from the sovereign state, with further incentivizes banks to issue mortgage loans. Based on these institutional conditions, in many cases based on long-term industry policies agreed on across the political spectrum, Sweden apparently combines low income inequality (as stipulated by a social democratic ideology) and considerably higher wealth inequality. The allegedly high degree of fiscal discipline in the Scandinavian countries (see, e.g., Jakobsen, Jakobsen, Kleven, and Zucman, 2020) is presumably maintained on the basis of the intuitive understanding among high net-worth households that income inequality is eventually compensated by housing equity benefits mirrored in the wealth inequality differentials reported by Pfeffer and Waitkus (2021: 591).

Under all conditions, Pfeffer and Waitkus (2021: 591) call for future research that examine the different modes of "housing market financialization" in different countries and regions.[2] Such studies may include what Pfeffer and Waitkus (2021: 591) refer to as "meso-level approaches," including, e.g., a comparison of the role of banks and asset management firms, the real estate industry, or other intermediaries involved in "expanding and intensifying mortgage credit." Pfeffer and Waitkus (2021) show that housing policy, and not least affordable housing policy, may be successful in providing qualitative housing (but whether that is a case is of course an empirical question to be examined, and in turn premised on how housing quality is defined and operationalized), but fails, at least in the case of Scandinavian countries, to even out differences in aggregated household wealth. Housing equity on the household level is largely a matter of how the mortgage lending industry acts and assesses the market value of housing assets, and such finance industry activities are in turn premised on policy making and institutional conditions. As will be discussed in the second chapter of this volume, the entanglement of state-based policy making, implemented and enforced by state agencies, finance industry interests, and household investment decisions are also determined by the global finance industry's demand for safe assets—financial assets such as mortgage loan contracts that are backed by sovereign states. In this expanded view of mortgage lending, significant wealth inequality derived from housing equity differentials may be difficult to escape altogether, or at least, it is a policy issue associated with significant difficulties and political costs.

The socio-economic and cultural context of housing policy

One policy making dictum frequently reiterated is that "the rising tide lifts all boats," that is, when the business cycle is in an upward movement, it benefits each and every one being part of the economic system—when the sun rises, it shines over the entire field. Such assertions do, however, say very little regarding those who are not fully included in the economic system, who lacks "economic citizenship" (with Krippners, 2017: 2, apt phrasing). Taking such concerns aside, "housing-based wealth" can be measured as the differential between housing valued at current market prices and mortgage debt, i.e., whether the household can factually account for a genuine ownership proportion of their real estate.

Fuller (2015) notices that the "sectoral allocation of credit" has "changed dramatically" over the past several decades in advanced economies. The share of the total stock of debt accounted for by governments and private non-financial enterprises has shrunk (Fuller, 2015: 245), whereas the debt of consumers and financial corporations has grown to a significantly larger share; "Households and banks have increasingly displaced non-financial businesses and governments as the primary debtors in modern capitalist economies" (Fuller, 2015: 242). Fernandez and Aalbers (2016: 73) argue that housing-based wealth has "risen to historically unprecedented heights," which implies that real estate has become "more important as store-of-value for household." In the Eurozon, Fernandez and Aalbers (2016: 73) write, "housing wealth grew from €3.7 trillion in 1980 to €13.2 trillion in 1999 and €24.2 trillion in 2006" (in constant monetary value). If these figures are taken as a proxy for the robustness and economic rationale of private home ownership policies, pursued in a variety of jurisdictions, it may be concluded that accepting the risks associated with home ownership pays off very well on average for individual households. This does not means that each and every presumptive home mortgage lender is equally successful in their investment strategies, especially not during housing bubble episodes wherein the households themselves may also act as speculators to make a return on investment. Furthermore, studies of how what Dickerson (2009: 219) refers to as the "mortgage industrial complex" become established in new jurisdictions indicate that the households are exposed to market risks that they cannot rationally be assumed to fully assess, anticipate, or counteract.

Ethnical and racial factors

In many parts of the world, not least in the US, housing policy has failed to counteract economic and social inequality wherein primarily black and Latin communities face the hardest challenges in terms of securing qualitative affordable housing. Not only is the situation problematic, it was even worsening during the decade following the 2008 finance industry crisis. In 2007, the year before the crash, the median white family had "eight times the wealth" of the median black family in the US; by 2013, this figure stood at 11 times, and "it has tapered off only slightly since" (Taylor, 2018: 23). As home ownership is one of the foremost sources of household wealth, the disfavoring, or even exclusion of black and Latin communities in the housing market is mirrored in official statistics. "Blacks, Hispanics, and Asians all had lower homeownership rates than their white counterparts" (Goodman and Mayer, 2018: 38). In fact, homeownership rates for black households "have fallen every decade for the last 30 years," both unconditionally and after controlling for income and demographics (Goodman and Mayer, 2018: 32). In 2015, close to a decade into the Great Recession that hit medium to low net-worth households particularly hard, "black households with a college education are less likely to own a home than white households whose head did not graduate from high school" (Goodman and Mayer, 2018: 32). Taylor (2018: 23) argues that African Americans were given promises in the 1990s to finally access "the robust housing market that had fueled the ascension of the white middle class in the second half of the twentieth century," but instead they were subjected to "rapacious lending and real-estate practices that extended familiar patterns of discrimination." For instance, at the housing bubble peak in the 2003–2007 period, African Americans were "50 percent more likely than their white peers to receive a subprime loan" (Taylor, 2018: 23–24). In addition, African Americans have been subject to "rent-to-own schemes" wherein poor and working-class households, not qualified for any other forms of mortgage lending, have made expensive payments for "substandard properties" (Taylor, 2018: 24).

Unsurprisingly, the exclusion from the robust housing market affects the quality of life of African Americans and Latin households. Harding's (2009) study of poor neighborhoods in Boston shows that compared with their counterparts in more "advantaged neighborhoods," adolescents in disadvantaged neighborhoods "are more likely to spend time with older peers" (Harding, 2009: 446). Not a problem per se, the closer ties between adolescent boys and grown men is indicative of the higher degree of "neighborhood identity" in disadvantaged neighborhoods, which in turn is caused by the higher risk of being exposed to violence when spending time away from the local neighborhood.

> Simon, a 16-year-old Franklin [a disadvantaged neighborhood] resident who has experienced many altercations with adolescents from other neighborhoods, rarely leaves his neighborhood anymore. He explains how leaving can easily lead to a violent confrontation if he is not with a group of friends.
>
> (Harding, 2009: 455)

By contrast, adolescent boys of Lower Mills, an advantaged Boston neighborhood, do not link identity and community membership to their local neighborhood in the same way. Harding argues that that risk of violence leads to a situation wherein grown men feel the obligation to protect the community, which in turn creates tighter bonds between adolescent boys and their elderly peers:

> Why do older adolescent males and young adults in Franklin and Roxbury Crossing attend to younger teens? First, they see it as their duty to look out for the younger adolescents and children in the neighborhoods with which they so strongly identify … They learned this behavior from adults and from the youths who came before. They also see this guardian and friendship behavior as a way to keep the neighborhood safer, to keep the peace and prevent the drama that conflicts can create.
>
> (Harding, 2009: 457)

While the very rationale for creating closer bonds across age groups in the local neighborhood mirrors the failure to provide a robust housing market, i.e., the risk of violence is what in fact restricts the geographical movement of adolescent boys, there are additional undesirable effects. Adults who go to work or participate in educational activities spend less time in the neighborhood, and are thus less visible.[3] In contrast, Harding (2009: 459) says, the older peers who are available and visible, and who can provide some measure of protection, are seldom positive role models, "although not for lack of good intentions" (Harding, 2009: 459). Harding argues that this bias in with whom adolescent boys forge relations with has many consequences, including expectations regarding romantic relationships with girls. Adult men in disadvantaged neighborhoods tend to take a skeptical to negative view of girls and women as they themselves have negative experiences in many cases. The boys in the disadvantaged neighborhoods thus tend to "approach potential girlfriends with hesitation, expecting them to try to take advantage of the relationship in some way" (Harding, 2009: 460). In contrast, the boys in the Lower Mills approach these relationships with "more positive expectations, expecting most girls to be 'good girls'" (Harding, 2009: 460).

Harding's (2009) study show that the exclusion from robust housing market affects African American and Latin communities far beyond concerns regarding the cost and quality of the housing facilities as such. In poorer neighborhoods, the imminent risk of being exposed to violence are supportive of neighborhood identities that may restrict the residents' capacity or willingness to participate in extramural social activities, which thus create a culture or an identity wherein a negative view of outsiders and xenophobia are nourished. The closer ties between adolescents and adults in disadvantaged neighborhoods may also affect the very family structure and the expectations regarding romantic relationships as younger boys are socialized to have low expectations regarding their relationships with girls and women on the basis of the previous (negative) experiences of the adult men being visible and available in community. In summary, it is possible to draw the conclusion that sub-optimal housing markets shape everyday life of low-income communities in a variety of ways, at times directly, but in most cases more indirectly as the overrepresentation of individuals with a checkered track record in the labor market and in social life more widely may create low expectations, not only on individuals but also in the neighborhood itself. Such vicious spirals are complicated to stop once they have gained some traction, and consequently housing policy needs to consider many conditions and effects to avoid a situation that discriminates individuals regardless of their personal merits and aspirations.

If Harding (2009) shows that residents in disadvantaged neighborhoods individually choose to restrict their geographical movements as the risk of being exposed to violence is a factual condition that needs to be handled, several studies show that outsiders, such as real estate agents, also contribute to segregation and the undesirable effects it causes. Besbris and Faber (2017: 861) show that real estate agents are incentivized to increase home values as they are compensated on the basis of the price paid for the properties they sell, but this wealth generation is itself contingent on racial and ethnic segregation as social homophily is assumed to be the dominant preference among home buyers. That is, individual real estate agents may dislike racism or segregation in private, but in their professional work, such beliefs or preferences matters little for the outcome, which perpetuates the geographical separation of racial and ethnic communities. Korver-Glenn (2018) shows that in some cases, the risk assessment tools, based on algorithms that are concealed from outsiders and used by mortgage lending companies, serve to preserve racial and ethical segregation in a similar manner. Fannie Mae, one of the major US federal mortgage lending institutes, has developed software called Collateral Underwriter that many mortgage lending companies use in their day-to-day work. The Collateral Underwriter flags any deviation from what is regarded as a regular home purchase (e.g., a Latino family buying a home in a neighborhood with primarily Latino residents), i.e., what is consistent with available market data. The mortgage underwriting process, part of the purchasing family's access to the credit that is necessary for closing the deal, is thus premised on historical home purchasing records, and that record is for historical reasons ethnically biased. What was originally intended to serve as a tool for the mortgage lending company thus tends to amplify racial and ethnic segregation in ways that the developer of, e.g., the Collateral Underwriter software presumably never intended, and possibly not even though of as a plausible scenario. Nevertheless, under all conditions, throughout the housing sales process, real estate agents generate substantial effects. In what Korver-Glenn (2018: 650) calls "minority areas," "a narrowed pool of competition for for-sale homes" results in lower home sales prices, which in turn is fed back into the algorithms that determine the risk assessment calculation of mortgage lending institutions. In contrast, in "white neighborhoods," a "broad pool of competition for for-sale homes" results in higher prices and higher ratings in terms of risk management calculations, which creates "systematically higher home values" that "interlock and compound advantage" (Korver-Glenn, 2018: 650–651).

Korver-Glenn (2018) here points at one of the major challenges in societies wherein racial and ethnic prejudice has been the case, that even in the case wherein individual actors such as real estate agents do not have racist beliefs, or preferences supportive of racist beliefs, i.e., they are neither "consciously racist, nor hostile toward minorities" (Bartram, 2021: 766), they may nonetheless act within social and institutional structures that produce "racism without racists" (Bartram, 2021: 766). As in the case of the Collateral Underwriter, presumably developed to act as a device supportive of the home mortgage lender who is incentivized to either minimize risk, or to keep calculated risk at a predefined level, but de facto participating in a chain of activities that in the end preserves racial and ethnic segregation, algorithm-based decision making has performative qualities that need to be examined after the fact and on an aggregated level.

Fortunately, not all participants in housing market activities actively but unintendedly contribute to the preservation of segregation. Bartram (2021: 760) studies the role of building inspectors in the Chicago housing market, and proposes that this occupational community actively contributes to a housing market that is fairer by assessing repairment and refurbishing needs based on what they regard as what is practically possible to accomplish, rather than on the basis of strictly adhering to what legal frameworks and regulatory statutes prescribe. Bartram (2021: 760) here distinguishes between what he calls *malign neglect*, what the inspectors regard as the property owners' failure to maintain their housing stock as expected, and *defensible disrepair*, the inspectors' tolerance of minor failures to follow the protocol, yet being excusable as the owners of the property has low or moderate income. This means that the inspectors would regard, say, a broken window in a "wealthy, single-family homes in White neighborhoods" as being more problematic than in a house in a low-income minority neighborhood. Some would say that the inspectors' lower tolerance for neglect in wealthy neighborhoods is itself mirroring the lower expectations held regarding self-discipline, law and order, etc. in low-income neighborhoods, thus being a form of racism or ethnic prejudice, but Bartram (2021) defends the operative distinction between malign neglect and defensible disrepair on the grounds that the inspectors have a detailed understanding of the local housing market and the consequences for the tenants if the property owner fails to follow the formal instructions. In some cases, the social welfare is optimized if there is a more lenient assessment of the property owners' facilities management performance. "[I]nspectors are more likely to infer defensible disrepair in communities of color" (Bartram, 2021: 780). This means that the inspectors' assessments are "racialized," but in a way that "protects low-income communities of color, in the short term at least" (Bartram, 2021: 780).

In the end, building inspectors play an important role in preserving qualitative housing in more advantaged neighborhoods, while keeping the housing stock habitable and safe in disadvantaged neighborhoods. The latter objective is contingent on the racial segregation of the Chicago housing market, but rather than further depressing the household economy of the tenants in such neighborhoods, the inspectors can tolerate evidence of defensible disrepair if they, e.g., believe that the property owner would raise the rent if renovation work is made, as the property owner lacks the funds needed to finance the activities, and that higher rents would result in evictions. As eviction cases would reduce housing welfare for certain household in excess of the housing welfare benefit that the renovation work generates for the tenants having the capacity to pay the higher rent, inspectors choose to make a more lenient assessment of the state of the property. In summary, American housing markets and housing markets elsewhere may be marked by racial and ethnic segregation on a structural level, but it does not mean that each and every social actor participating in housing markets has racist beliefs or preferences derived from such beliefs, in private. On the contrary, it is quite likely that structural conditions, path dependencies, and various forms of lock-in effects are the primary sources of the unequal housing markets that Taylor (2018) calls attention to.

Market practices in the shadow of housing market policy

Households as housing markets speculators

It can be safely assumed that housing ownership policy is designed on the basis of the "one household-one home" ideal, i.e., there is a diminishing return on investment in policy promoting home ownership beyond the primary residential home. Policy makers may not actively object to or oppose the ownership of, say, cabins and summer homes, but the primary political benefits from home ownership can be stipulated to be secured on the basis of the first residential home being purchased. Despite the lack of policy-based incentives, studies from, e.g., the US show that households at times regard the housing market as a platform for the investment of surplus finance capital (rather than investing in stocks, bonds, collectable items, etc.). This in turn creates systemic risks in the economy if private speculators may not only invest the residual finance capital but may in fact jeopardize their household economy. If this is a marginal phenomenon that would not affect housing prices on a systemic level, individual choices to speculate in housing leave regulatory agencies indifferent and/or agnostic regarding such speculation, but if the speculation is widespread and systematic, it may generate undesirable financial or even macroeconomic consequences.

Kaplan, Mitman, and Violante (2020: 3288) provide evidence that shows that "expectations about future house price appreciation" played a central role for the "macroeconomic dynamics" that resulted in the Great Recession. As Kaplan, Mitman, and Violante (2020: 3289) remark, "direct evidence" indicating the role of expectations in the boom and bust of housing market "is scarce," but the evidence that exists points convincingly to widely shared optimistic expectations among households, investors, and lenders (Kaplan, Mitman, and Violante, 2020: 3289). Also the media (Soo, 2018) and financial traders (Cheng, Raina, and Xiong, 2014) shared this optimism regarding soaring housing market price. Kaplan, Mitman, and Violante (2020: 3287) show that shifts in beliefs about future housing demand are the "dominant force" behind documented swings in house prices. This is turn increases the incentives to purchase homes as the cost of renting a residential home become relatively higher if housing price appreciations are considered. An additional effect of overoptimistic expectations regarding future housing market prices is that households owning their residential homes regard their non-liquid asset holdings as a source of wealth, and thus expand their consumption accordingly. Kaplan, Mitman, and Violante (2020: 3287) find that "the boom and bust in house prices" directly accounts for roughly half of the corresponding boom and bust in nondurable expenditures, which means that housing markets dynamics, including periods of turbulence, have repercussions throughout the economic system (see, e.g., Mian and Sufi, 2018). In addition, sheer speculation of housing markets further propels the boom-bust cycle, an issue that Goldstein (2018) explores.

Goldstein (2018) reports that in 2003, the US residential loan origination reached its local peak at $3.9 trillion in debt, which represented "a 600 percent increase over 1995 levels." Anecdotally, Goldstein (2018: 1109) writes, at the height of the housing boom in 2005, "there were more real estate agents than farmers in the United States": the harvesting of housing markets replaced the harvesting of fields. Goodman and Mayer (2018: 46. Table 4) show that such an upsurge in speculation was primarily driven by soaring housing market prices and revenues collected on housing asset holdings. In 2006, at the height of the housing market boom, the return on housing ownership and resell was estimated to be 24.9 percent (30.6 percent after tax benefits); in comparison, the return on an indexed S&P500 stock holding portfolio was 12.5 percent, and an average bond portfolio return was 5 percent. Entering and exiting the housing market, or any other high-speculation market, can be very profitable if the asset holding period is optimized.

As Goldstein (2018: 1109) remarks, investors in real estate need to both examine the actual location "in a concrete social place," including its local and regional labor market, amenities, and income levels, and economic prospects for the region wherein they invest. Furthermore, real estate investors also need to pay close attention to second-order constructs of relevance for their investment, i.e., they need to assess how much they believe *other* investors or home buyers would be willing to pay for housing assets. This means that housing speculation is largely a local affair, that is, it is possible to detect regions and local areas wherein housing asset speculation has been rampant, and, potentially, to explain such local housing bubbles on the basis of specific market expectations related to local and regional condition.

Goldstein (2018) examines the local housing market in 1,566 US municipalities over the 2000–2006 period, and finds that that the more "laissez-faire development style" in the region and in the municipality housing market, the higher the proportion of "non-professional investment" (NOI) (Goldstein, 2018: 1127). Las Vegas, Nevada, was the fastest growing US city in the first decade of the new millennium, and the identity of the city has been that of "a site of unfettered economic freedom, where risk-takers can gamble and make it" (Goldstein, 2018: 1116). Such local political cultures encouraged NOI. Goldstein (2018: 1131) also found a "sizable autoregressive effect" inasmuch an initial growth in NOI resulted in an additional 6.6 to 7.5 percent activity during the subsequent year. Bayer, Mangum, and Roberts (2021: 611) examine the role of such "investor contagion" in housing markets, being part of what Burnside, Eichenbaum, and Rebelo (2016: 1089) refer to as the "social dynamics" of housing market booms and busts, on the basis of a sample of "nearly five million housing transactions" in the Los Angeles metropolitan area in 1988–2012, complemented by two samples from San Francisco and Boston, including 1.1 million and 584,000 transactions, respectively. In the sample, *circa* 45 percent of all purchases are made by institutions and are consequently excluded. In the US, during the housing boom of 2003–2006, it is estimated that 40–50 percent of all homes purchase in states that experienced the largest housing booms were "investment properties" (Bayer, Mangum, and Roberts, 2021: 610). Furthermore, consistently with Goldstein's (2018) results, "[m]uch of this investment was made by new investors," including, e.g., households speculating on rising housing prices (Bayer, Mangum, and Roberts, 2021: 610). The analysis of the empirical material reveals "sizable contagion effects," i.e., households that experience local speculation purchases (defined as investment made within 0.10 miles from the residential home) are more likely to invest in housing. Households located in areas where housing speculation is taking place have a higher probability of investing at 8 percent within the next year and up to 14 percent over three years (Bayer, Mangum, and Roberts, 2021: 612). Such measures are indicative of the self-propelling growth of NOI as more non-professionals are eager to jump the gravy train. Taken together, the mid-2000s' housing bubble, wherein "hundreds of thousands of Americans" became real estate entrepreneurs, "buying millions of homes for short-term profit" (Goldstein, 2018: 1137), was predicated on "broad institutional changes that made investment an increasingly dominant idiom of economic action and reconceived houses as financial assets" (Goldstein, 2018: 1137).

What Goldstein (2018) refers to as laissez-faire political and economic doctrines thus played a key role in promoting NOI, which prior to the financial crisis generated wealth for certain private investors but also generated much economic and political turmoil and served to transfer economic value from primarily low-income household to housing mortgage lenders. An important policy issue question is then if speculation is conducive of economic welfare or if it needs to be subject to regulatory practices. Simsek (2021: 360) reviews the literature on speculation in finance markets and concludes that there are "negative externalities that the speculators induce on the rest of society." One study indicates that individual investors who trade too frequently tend to have a poor investment performance relative to investors with a well-diversified portfolio, due to "excessive risks, transaction costs, and poor timing to buy or sell" (Simsek, 2021: 360). A study examining Taiwanese market data suggests that individual investors trading losses amount to no less than 2 percent of Taiwan's GDP over a five-year period (Simsek, 2021: 360). Such results indicate that finance market traders are not rational decision makers as has been proposed in, e.g., the free market theory literature. On the contrary, speculation generates externalities that reduce the economic welfare and incur costs for other market actors, and consequently Simsek (2021: 362) suggests that the scholarly literature provides only "a weak rationale for allowing unrestricted speculation."

The supply side view: legal reforms and managerial practices

One legal device used in many American states and cities to promote the supply of affordable housing is Installment Land Contracts (ILCs). An ILC is a so-called "rent-to-own housing contract," being "a seller-financed agreement" wherein the buyer pays "[a] relatively small down payment and then pays off the remainder of the purchase price plus interest in installments, while the seller retains title until the loan is repaid in full" (Miltko, 2020: 2276). Under these agreements, the tenant-buyer should have the full protection of the landlord–seller during the period of the lease, but in practice, studies show, that is not always the case as law enforcement is weak. ILCs became popular in the second half of the nineteenth century, when railroad companies began to sell off the land they had acquired in the course of the building of the transcontinental railways (Miltko, 2020: 2282). Eventually, ILCs were used in cities with a great demand for affordable housing facilities, and in, e.g., Chicago, between 1934 and 1968, an estimated 86 percent of all homes purchased by black families were based on ILCs (Miltko, 2020: 2283). After the financial crisis of 2008 and the Great Recession that lingered on for a decade, ILCs have again become a more widespread housing finance device (Miltko, 2020: 2291), and studies reveal substantial evidence of predatory lending practices in the period (Akers and Seymour, 2018).[4] For instance, tenants with ILCs have paid interests rates in the 8–10 percent span, being roughly twice the interest rate for the federally backed bank loans provided by Government State Enterprises such as Freddie Mac and Fannie Mae (Miltko, 2020: 2291). Furthermore, the housing stock subject to ILCs is often in a state of disrepair, Miltko (2020: 2291) writes: "The homes being sold via ILC are often substandard—rotting wood, black mold, broken windows, and failing foundations are just a few of the concerns faced by ILC buyers." These material conditions taken aside, there is also limited evidence that ILC housing financing is effective in transferring home ownership rights to low-income households. A study showed that in one county, since 1989, less than one-fifth of ILC buyers had managed to finally purchase their homes. In contrast, of the mortgage loans originated between 2004 and 2008, only 6.4 percent of mortgagors nationwide had lost their homes by February 2011, two and a half years after the financial crisis (Miltko, 2020: 2301–2302).

The poor track records of ILC in terms of providing affordable housing and being supportive of home ownership is partially explained by weak legal protection of the tenants/tenant-buyers and an inadequate law enforcement. As Miltko (2020: 2310) notices, there is a factual difference between law as it is written and the law "on the ground": "[B]ecause of the differences in how landlord-tenant law is written and how it is enforced, the various protections provided by statutes and judicial decisions are nearly meaningless for most tenants" Miltko, 2020: 2311). Furthermore, the informational costs related to the ILC housing finance device further complicates the situation, which means that tenants/tenant–buyers oftentimes require legal counsel to have their rights protected. In the state of Texas, there are in fact strong protections against predatory business practices in state law, but despite such statutes, the law on the ground has failed to "meaningfully protect buyers in part because they lack information about their legal rights" (Miltko, 2020: 2316). Based on such evidence and conditions, Miltko (2020: 2318–2319) advocates that ILC housing finance should be subject to the same strict regulation that applies to other forms of housing finance contracts. To a high extent, the current ILC housing finance model relies on mandatory disclosure and complex legal schemes that de facto undermine the legal protection of tenants/tenant–buyers. "As it stands now," Miltko (2020: 2319) writes, "the ILC exists as a uniquely exploitative tool for sellers." Therefore, policy makers, judges, and scholars should be aware that currently sellers appear to be attracted by ILCs as it provides them with possibilities to lend money on predatory terms, which add costs for several constituencies throughout the economic system.

Technological changes and new market conditions as the drivers of the decline of affordable housing

In scholarly circles, there has been a comparably modest interest in the loss of affordable housing and in its consequences (Desmond and Bell (2015: 16). This is surprising given mounting evidence that points at the loss of social and economic welfare derived from soaring housing costs. In fact, the lack of affordable housing is "among the most pressing issues facing the urban poor" (Desmond and Bell, 2015: 16). Furthermore, the American housing market is by and large unregulated, with only 1.7 percent of all renter-occupied units being rent controlled by 2013, according to the American Housing Survey (Desmond and Bell, 2015: 17). This is unfortunate from the view of the tenants as empirical evidence indicates that housing conditions have improved considerably in American cities that increase the regulatory control of housing markets and that enforce the existing legislation (Desmond and Bell, 2015: 21). In the absence of regulatory oversight, American households are largely exposed to the whims of landlords, and, e.g., so-called "informal evictions" wherein landlords are "[f]orcibly removing tenants (e.g., by demanding them to move, changing their locks) beyond the purview of the court" (Desmond and Bell, 2015: 24) are relatively common. In many cases, families that include children are affected, and empirical evidence suggests that households with children are almost three times more likely to receive an eviction judgment than adult-only households, after a number of factual conditions are considered (Desmond and Bell, 2015: 25). The UN Declaration of the Rights of the Child (enacted in 1989) is apparently neglected in such cases.

Recently, platform economy actors such as Airbnb, aggressively promoting what is called a "sharing economy" model, have further contributed to a situation wherein affordable housing is in dramatic decline. Airbnb has a "corrosive effects on fair and affordable housing," Lee (2016: 253), discussing the case of Los Angeles, argues (for the case of Sydney, where a similar situation is observed, see, e.g., Gurran and Phibbs, 2017). It is noteworthy that urban studies scholars and legal scholars dispute the legitimacy of Airbnb's business practices and their consequences. Similar to the case of the mobility services provided by the ride-sharing platform company Uber, several legal scholars tend to take a more affirmative view of Airbnb. In contrast, critics argue that Airbnb has "[e]nabled tourism accommodations to penetrate residential neighborhoods, which creates conflicts between visitors and residents, displacing permanent accommodations in high-demand cities and exacerbating affordability pressures for low-income groups" (Gurran and Phibbs, 2017: 80). Edelman and Geradin (2016: 314), two legal scholars, argue that the negative externalities of the Airbnb business model "seem modest"—mostly in terms of a bit of extra traffic, or an increased presence of strangers in the neighborhood—and that these intrusions primarily affect public spaces. Furthermore, as residential homes are also financial assets (which the critics are the first to admit as that condition is part of their primary argument against sharing economy platforms such as Airbnb), a prohibition on occasional short-term rentals would infringe on the legal rights of the owner of the house and would potentially affect the resell value of the house (Edelman and Geradin, 2016: 314). Based on this line of argument, locating contractual rights as stipulated by contract law and the integrity and property law rights of the owner of real estate, a ban on Airbnb would overreach the limits of political and regulatory authority.

Kaplan and Nadler (2017: 106) take an alternative perspective and argue that Airbnb's growth does not of necessity "come at the expense of the hotel industry." On the contrary, it may be the case that the size of the pie grows overall, so that also other industries can obtain a larger slice. Empirical evidence from, e.g., New York City indicates that Airbnb guests stay longer, and spend larger nominal sums of money than regular hotel guests do (Kaplan and Nadler, 2017: 105). Furthermore, Kaplan and Nadler (2017: 107) argue that new entrepreneurial companies that are regarded as a threat to incumbent businesses are likely to face resistance from, as in this case, "well-funded coalition of landlords and hotel-industry insiders, which plans to spend millions of dollars on a public campaign criticizing Airbnb." For instance, the hotel industry has "stiffly resisted Airbnb's voluntary efforts to facilitate tax collection on behalf of its hosts," despite having initially criticized Airbnb for supporting tax avoidance for its own benefit (Kaplan and Nadler, 2017: 110). This campaign to undermine Airbnb's attempt to correct a situation that generate market disadvantages suggests that the hotels industry's opposition is "rooted in protectionism rather than principle," Kaplan and Nadler (2017: 110) propose. In summary, similar to the case of Uber, Kaplan and Nadler (2017) are concerned that innovative business models and sharing economy platforms that provide individual car owners and house owners with a market making device that they can benefit from financially will be fiercely resisted by incumbent industries with deep pockets and considerable political connections, which in the end will protect the status quo, and thus reduce the dynamics of the economy in both the specific industry and on the aggregated level.

Unsurprisingly, low-income households are struck the hardest by housing market changes derived from technological developments, but studies of, e.g., the Italian housing market indicate that middle class households today also rely on "intergenerational" support to enable home ownership (Manzo, Druta, and Ronald, 2019). "For many [younger Italians], the tradition of buying a home before marriage has thereby become an unachievable aspiration, marking a shift from previous generations" (Manzo, Druta, and Ronald, 2019: 523; see also Forrest and Hirayama, 2018). Crawford and McKee (2018) argue that these differentials in intergenerational housing welfare may generate considerable consequences in terms of the trust in and reliance on civic institutions and state-controlled authorities. Crawford and McKee (2018: 184), studying the Scottish housing market, introduce the concept of "housing aspirations" to denote the socio-economic expectations (including, e.g., home ownership) that families located in different social strata can justify on reasonable grounds. Furthermore, Crawford and McKee (2018: 185) introduce the term *hysteresis* (adapted from Pierre Bourdieu, but generally meaning the incapacity to adapt to changing conditions) to denote the situation wherein housing aspirations are not consistent with current housing market conditions, i.e., a gap emerges between "what individuals and groups subjectively want, and the objective chances of their realization." Under current conditions, there is a marked intergenerational decline in "housing welfare" in Scotland, Crawford and McKee (2018: 187) report:

> 'Marginal professionals' [e.g., freelance workers with limited possibilities for predicting long-term income] can today only dream of the home ownership opportunities which were readily available to the working classes during the period of transition from an industrial to a financially based economy.

For policy makers, the failure to regulate the housing market so that median income households can afford a housing standard that is consistent over generations is a key challenge as it may harm the belief in the virtue of fiscal discipline and other social norms supportive of the welfare state model. "Hysteresis, the gap between subjective expectations and objective possibilities … will undoubtedly result in growing disappointment for those increasingly unable to realize their dream of home ownership," Crawford and McKee (2018: 194) predict.

The challenge to provide legal protection of low-income households' housing welfare

Given a shrinking pool of affordable housing units, and alternative uses of the available housing stock derived from platform economy innovations, the legal protection of, e.g., tenants become a key issue for policy makers to consider. Unfortunately, studies show that tenants enjoy limited legal protection, even in the case where they are represented by a lawyer. Summers (2020: 149) examines a data set from New York City, the largest rental market in the US, wherein tenants have the right to rent abatement on the basis of the so-called warranty of habitability clause in US legislation, intended to protect tenants against landlords that neglect their property. The analysis reveals that less than 2 percent of tenants who had "meritorious claims" received rent abatements. Even in the case where the court ruled that landlords were held responsible for "hazardous," or even "immediately hazardous" Housing Code violations, only 7 percent of the tenants needed to pay lower rents. New York State courts have broad authority to order the Housing Code enforcement agency "to perform an inspection of the unit" (Summers, 2020: 201), but despite the legislator's intention to protect tenants, in the end, "landlords are rarely facing financial consequences for neglecting their properties" (Summers, 2020: 193). Summers (2020: 149) calls attention to what she refers to as the "warranty of habitability operationalization gap" in US legislation, being indicative of how law enforcement is prevented by the unwillingness of landlords to cooperate with courts, and their failure to honor the legislator's intentions.

The decline of affordable housing is also associated with homelessness. Desmond and Bell (2015: 27) report that in 2013, roughly 1 in 500 Americans were homeless. At the same time as the stock of affordable housing is in decline, homelessness has also declined in the US: between 2007 and 2013, for example, "unsheltered homelessness declined by 23%" (Desmond and Bell, 2015: 27). Such evidence is puzzling and merits further scholarly inquiry. At the same time as homelessness was reduced in the period, economic welfare declined considerably for a number of groups, and not least for black and Hispanic families: between 2007 and 2010, during the Great Recession, the average black family experienced a 31 percent reduction in wealth, and the average Hispanic family experienced a comparable reduction of 44 percent. In comparison, the average white family experienced an 11 percent reduction in welfare.

Regardless of the decline in economic and social welfare caused by the decline in affordable housing, the legal system is unsupportive of more strict regulatory control. For instance, in the case *Lindsey v. Normet* (1972), the US Supreme Court stated that:

> We do not denigrate the importance of decent, safe, and sanitary housing. But the Constitution does not provide judicial remedies for every social and economic ill. We are unable to perceive in that document any constitutional guarantee of access to dwellings of a particular quality.

The conventional wisdom is that this Supreme Court decision foreclosed any federal constitutional positive right to housing (Desmond and Bell, 2015: 27). In the US then, housing is a matter of market pricing and contractual relations outside of the realm of constitutional rights, i.e., housing policy "drifted into shadowy realms of the marketplace" (Peterson, 2019: 1185) wherein it is subject to only limited public oversight, with certain consequences. Taken together, the current situation wherein the loss of affordable housing is at a critical level, there would perhaps be some room for legal or regulatory reforms to better adjust the regulatory system to changes in, e.g., the global finance industry, wherein mortgage lending and the securitization of financial assets with long maturation (say, in the range of 30 years) are today standard business practices. The interest for political reform still seem modest, so significant changes are unlikely to appear anytime soon.

Legal and regulatory reform and corporate activities derived therefrom in housing markets

The insights that affordable housing has been undermined by deregulatory reform that per se was intended to promote home ownership is indicative of how policy making generates unintended or unanticipated consequences. To just explain the decline of affordable housing on the basis of failed or inadequate policy making would still be to exclude business practices "on the ground," and to ignore how policies are translated into business models and practices that directly affect households and their financial situation. Consistent with Riles' (2010: 797) claim that finance industry practices need to be understood as a form of "explicit politics" that reveal a "candid, pedestrian, and on-the-surface quality," being scholars' domain of expertise to examine, the decline of affordable housing cannot only be explained on the basis of some "grand theory of capitalism," derived from a finance theory enactment of economic relations (Riles, 2010: 795). Instead, corporate practices, largely justified by legal and regulatory reform, are to be examined to shed light on why housing prices reach unprecedented levels across of variety of jurisdictions.

Policy makers are fond of using market-based reforms to promote affordable housing policies and to translate abstract policy decisions into business practices. As the credit-supply shock explanation for rising housing prices has been firmly established, a corollary question is how the increased credit supply committed to housing production and mortgage lending actually trickles down to market level interactions and contracts. One condition comparably little attended to in the scholarly literature is the growth of alternative ways to incorporate business ventures in the finance-led economy. Soener and Nau (2019) examine the growth of the "Limited Liability Company" (LLC) and the Limited Partnership (LP) as comparably new vehicles for business practices. As Soener and Nau (2019: 400) remark, the growth of these legal entities was considerable in the 1990–2012 period: "Between 1990 and 2012, the number of limited liability companies (LLCs) and limited partnerships (LPs) in the United States increased by more than 750 per cent—far faster than other forms of economic organization including traditional corporations."

Soener and Nau (2019: 401) portray LLCs and LPs as a specific species of "hybrid businesses" that provide many of the benefits that a limited liability corporation granted by the state includes but that ensure secrecy that benefits certain owner interests; the "legal-organizational structure" of LLCs and LPs combines benefits of corporate status like limited liability but without burdens like "full public disclosures, rigid governance structure and double taxation" (Soener and Nau, 2019: 401). The rise of these legal entities is by no means "an inevitable process," Soener and Nau (2019: 402) suggest. On the contrary, the legal entity LLC was developed in Panama, a well-documented tax haven, and in 1977, the State of Wyoming, following an intense lobbying campaigns, passed laws that enabled LLCs to be incorporated in the state (Soener and Nau, 2019: 402). Like in many other cases of corporate legislation, grievances from legal and economic institutions that compete over incorporated businesses result in a "race to the bottom" phenomenon (with Cary's, 1974, much-cited term), wherein states and overseas jurisdictions gradually bet lower to attract new businesses. More specifically, legal scholars have been concerned with the "weak governance rules" that applies to both LLCs and LPs on a stand-alone basis (Soener and Nau, 2019: 410). Needless to say, corporate restructuring has been widely applied to benefit corporate interests. Soener and Nau's (2019: 412) review of the annual reports of all publicly traded Fortune 100 companies for the years 2014–2015 revealed that 90 percent of these companies have at least one LLC subsidiary, and that nearly 50 percent have at least one LP subsidiary. On average, Fortune 100 firms have no fewer than 28 LLC subsidiaries (and with great variation in the sample) and just over two LP subsidiaries (Soener and Nau, 2019: 412). Such evidence underlines the role of corporate restructuring on the basis of legal reform.

Travis (2019) more specifically examines the role of LLCs in the US home rental market, in many cases being the only possible housing form for low-income families in many jurisdictions as their real wage income excludes them from home ownership when housing prices escalate. First, Travis (2019: 143) documents a growth in corporate interest in rental properties over the 1991–2015 period in the US. Over the period, the proportion of rental properties owned by unincorporated individual has declined from 90 to 75 percent. In the same period, LLCs have become more prevalent owners of rental properties, and by the mid-2000s, "the LLC had become the most popular business organization in the United States, with more new LLCs formed each year than corporations" (Travis, 2019: 146). LLCs provide many benefits for rental properties owners, and they are often viewed as "an easy-to-use legal tool that allows owners to circumscribe liability and protect their assets" (Travis, 2019: 147). Travis' (2019) study shows that LLCs are used to protect real estate owners against legal claims made by the tenants, or city planners and building inspectors. These problems are particularly pronounced in low-income neighborhoods, Travis (2019: 163) remarks: "Adverse selection on property characteristics, which concentrates LLC ownership among low-end properties and in high-poverty neighborhoods, suggests poorer tenants are most likely to face diminished legal recourse." On balance, LLC ownership is "positively associated with indicators of property neglect" (Travis, 2019: 164). This condition is not merely accidental as the choice of the LLC as a legal entity provides both anonymity and liability protections for LLC owners, and consequently, cities and municipalities, acting on behalf of tenants, therefore encounter considerable obstacles when they seek to hold landlords accountable for "substandard housing conditions or tenant abuse" (Travis, 2019: 165). The concern derives from the fact that cities and municipalities in many cases adopted LLC statutes as a means to attract finance capital to renew the urban environment. Limited liability has long been regarded as a mechanism that attracts capital to risky entrepreneurial projects, but when subsidies and insurances tip over in the favor of, e.g., LLC owners, the net social and economic welfare generated on such public investment becomes marginal, or even results in a transfer of wealth from, e.g., taxpayers to private businesses. In an economic regime that operates under such conditions, limited liability becomes "a source of moral hazard," Travis (2019: 144) proposes.

The corporate restructuring in European and Australian housing markets

The increased use of new corporate entities such as LLCs and LPs has also been observed in European housing markets. Fields and Uffer (2016) report that when Goldman Sachs' real estate arm Whitehall Funds started to operate in the lucrative Berlin housing market in 2004, they created a "a herd-like movement of international investment firms following the money to Berlin's rental housing." In the 2004–2007 period, ending with the global finance industry stalemate in 2008, a veritable self-reinforcing speculation bubble occurred in the Greater Berlin area. This speculation boom did not benefit the Berlin residents as the high-leverage investment strategies favored by international investors were associated with "reduced maintenance, physical and social deterioration, and the increasing isolation of low-income households unable to move to better housing" (Fields and Uffer, 2016: 1498). The greater Berlin area may be an idiosyncratic case for apparent historical reasons, but studies of other German regions indicates a similar inflow of global finance capital in the period. Botzem and Dobusch (2017) show that three major international finance institutes, UK-based Terra Firma, Fortress, and Cerberus/Goldman Sachs, had acquired ownership over 190,000, 150,000, and 90,000 apartments, respectively, by 2007. All three companies applied the same business model: they acquired undervalued properties, quickly built up a sizeable asset portfolio "with a high degree of borrowed capital," and, in a relatively short period of a few years, organized "a sale or IPO of the entire firm" (Botzem and Dobusch, 2017: 35). In the 2006–2007 period, roughly half of all apartments being sold in Germany were "resales," i.e., one investor bought a bundle of rental apartments from another investor to keep it for a relatively short period to speculate on rises in housing prices (Botzem and Dobusch, 2017: 35).

Botzem and Dobusch (2017) pay specific attention to the German company IMMOFIRM (a pseudonym), which closely followed the business model prescription presented above. As the primary goal of the business activities was to "assemble a sufficiently large stock of real estate assets that was to be taken public," the costs spent on renovation and modernization of the housing facilities "were kept to an absolute minimum" (Botzem and Dobusch, 2017: 36). Next, to minimize the equity needed to acquire a portfolio of real estate assets, most business practices were outsourced, including facility management for nearly all properties, and the handling of cashflow reports to a loan servicing firms (Botzem and Dobusch, 2017: 39). Furthermore, IMMOFIRM's legal holding company was headquartered in an offshore tax haven, primarily for tax reasons, and the business activities relied on an auditing firm that certified the value of the portfolio of residential property. This certification emphasized two main criteria: operative cash flow and market value. It is noteworthy that each of these two criteria depend heavily on assumptions (e.g., with regard to expected percentage of rental vacancies) and reference values (e.g., market prices paid for similar properties) (Botzem and Dobusch, 2017: 40). Regardless of the risk of inflated market evaluations of the portfolio holdings, the auditing firm's estimates were central to the operational business model. Based on all these business practices and corporate governance choices, IMMOFIRM managed to acquire a portfolio of property assets worth roughly 1 billion euros over a three-year period. It is symptomatic that this accomplishment was made with "virtually no net equity" (Botzem and Dobusch, 2017: 40). In summary, IMMOFIRM is representative of the new return-on-equity driven business, wherein real estate assets are managed like any financial asset. Unfortunately, this business model is at risk to run counter to the interest of city and municipality governments and tenants, as economic values are extracted on the basis of the minimized costs to maintain the housing stock, and tax evasion.

Bryan, Rafferty, Toner, and Wright (2017: 502) discuss the commercial property market situation in Australia, and they notice that, e.g., retail space, warehouses, and similar property intended for business practices have been "integrated into global capital markets." Thirty years ago, the major clients of commercial builders were governments, large corporations, and insurance companies, who typically "built-to-own or built-to-occupy or manage" (Bryan, Rafferty, Toner, and Wright, 2017: 502). Over time, finance market actors such as pension funds and hedge funds without any necessary direct connection to the local and regional industry have become more active as commercial property owners. Their primary interest is to take advantage of the "financial performance of buildings," but they are, unlike the traditional property developers and owners, less concerned with the responsibilities that are assumed to be included in direct ownership of such assets. More recently, securitized investment vehicles such as Real Estate Investment Trusts (REITs), which examine real estate property as a specific asset class to be compared with any other investment, have entered the market. The managers of these REITs are less incentivized to be concerned with the overall economic and social welfare of the community than the traditional property owners were, who oftentimes conducted business on a local and regional basis, and therefore could not take advantage of global property asset investment opportunities. In Bryan, Rafferty, Toner, and Wright's (2017) account, a finance theory model propels the property development and ownership industry, and such a business model is less concerned with the user-value of real estate.

Wijburg and Aalbers (2017) identify "three waves" in the restructuring of the German housing market over time. As they remark, the German "housing system" is often regarded as being somewhat dull and uneventful as it relies on corporatist and non-financialized agreements rather than open finance market activities. In this view, the German housing market is pitted as a counterexample to the more liberal and financialized US housing market (Wijburg and Aalbers, 2017: 968). Subscribing to the "varieties of financialization" perspective (which Van der Zwan, 2014, advocates), Wijburg and Aalbers (2017: 970) propose that financialization is "not a singular, teleological process that unfolds in the same way everywhere," but should rather be understood as being "variegated across time and space and triggers alternative trajectories of change." The first wave of German housing market financialization occurred between the mid-1980s (in the former *Bundesrepublik*, prior to the German unification) and the late 1990s, which naturally called for new housing finance market activities and market regulation reforms to increase the supply of credit to prospect homebuyers. The second wave, which Wijburg and Aalbers (2017: 970) refer to as "financialized privatization," began in the end of the 1990s and included a major structural reform as large parts of "the former social housing sector" were sold to private equity firms and hedge funds. This second episode is by and large consistent with the mainstream (critical) view of housing policy and housing finance activities, which overstate housing units and real estate as a financial asset and as a storage of value. However, at least in the various jurisdictions of the German *Bundesländer*, "making money on subsidized rental housing turned out to be harder than expected" (Wijburg and Aalbers, 2017: 981). Such insights paved the way for the third wave of housing investment, following the finance industry crisis and the Great Recession. In this third regime, a housing boom in German cities coincides with the market entry of a small number of very large real estate companies, all being listed on the stock exchange. The third wave of housing market financialization is thus premised on the rules of the stock market, which makes it easier for regulatory agencies to monitor market fluctuations and systemic risk, conditions that were largely ignored by regulatory agencies and policy makers in the 2003–2007 period, not least in the US. In summary, the most recent prospect for providing affordable housing for German households is to rely on public companies in the real estate sector, which regard such services as being conducive to long-term competitive advantage and bottom line results, most likely assisted by a variety of federal or state-based subsidies and tax exemptions that transfer wealth from tax payers to both individual households and the corporate sector.

Wijburg, Aalbers, and Heeg (2018: 1099) suggest that the financialization of the European housing market has now reached the end of the road inasmuch as several private equity firms' real estate acquisitions are so "over-leveraged" that "the average rent per unit is lower than the cost of servicing the debt per unit." As this is an unsustainable business model, based on speculative investment in markets with high-paced real estate valuation growth, Wijburg, Aalbers, and Heeg (2018) speak about a shift from "Financialization 1.0" to "Financialization 2.0." Whereas the "1.0 phase" business model was geared towards generating revenues on the basis of purely speculative investment strategies, the "2.0 phase" business model increasingly regard housing as a "mainstream commodity" that demands investment, management, and solid public relations: "Unlike private equity funds, listed real estate companies adopt a mid- to long-term approach of managing and maintaining income-producing real estate assets" (Wijburg, Aalbers, and Heeg, 2018: 1003). A new generation of listed real estate companies works on the basis of two complementary strategies to generate a return on equity: they sell housing units at a lucrative price or they rent them out while improving the net value of the portfolio (Wijburg, Aalbers, and Heeg, 2018: 1007). Even though real estate companies are eager to play by the rulebook, and make declarations that they are long-term investors in housing facilities for the benefit of, e.g., tenants, Wijburg,

Aalbers, and Heeg (2018: 1014) still propose that these business practices are neither of necessity more "friendly," nor "patient" as the primary consideration is nonetheless to generate shareholder value. Still, the Financialization 2.0 business model is indicative of how the real estate market has shifted gears as asset holdings are valued on the basis of a more long-term business commitment.

Taken together, the development of new corporate entities such as LLCs and LPs in combination with a low-equity investment strategy have transformed the housing and commercial property markets in ways that on the aggregated level reduce the stock of affordable housing. As in the case of IMMOFIRM, the combination of outsourcing, the use of a overseas tax haven as the domicile for the business operations, and auditing practices based on Fair Value accounting principles (for an overview, see Barker and Schulte, 2016; Power, 2010) that rely on estimates on the basis of fictive or extrapolated market information, is a business school textbook case of how to build a portfolio of assets on the basis of minimal equity investment. Although impressive in terms of economic value creation *ex nihilo*, such business practices arguably run counter to policy makers' intentions to promote home ownership, and, in the absence of possibilities for the former, to provide affordable housing as welfare provision. In the current situation, critics contend that subsidies and lax regulatory control of the housing market directed towards real estate developers and property owners do not optimize social and economic welfare (e.g., Desmond and Wilmers, 2019). The loss of affordable housing is therefore a concern that can be explained on the basis of firm-level business practices, which ultimately serve to demystify the unprecedented rise of housing prices that many policy makers and commentators appear to believe is best explained on the basis of macroeconomic conditions such as demographic conditions or, more simply, a mismatch between supply and the demand in housing markets.

Summary and conclusion

By and large, over the post-World War II period, housing policy has emphasized private ownership but has also recognized the need for handling low net-worth households' need for qualitative housing. Despite the best of intentions, there is today an endemic shortage of affordable housing, and this in turn risks reducing the overall economic welfare as, e.g., highly productive individuals (e.g., educated younger people) cannot afford to "move to opportunity." This policy concern calls for a wider perspective on how political processes may need to be assisted by other economic and financial activities to result in housing welfare in the way stipulated by the policies being enacted and implemented. In the next chapter, this question will be examined in detail. Given the expanding instrumental and structural power of the finance industry (Braun, 2020), it may be that housing policy has overstated the role of the supply of credit, which has been in the interest of housing finance actors, but at the expense of the question regarding how to increase the supply of housing units, especially in metropolitan areas wherein the demand for housing is considerable. This question is of particularly relevant when considering a more general critique regarding the privileges and authority of the finance industry in the contemporary economy, wherein some scholars argue that the finance industry—similar to all other industries in the economic regime of competitive capitalism—is primarily concerned with preserving itself, and to optimize the return on investment, given the current legal, regulatory, and norm-based frameworks. According to Stein:

> The role for financial stability policy arises because the private choices of unregulated banks with respect to money creation are not in general socially optimal. When banks issue cheaper short-term debt, they capture its social benefits, namely, the monetary services it generates for households. However, they do not always fully internalize its costs.[5]
>
> (Stein, 2012: 58)

The finance industry provides credit, which enables households to borrow money to purchase homes, but to only emphasize the credit supply side of the equation—especially since one part has strong incentives to maximize the mortgage lending stock—and to ignore the supply of housing units only results in inflated housing prices, i.e., the affordability of housing evaporates, especially in the "open auction" model that is the standard in, e.g., the Swedish housing market. Prospective house owners face challenges in organizing themselves against, e.g., overlending or to promote a posted price model (as is the case for newly built housing units in Sweden, for the most part) as they have few joint interests besides seeing a more tempered housing finance market being established. Consequently, the instrumental and structural power of the finance industry gradually diminishes the affordable housing stock as the supply of credit is considerable in the financialized economy. In the next chapter, the housing finance nexus (with Fligstein, Brundage and Schultz's, 2017: 884, apt phrase) will be examined in more detail, being the central explanatory model for the affordable housing policy challenge facing policy makers in most Organization for Economic Co-operation and Development (OECD) countries.

Notes

1 Dang, Gorton, and Holmström (2020: 55) report that ABS and MBS are generally treated as safe assets, i.e., they are commonly rated AAA by credit rating agencies. A study published in 2012 demonstrates that, on average, 86.3% of an ABS/MBS deal was rated AAA (Dang, Gorton, and Holmström, 2020: 55).

2 Blackwell and Kohl (2018) examine what they refer to as "national housing finance systems," and identify three different systems, differing in the degree of "credit centralization." First there is the *bond-based finance mode*, wherein housing finance institutions are operating on the basis of finance market lending. This is the most widespread model in coordinated market economies (CMEs), e.g., Germany and the Scandinavian countries, which rely on bank-based mortgage lending, and on the bond market in particular. The second model is the *deposit-based finance mode*, which dominates in liberal market economies (LMEs), including the US, UK, Canada, and Australia. In this mode, deposit-based mortgage institutions that operate off the finance market are the primary mortgage lenders. Third and finally, the *state finance mode* is a model used in Southern

Europe, where the sovereign state provides finance capital, acting through its agencies. The interesting finding is that the LMEs, otherwise characterized as being "market-based," rely on off-market financing activities, whereas CMEs, comparably less reliant on free market transactions, have developed a bond market-based housing finance system, first developed in East Prussia in the nineteenth century and then spreading to, e.g., Denmark and Sweden (Blackwell and Kohl, 2018: 52). Blackwell and Kohl (2018: 51, emphasis in the original) summarize their findings: "*Market-based* countries thus developed housing finance systems which were ostensibly *off market*, whereas the *bank-based* countries developed *bond-based* systems which were very much *market-based*." Based on such counter-intuitive results, further scholarly research on national housing finance systems is welcome.

3 The increased emphasis on neighborhood identity that Harding (2009) emphasizes needs to be contrasted against Browning et al.'s (2021: 214) empirical study material that shows that "household income is positively associated with time-in-neighborhood." That is, the poorer the neighborhood, the less time children spend in the neighborhood. That neighborhood identification is more pronounced at the same time as residents spend more time elsewhere in comparison to more advantaged neighborhoods is unexpected, and needs to be explained on the basis of plausible theory (as in the anecdotal case of expatriates who maintain an overtly romantic and positive image of their former homeland, but without spending much time there). Browning et al. (2021: 214) suggest that their result is robust: "A move from the 10th to the 90th percentile on neighborhood concentrated disadvantage is associated with a 59.6 percent decrease in the expected count of minutes in the neighborhood, corresponding to about 48 minutes at the day level." This translates into a differential of 5.61 fewer hours in the local neighborhood, all things equal, between disadvantaged and "low-disadvantaged" neighborhoods.

4 The conventional wisdom has been that the 2008 financial crisis was the event that triggered a wave of foreclosures when borrowers in sub-prime segment could no longer pay their interests. *The Washington Post* published an article in 2018, arguing that "The housing market was ground zero of the crisis" (Renae Merle, "A Guide to the Financial Crisis—10 Years Later," *Washington Post*, Sept. 10, 2018), cited in Miltko, 2020: 2289). Merle continues: "The market crashed as homeowners with subprime and other troublesome loans defaulted at record levels. Home prices dropped, and millions lost their homes to foreclosure." While this account is substantiated by robust empirical evidence, in the low-end of the US housing market, foreclosures were a systemic feature also prior to 2008, Akers and Seymour (2018: 132) show: "Between 2005 and 2007 mortgage foreclosure inventories ballooned nationwide": "Private entities (i.e., banks and servicers) saw a 156% increase in the number of properties acquired through foreclosure. The GSEs [e.g., Freddie Mac and Fannie Mae] saw their inventory grow 87% while HUD [U.S. Department of Housing and Urban Development] experienced an increase of 56% … With swelling inventories, banks and GSEs accelerated sales on foreclosed homes." Such foreclosures have a devastating effect on local communities, Piskorski, Seru, and Vig (2010: 395) notice, and, they continue, "the reduction in collateral prices can further aggravate financial distress" that affect the wider financial system. That is, Piskorski, Seru, and Vig (2010: 395) argue, "the foreclosure bias" in decisions of servicers of securitized loans may have "exacerbated these social costs of the crisis, warranting intervention." Such calls for the consequences of predatory lending and predatory housing practices have received only limited attention from policy makers. As the immediate effect of such inaction and inertia in policy making and legislative quarters, "[c]hronic eviction is an essential component of the low-income housing market," Akers and Seymour (2018: 129) contend.

5 Stein (2012: 90) emphasizes how the instrumental and structural power of finance industry actors would leave them protected against default and bankruptcy on the basis of the ex post resolution activities organized by the sovereign state or transnational agencies, including bailouts (as being used in 2008; see, e.g., Levitin, 2011): "While society

benefits from this private money creation, banks' private incentives lead them to overdo it, since they do not fully internalize the fire-sales costs that are a by-product of their maturity transformation activities" (Stein, 2012: 90). This condition, which Stein (2012: 90) refers to as "the externality associated with excessive private money creation," justifies robust financial stability regulation; without such steadfast regulatory control and when "left to their own devices" (Stein, 2012: 58), "unregulated banks may engage in excessive money creation and may leave the financial system overly vulnerable to costly crises."

2 The credit formation process and the role of housing production and financing

Introduction

As the previous chapter demonstrates, in the welfare state model, housing policy is intended to provide affordable housing for citizens, but in many cases a failure to accomplish this policy goal has been observed in a number of regions and cities. This policy failure could be interpreted as an indication of a receding welfare state, now increasingly substituted by a "neoliberal" economic policy model that several scholars dismiss *in abstracto* (see, e.g., Rolnik, 2019). However, such a generalized and sweeping explanation for the affordable housing policy failure is unsupported by empirical data. Kerstenetzky and Guedes (2021: 174) show that between 2007 and 2013, in the immediate aftermath of the global finance industry crisis, public social expenditure climbed from 56.6 percent to 58.5 percent of "total government expenditures" in the OECD countries. Furthermore, in the same period, there was a "slight growth in the tax burden," rising from 33.7 percent to 34.5 percent of GDP (Kerstenetzky and Guedes, 2021: 174). The primary critique of neoliberal economic doctrines, that they either hinder domestic redistribution mechanisms or render them theoretically and practically suspicious (see, e.g., Friedman and Rosen, 2020), is not supported by such evidence. On the contrary, the welfare state has played a key role in making "extra effort" in the post-crisis period to keep pace with "the evolution of market poverty" in OECD countries (Kerstenetzky and Guedes, 2021: 185).

Despite the extraordinary efforts to keep poverty levels at bay, the post-crisis period has been characterized by soaring housing prices. Goda, Stewart, and García's (2020) study of economic inequality and housing prices establishes positive correlation and causality between "absolute inequality" and real house prices. Examining the period 1975–2010, Goda, Stewart, and García (2020: 960) propose that increasing income inequality "contributed to the rise in real house prices" in 15 OECD countries. What is important is that increased income inequality and rising real housing prices are not only associated, but that the causality goes in the direction from increased income inequality to housing prices. While rising real housing prices do have positive economic policy effects, not least from a perceived increase in economic welfare on the household level (as discussed above), starkly rising prices render housing unaffordable, being a particularly accentuated concern in the most productive urban areas wherein younger and aspiring individuals,

DOI: 10.4324/9781003244417-4

looking for housing, face considerable difficulties. Furthermore, from an economic inequality perspective, low-income households tend to be excluded from the housing market via limited access to credit in the form of limited mortgage lending (Goda, Stewart, and García, 2020: 943). When combining the results of the studies presented by Kerstenetzky and Guedes (2021) and Goda, Stewart, and García (2020), housing policies and political intentions appear to have limited effect in terms of the supply of affordable housing. That is, rather than primarily being an administrative matter of political deliberations and policy making, affordable housing supply appears to be an economic and, more specifically, a financial concern, derived from the combination of housing supply (including new production of housing), finance market lending to real estate companies, construction industry actors, and households, and the role played by the state-controlled agencies that are supportive of welfare state policy. Unfortunately, to unwind and sort out all the relationships, mutual dependencies, transactions, and interrelations in this field of housing production is a non-trivial challenge. This chapter seeks to point at some of the constitutive features of the housing market that on the one hand is based on the preservation of welfare state's responsibilities vis-à-vis its citizens, while, on the other hand, it generates economic inequalities that result in soaring housing prices and, *eo ipso*, a shrinking pool of affordable housing. In this account, general ideas about "neoliberal" ideas undermining the welfare state are contrasted against a more comprehensive view of a legal-financial economic regime wherein housing assets serve a central role as collateral in the global credit formation process that serves as the vital infrastructure—a bloodstream of sorts—of competitive capitalism. The centrality of housing asset *qua* collateral is, in other words, the key concern for housing policy makers who wish to push down housing prices to benefit either economic growth as highly productive (and oftentimes younger) individuals can afford to settle in metropolitan areas (see, e.g., Florida, 2017; Schleicher, 2017), and to support low-income families' housing welfare.

Prolegomena: finance capital coded in legal contracts

In order to examine the credit formation process, and how housing production and financing are elementary components in this framework, credit needs to be understood as a device within the legal framework established by the sovereign state. In the legal institutionalism view, capital is coded in law, i.e., there is no freestanding credit formation outside of the legal framework. Pistor (2020: 165) here talks about *intangibles*, including, e.g., intellectual property rights (IPRs) or financial assets (say, corporate bonds, US Treasury bills), which are coded in law and "backed by the coercive powers of the state": "[I]ntangibles are wealth producing assets that are coded in law; in the law of contracts and property with additional protections that come from trust, corporate, or bankruptcy law" (Pistor, 2020: 166). The foremost purpose of law is to ensure that the credit formation process runs smoothly, and to protect market actors (both creditors and debtors) against fraud, opportunistic behavior, and other illicit or undesirable acts that impose costs for all agents.

The legal institutionalism view, wherein credit is legal device and formally speaking a contract, is in turn premised on what Ricks (2018: 758) calls the *intermediation paradigm*, a finance industry model wherein banks are primarily (but not exclusively) regarded as intermediaries that are in the business of "'taking funds' from depositors and then 'lending them out.'" In this role, banks and other financial institutions are assumed to play a relatively passive role in terms of channeling finance capital from savers to investors lending finance capital to fund their business projects. According to Ricks (2018), the intermediation paradigm provides an incomplete image of what financial institutions de facto and de jure do, and therefore Ricks introduces what he calls the *money paradigm* to better explain the credit formation process. In this complementary view, financial institutions such as banks do in fact not only distribute a finance capital surplus in the economy but also actively create money as part of their business operations; banks "augment the money supply," Ricks (2018: 758–759) proposes. Fuller (2015), here cited at length, summarizes how housing assets are coded in law, as prescribed by Pistor (2020) but also operating according with what Ricks (2018) calls the money paradigm model:

> When a household receives a mortgage from a bank, it creates an asset that a bank can then sell. But that one transaction for the household could then feed a number of financial sector transactions. In the labyrinth of contemporary financial markets, a bank could borrow from another bank to create a mortgage, chop up that mortgage into a structured financial product, sell it to an off-balance-sheet vehicle, insure the resulting product through a credit derivative, chop that financial derivative into a new structured product, and sell it to another bank—which could purchase it with its own borrowed funds. This process may be confusing, but the end result is simple; many layers of financial sector debt—both on and off balance sheets—can be underpinned by a single household transaction.
>
> (Fuller, 2015: 243)

The differences and divergences between the two paradigms, of great importance for, e.g., policy making and regulatory activities, are noticeable. The intermediation paradigm portrays banks as private institutions, and consequently the finance market activities should be regulated on basis of this proposition, e.g., bankruptcy law would be the foremost legal mechanism to eliminate defaulting businesses. In contrast, the money paradigm emphasizes that the credit formation process has a "public dimension," i.e., the credit formation process (e.g., money supply) is a concern for the sovereign state and its regulatory agencies including the central bank, and therefore credit formation activities are practically speaking outsourced to financial institutions (Ricks, 2018: 765–766). Financial institutions make returns on a combination of fees collected in the credit formation process, and their ability to leverage their holdings, i.e., banks are incentivized to increase the supply of credit, and this may result in, e.g., overlending. This was the case in the 2003–2006 period in the US, when the subprime housing finance market quickly expanded. Based on the incentive to increase credit supply, the sovereign state needs to ensure that there are ex ante regulation and ex post resolution systems that ensure that the credit formation process is managed in a prudential and controlled manner.

Similar to Ricks (2018), Hockett and Omarova (2016: 147) regard the contemporary financial system as a public–private partnership, which they portray as a "franchise arrangement" wherein the sovereign state delegates the credit formation process to private financial institutions. These private financial institutions in turn receive a variety of insurances, tax exemptions, and other rights from the state. "Pursuant to this arrangement, the sovereign public, as franchisor, effectively licenses private financial institutions, as franchisees, to dispense a vital and indefinitely extensible public resource: the sovereign's full faith and credit" (Hockett and Omarova, 2016: 147). That is, in the credit formation franchise model, the sovereign state, operating through its regulatory agencies and not least the central bank, in most cases separated from the influence of democratic entities such as parliaments, acts as the principal and the financial institutions act as agents, in the agency theory vocabulary. More specifically, in the franchise model, financial institutions participate in three distinct activities: "(1) credit-*intermediation*; (2) credit-*multiplication*; and (3) credit *generation*" (Hockett and Omarova, 2016: 148). Credit-intermediation basically denotes the activities that are part of Ricks' (2018) intermediation paradigm, wherein, e.g., banks act as intermediaries between savers and borrowers. Credit multiplication denotes all finance market activities wherein existing credit relations (say, a mortgage loan) are transformed into financial assets (e.g., securities) that can be traded to distribute risks, and to generate a secondary finance market on the basis of assets held. In this case, e.g., mortgage-backed securities are created on the basis of a stock of mortgage loans, which is a procedure that makes it more lucrative to lend money as there is a secondary market wherein such assets can be traded as derivative instruments asset classes. Third and finally, the franchise model includes credit generation, which denotes the situation wherein, say, a bank creates money on the borrower's account to, e.g., finance a home purchase. In these different credit formation activities, private liabilities are monetized so that legal contracts representing various financial asset classes can be traded, which in turn, ideally, results in a better supply of credit, beneficial for a variety of actors who want to realize their business prospects or to borrow money to purchase, e.g., a private home.

When the credit formation is managed in a responsible manner so that, e.g., credit default risks on part of the borrower are carefully assessed so that the risk of future credit losses would not imperil the finance system, the money paradigm and the franchise model work as prescribed by theoretical models, and as intended by policy makers and regulatory agencies. The concern is, again, that the sovereign state's delegation of the credit formation process to private companies easily results in dysfunctions such as overlending. Consequently, both the legal and economic theories that guide and structure the policy making process and the regulatory activities, and the policies implemented need to include mechanisms that account for behavioral bias, and the risk of opportunistic behavior—two all-too-human conditions that easily result in increased systemic risks when financial activities are amplified and expanding over time. Furthermore, as a lender can reasonably be assumed to know more about the finance market than the generalized borrower, the risk of moral hazard needs to be recognized (see, e.g., Acharya and Viswanathanm, 2011; Baker, 1996). In the end, quite detailed but precise regulatory activities must be implemented and effectively applied to avoid disturbances in the credit formation process (Bubb and Prasad, 2014; Gubler, 2014).

Housing as investment asset: the long-term perspective

Housing policy and housing ownership rates are of relevance for macroeconomic policy and for economic policies more widely for at least three reasons. First, housing assets are "[t]ypically the largest component of household wealth," and they serve as "key collateral" for bank lending, which in turn influences "long-run trends in wealth-to-income ratios" and the size of the financial industry (Knoll, Schularick, and Steger, 2017: 331–332). Second, home ownership affects how individuals "interact with the tax system," how they perceive the welfare services their taxes are being spent on, how they perceive "their wealth, social worth, and the health of the economy," and how individuals interact with their local governments and other authorities and agencies—"even their own family" (Johnston and Kurzer, 2020, 276). Third and finally, housing policy is a key component in the welfare state, but unlike most other welfare programs, the key entity in questions, the individual home is a "consumer commodity" that can be bought and sold, serve as an investment, and as a storage of economic value (Johnston and Kurzer, 2020: 281). These three conditions makes housing policy a key component in any economic policy implemented by the government. Housing ownership is thus at the intersection of private economy consideration and a public responsibility, a condition that creates tensions, not least if evidence indicates a substantial inequality in housing wealth (and thus aggregated wealth) over time, being a condition that is likely to be noticed and rendered problematic.

Under all conditions, housing assets are important financial assets in advanced economies. On average, Jordà, et al. (2019: 1226) write, housing wealth represents roughly "one-half of national wealth in a typical economy." Despite this weight in the household asset portfolio, and the role of housing assets in the economy more widely, Jordà et al. (2019: 1231) propose that in fact, "very little has been known about long-run returns on housing." Using a number of data sets, collecting the returns on housing, equity, and so-called safe assets (government bonds and corporate bonds) over the 1870–2015 period, Jordà et al. (2019) shed light on the centrality of housing wealth and its return over time in several economies. The analysis of the data shows that there is a higher return on risky assets vis-à-vis safe assets, but the differential is lower than what may have been predicted; the risk premium for risky assets stands at 5.9 percent when using arithmetic means and 3.8 percent when using geometric means (Jordà et al., 2019: 1244). This result is consistent with the conventional wisdom that assets with less volatility, i.e., associated lower risk, generate a lower return. When examining the class of risky assets, the data indicate that the investment in "residential real estate," and not equity (e.g., corporate stocks and other instruments), has been "the best long-run investment over the course of modern history" (Jordà et al., 2019: 1242). The two asset classes of residential real estate and equity generate a return in the range of 7 percent annually and over time, but the standard deviation of the return on housing (i.e., the calculated parametric risk) is "substantially smaller" for housing assets (*circa* 10 percent for housing, versus 22 percent for equities) (Jordà, et al., 2019: 1242). When calculating the geometric average, i.e., the "compounded return," housing assets actually outperform equity investment, with housing assets generating a 6.6 percent return against 4.7 percent return for equities (Jordà et al., 2019: 1242). From an economic theory perspective, this result is puzzling and calls for a theoretical explanation. In mainstream economic theory, marginal returns are predicated on higher risks, but in the case of housing ownership, there are a variety of policies and mechanisms that reduce the risk, which would predict that the return on housing would be lower for housing assets than for equity. "This finding appears to contradict one of the basic tenets of modern valuation models: higher risks should come with higher rewards," Jordà et al. (2019: 1242) contend.

As housing assets are not only an investment object for households but also for finance industry actors, Jordà et al. (2019: 1262) calculate the return of real estate investment trusts (REITs), investment funds that specialize in the purchase and management of residential and commercial real estate. The data indicate that the long-run levels of "unlevered REIT and housing returns" are "remarkably similar" (Jordà et al., 2019: 1263), i.e., REIT portfolios include assets with the highest returns and the lowest risk. Furthermore, the analysis of the data set demonstrates that in contrast to equities, cross-country housing returns have remained relatively uncorrelated, a condition that is potentially explained on the basis of housing assets are less "globally tradable" than equities are (a fact that Johnston and Kurzer, 2020: 278, also emphasize), or because housing assets are more exposed to "idiosyncratic country-level shocks" (or combinations thereof), Jordà et al. (2019: 1272) speculate. In the end, the result is fairly straightforward and robust for the 1870–2015 period, summarized accordingly:

> [H]ousing has been as good a long-run investment as equities, possibly better. Housing has offered a similar return to equity in the majority of countries and time periods. In the long run, housing outperformed equities in absolute terms in six countries, and equities outperformed housing in five.
>
> (Jordà, et al., 2019: 1274)

Regarding the implications for housing policy and economic inequality reducing initiatives and reforms, it is apparent that housing wealth is unevenly distributed (as indicated in Chapter 1), but at the same time, Jordà, et al. (2019: 1292) remark, "housing wealth is more equally distributed than, for instance, equities." Furthermore, as opposed to equities, housing assets have a user value that cannot be ignored. In the end, policies and legislation that are supportive of private ownership are arguably justifiable within a general welfare state model.

The convergence of housing asset returns and equity returns despite housing asset's lower volatility is an empirical condition in search for a theoretical explanation. Knoll, Schularick, and Steger (2017) examine a data set for the 1870–2012 period and including 14 advanced economies, and they find a close correlation between soaring housing prices after *circa* 1980 and growing land prices: "Our decomposition shows that more than 80 percent of the increase in house prices between 1950 and 2012 can be attributed to land" (Knoll, Schularick, and Steger, 2017: 332). During the period 1980–2012, construction costs have remained broadly stable after correcting for inflation, whereas housing prices have grown remarkably. When increased new production costs have been eliminated as a plausible explanation for rising housing asset prices, the price of land, which is naturally limited, provides a better explanation: "Since 1980, residential land prices have approximately doubled" (Knoll, Schularick, and Steger, 2017: 346).

Knoll, Schularick, and Steger (2017) establishes a credible *association* between growing land prices and housing prices, but this association does not explain the growth of land prices themselves. Kohl (2021) investigates housing prices not by turning to the supply of land but to finance capital supply. Using a similar long-term data set, including housing production and mortgage credit data for the 1913–2016 period (i.e., roughly the similar period as Knoll, Schularick, and Steger, 2017, use), Kohl's analysis shows that from the mid-1970s, real housing supply indicators (e.g., new construction, building costs, residential capital formation) and housing finance indicators (e.g., prices, mortgages) were decoupled:

> While more mortgages generally increase building activity up to a certain point, the unique explosion of private mortgage credit since the 1970s is associated not with a proportional expansion in new construction but rather with house price inflation and construction-depressing effects. The relation between mortgage debt and construction (investment) is approximated by an inverted U-shaped curve in most countries.
>
> (Kohl, 2021: 414)

Kohl thus indicates that the supply of mortgage lending services, associated with finance industry expansion, becomes uncorrelated with housing production indicators. In the mainstream view of housing finance, an increased supply of finance capital to enable real estate purchases on the household level is associated with favorable economic conditions and prospects, but Kohl proposes that there can in fact be too much finance capital injected into an industry, as an inverse U-shaped curve indicates:

> [A]n inverse U-shape best describes the relationship between mortgages and construction within countries … [U]p to a certain threshold of mortgage indebtedness per GDP, a positive effect of higher mortgage indebtedness levels on house construction or residential capital formation can be observed. Beyond this threshold, however, the effect becomes negative.
>
> (Kohl, 2021: 420)

That is, whereas Knoll, Schularick, and Steger (2017) show evidence that growing housing asset prices are caused by growing land prices, the growth of land prices must itself be explained on the basis of empirical data and robust theoretical model. Kohl (2021) proposes that the increased supply of finance capital, serviced by an expanding global finance industry, is the underlying mechanism that explains both the sharp rise in housing prices and land prices.

This result is of theoretical significance and matters for housing policy as it indicates that there is a separation of housing finance and housing production, i.e., "those taking out new mortgages are not necessarily those contributing to new construction" (Kohl, 2021: 432). Policy makers are not only concerned with housing welfare and housing welfare equality but are also held responsible for job growth and other economic performance measures. The construction industry sector accounts for up to 10 percent of employment in OECD countries, including not least blue-collar jobs that are of great importance for economic welfare and equality. This means that lower construction production activity (during e.g., recessions) become a prioritized political question as it generate a variety of macroeconomic problems (Kohl, 2021: 434). Therefore, Kohl's (2021) findings are far from good news for policy makers, oftentimes treating a growing stock of mortgage lending as an index of an economy being in a healthy stage. The inverted U-shape relationship between housing production and housing finance supply may be interpreted in less benign terms, in turn justifying policy reforms or even legal or regulatory changes, Kohl (2021) proposes.[1] Based on this proposition and the empirical evidence it rests on, the next section examines the role of what has been referred to as the "household lending channel" and its key importance when explain the housing–finance nexus.

The macroeconomic perspective: the household-lending channel and the demand for safe assets

The intricate relations between housing production, mortgage lending, and the safe asset device in the contemporary economy need to be discussed to set the stage for affordable housing policies. Since 1980, Mian and Sufi (2018: 53) write, advanced economies have experienced four trends: (1) there has been economic growth, and a marked growth in economic inequality; (2) borrowing costs have fallen "dramatically"; (3) household debt-to-GDP ratios have "increased substantially"; and (4) the finance industry has grown as a fraction of the GDP. These four trends are interrelated, but in what way and through what mechanisms and channels is not a trivial issue to sort out. Economic theory provides a number of explanations and theoretical models, and what Mian and Sufi (2018) call the "credit-driven household demand channel" is one particularly important mechanism. To fully explain how, e.g., the second and the third trend listed above and the fourth trend are interrelated, the broader role of housing industry and mortgage lending are examined, and thereafter the individual household decisions to purchase a home are discussed.

Safe asset and the role of mortgage loans as collateral

Housing finance "naturally produces liabilities that function as money" (Min, 2018: 900). When a family decides to buy a residential home, they oftentimes acquire a mortgage loan with a contract period of *circa* 30 years (Levitin and

Wachter, 2020). In many advanced economies and welfare states, the government has enacted policies that are supportive of home ownership as such polices have benefits that extend beyond the mere utility of the housing facility as such. For instance, in the US, the two so-called Government Sponsored Entities (GSEs) of Fannie Mae and Freddie Mac (being shorthand anthropomorphic and mnemonic terms for a more hard-to-articulate acronyms) provide home mortgage loans. Min (2018: 901) shows that Fannie Mae and Freddie Mac have issued more than $5.3 trillion in "mortgage-backed securities, collateralized mortgage obligations (CMOs), and corporate debt" as part of their housing finance activities. These liabilities of the GSEs serve a wider role in the financial economy as what economists refer to as *safe assets*, i.e., financial contracts that are "understood to carry an implicit federal guarantee against losses that is nearly as robust as the 'full faith and credit' guarantee on US Treasury obligations" (Min, 2018: 901). Safe assets issued by American GSEs play a key role in the credit formation process as they leverage the credit supply of private-backed finance capital. Studies show that safe assets account for *circa* one-third of all assets in an advanced economy (Gorton, 2017), which means that the government plays a key role in supporting the credit formation process, otherwise primarily located to the privately owned finance companies. Min (2018: 901) suggests that American GSEs account for no less than one-tenth of the entire stock of global safe assets, which underline the centrality of the American federal institutions in the global finance system (Conti-Brown and Wishnick, 2021; Perry, 2020; Conti-Brown and Zaring, 2019).

Gorton (2017: 548) defines a safe asset as "an asset that can be used to transact without fear of adverse selection." That is, there are no concerns that "the counterparty privately knows more about the value of the asset." In this view, a safe asset is "informationally insensitive" inasmuch as there is a limited perceived risk that new market information being issued would depreciate the economic value of the asset. "A safe asset is a simple debt instrument that is expected to preserve its value during adverse systemic events" (Caballero, Farhi, and Gourinchas, 2017: 29). For instance, a pawn shop owner may regard a prestigious Swiss wristwatch as a high-quality collateral item as its market price is easy to determine and because the ability of the money borrower to repay the loan does not affect its valuation. In this context, the Swiss wristwatch is nominally treated as a safe asset by the pawn shop owner. Expressed in more technical terms, this information insensitivity of the asset is of great value as it makes the lender immune to "adverse selection in trading" (Gorton, Lewellen, and Metrick, 2012: 101):

> To the extent that debt is information-insensitive, it can be used efficiently as collateral in financial transactions, a role in finance that is analogous to the role of money in commerce. Thus, information-insensitive or 'safe' debt is socially valuable.
>
> (Gorton, Lewellen, and Metrick, 2012: 101)

In legal terms, of key importance as any financial liability is formally a contract, the concept of safe asset is based on what legal scholars and practitioners call *legal fiction*: "Unlike the Higgs boson, safe assets are not to be found in nature" (Gelpern and Gerding, 2016: 366). Safe assets exist only in economic theory and in "market vernacular": "'safe' in this context does not, and cannot mean genuinely risk-free, but rather 'safe enough' to ignore the risks for some purposes" (Gelpern and Gerding, 2016: 366). "All stores of value are not created equal," Caballero, Farhi, and Gourinchas (2017: 29) add. Assets that serves as stores of value differ in their "degree of liquidity," i.e., "the ease with which they can be traded," and their "sensitivity to various risk factors" (Caballero, Farhi, and Gourinchas 2017: 29). While the term "safe assets" indicates some kind of absolute or measurable degree of stability, such financial contracts are never "wholly safe," but only "safe enough" to make them reliable and useful in the credit formation process. That is, safe assets make finance actors believe they are sufficiently vigilant to manage the risks of certain asset classes efficiently (Gelpern and Gerding, 2016: 420).

Government sponsored enterprises, US Treasury bond supply, and the global savings surplus

Government sponsored enterprises have been described as the "cornerstone" or the "anchor" of the global financial system (Min, 2018: 912). The sharp rise of overseas savings in jurisdictions that export, e.g., energy (such as oil or natural gas), or that have benefitted from offshoring investment (as in the case of China) but that themselves lack sufficient local investment opportunities or sophisticated domestic finance markets results in the situation wherein the financial surplus generated has been invested in primarily the US, and in US Treasury bonds in particular, Caballero, Farhi, and Gourinchas (2017: 30) write:

> The capacity of a country to produce safe assets is determined by constraints in the financial sector, the level of financial (under-) development, the fiscal capacity of the sovereign, and the track record of the central bank for exchange rate and price stability. For these reasons, the supply of safe assets, private and public, has historically been concentrated in a small number of advanced economies, most prominently the United States.

As the collective growth rate of advanced economies supply safe assets has been lower than the world's growth rate (Caballero, Farhi, and Gourinchas 2017: 30), surplus capital is invested in a limited number of jurisdictions, such as in the US. What has been referred to as the international savings glut has thus served to propel the expansion of the finance industry in the US and Europe, and thereafter globally. Empirical evidence indicates that overseas investors prefer low-risk investments, and consequently the US Treasury bond market is today dominated by overseas investors, Favilukis, Ludvigson, and Van Nieuwerburgh (2017: 151) show:

> Foreign ownership of US Treasuries (T-bonds and T-notes) increased from 13.5 percent of marketable Treasuries outstanding in 1984 to 61 percent of marketable Treasuries by 2008. By June 2012, foreign holdings represented 52.5 percent of marketable Treasuries, driven by a large increase in foreign purchases between 2008 and 2012 and an even larger increase in the supply of

> marketable Treasuries. But foreign holdings of long-term and short-term US Treasury and agency debt as a fraction of GDP continued to increase in the 2008–12 period, from 31 percent to 40.6 percent of GDP by 2012.

By 2008, at the verge of the global finance industry crisis, so-called foreign official institutions (FOI) held "70 percent of all foreign holdings of US Treasuries" (Favilukis, Ludvigson, and Van Nieuwerburgh, 2017: 151–152), and by 2010, the bond market portfolio composition of FOI consisted of 78 percent US Treasuries. This means in practice that safe assets in the form of US Treasury bonds display a price inelasticity that reveals a preference for low-risk asset holdings among FOI fund managers:

> [D]emand for US Treasury securities by governmental holders is completely inelastic, implying that when these holders receive funds to invest, they buy safe US securities such as Treasuries or agencies, regardless of their price relative to other US assets. Foreign governmental holders have very deep pockets and will pay whatever price necessary to push nongovernmental holders out of the safe US bond market when their demand is not met with an equal increase in supply.
>
> (Favilukis, Ludvigson, and Van Nieuwerburgh, 2017: 152)

In Europe, a similar pattern is observed as German state-backed financial assets "sell themselves" (Gabor and Ban, 2016: 624), which means that the European Central Bank (ECB) can rely on Bundesbank, the German central bank, to act as its trusted and primary safe asset issuer, which benefits the credit-formation process in the European Monetary Union (EMU).

The global demand for safe assets has several implications for the US and global economy. First, at the low interest rate equilibrium that has been established for a considerable period of time and that is "expected to remain the case for the foreseeable future" (Blanchard, 2019: 1198), safe assets "acquire a public good dimension since their production helps stimulate output in other countries" (Caballero, Farhi, and Gourinchas 2017: 37). Caballero, Farhi, and Gourinchas (2017: 37) question whether the benefits of producing a public good can be "fully internalized by the economy that is issuing the safe assets," which means that the US economy does not sufficiently benefit from being the primary storage of value in the global economy. Second, which may counteract the disadvantage of being a primary provider of safe assets, the US dollar has maintained its central role in the global economic system, despite consistent predictions that it would soon lose this status. Lysandrou and Stassinopoulos (2020: 391) argue that the dollar's continuing "hegemonic position in the international currency system" needs to be compared with economic fundamentals that reveal the US economy's shrinking share of world production and "mounting trade deficits." Regardless of the marked weakening of the US economy, "dollar hegemony is as strong as ever" (Lysandrou and Stassinopoulos, 2020: 391). The explanation for the preference for the US currency derives from the US economy's role as the primary contributor to "global equity supplies," and its "even larger contribution to global bond supplies"

(Lysandrou and Stassinopoulos, 2020: 391). In the situation wherein global economic growth outpaces the supply of safe assets, backed by sovereign states that are deemed trustworthy, the global finance capital surplus has to go someplace, which leaves sovereign wealth fund managers who invest the finance capital generated in export-oriented economies with few choices than to invest in US dollar-nominated or euro-nominated assets (see, e.g., Alhashel, 2015; Aizenman and Glick, 2009; Pistor, 2009; Gilson and Milhaupt, 2008):

> Any one group of foreign institutional investors may choose to exit dollar assets for fear of the US's repayment abilities but that option is not open to all foreign institutional investors taken in the aggregate because there are simply not enough supplies of other currency-denominated securities that can serve as stores of value.
>
> (Lysandrou and Stassinopoulos, 2020: 391)

Just like Caballero, Farhi, and Gourinchas (2017) argue, Lysandrou and Stassinopoulos (2020: 391) propose that in an era of growing financialization of the global economy, it is the "national capital market size that is the ultimate determinant of a national currency's international status and power." This view is also consistent with the legal institutionalism proposition that finance capital is coded in law, and thus bound up with the sovereign state's capacity (acting through the central bank, albeit being formally separated from the political system and its capacity to determine fiscal policy) to protect the value of its currency, and the value of financial assets nominated in that currency.

Seen in this view, the credit formation process is dependent on two things: First, that the sovereign state, acting through its GSEs and similar agencies, or some transnational governance agency such as ECB, insures certain financial assets against losses so they de facto (albeit not de jure—safe assets are a species of legal fiction) can serve as safe assets in the financial system. Economists and policy makers dispute whether private-backed safe assets can substitute safe assets backed by the sovereign state. In the early 1950s, bank deposits were regarded as safe assets, but as the finance industry grew and became more sophisticated (or at least more risk-tolerant), the category of safe assets expanded to include money-like debt (such as commercial papers, money market funds, repurchase agreements) and private label AAA-rated asset-backed securities (Caballero, Farhi, and Gourinchas 2017: 40). In this process, the degree of "safety" of safe assets has been re-negotiated inasmuch as private-backed assets are now increasingly treated as safe assets. Caballero, Farhi, and Gourinchas (2017: 40) argue that it is "possible in principle" to create private-backed safe assets on the basis of "overcollateralization," but in the end, this model remains fragile as the private sector's ability to "insure against a truly systemic event is limited"—a lesson dearly learned during the 2008 financial crisis. In fact, the subprime mortgage lending business, which substantially contributed to the global finance industry stalemate, was based on the financial industry's attempt to "extract a (seemingly) "safe asset tranche from pooled lower-quality assets" (Caballero, Farhi, and Gourinchas 2017: 40). Unfortunately, Caballero, Farhi, and Gourinchas (2017: 40) continue, "even the most senior and seemingly safe tranches on private assets may contain some irreducible tail-risk," which make private-backed assets unsafe when truly systemic events unfold. Such evidence and episodes suggest that private-backed assets cannot substitute safe assets backed by the sovereign state—a proposition that has significant implications for the finance industry and the economy at large.

Second, safe assets cannot be produced *ex nihilo* but need to be supported by collateral, and housing assets are the near-perfect collateral as they have a long utility period, are supported by multi- or bi-partisan policies, and have a utility value beyond their role in supporting credit formation. The credit formation process is partially propelled by the international savings glut, wherein surplus finance capital is transferred from domicile jurisdictions to, e.g., the US or Europe as low-risk asset investments. To complete the circle, there is a need for households that hold mortgage loans and carry the risks that otherwise benefit a healthy, dynamic, and expansive credit formation process, and therefore increases the supply of credit, and thus lowers the financing costs for, e.g., venturing or entrepreneurial activities. This is the defining features of the credit-driven household demand channel. As Min remarks (2018: 932), the sovereign state plays a key role in stabilizing the otherwise protean and porous financial system, prone to crises and other forms of unintended consequences of purposeful action on all levels, and consequently, it is difficult and costly to replace "public safe assets with riskier privately created collateral"; "either a safe asset shortage or an increased shift to private money would increase the likelihood of financial crises," Min (2018: 933) summarizes.

Home mortgage lending in the macroeconomic perspective

The concern for policy makers and economists is that home mortgage lending generates a stock of safe assets that serves to leverage the credit supply, while excessive mortgage lending and increased household debt-to-GDP ratios are associated with financial turbulence and crises. This means that a primary policy goal is to ensure that the mortgage lending industry does not engage in overlending, i.e., issue credit, e.g., as mortgage loans to households that cannot hold their contracts until their maturation. Mian and Sufi (2018: 31) suggest that the expansion of credit qua safe asset primarily operates through household demand, and that credit expansion has served as an "important driver of business cycles." Furthermore, Mian, Sufi, and Verner (2017) and Mian and Sufi (2018) identify what they refer to as "credit supply shocks" as the foremost cause of financial crises. Mian and Sufi (2018: 32) define a shock as a change in policy, or new macroeconomic conditions that "leads to a rapid influx of capital into the financial system," and that oftentimes "triggers an expansion in credit supply." Justiniano, Primiceri, and Tambalotti (2019: 2322) reach a similar conclusion, based on a theoretical model and empirical data: "[A] progressive loosening of the lending constraint in the residential mortgage market increases household debt in equilibrium." There are several defined triggers of credit supply shocks, including a rise in economic inequality, a "rapid rise in savings" in emerging economies, and "banking deregulation episodes" (Mian and Sufi, 2018: 36). In the latter case, legal reform or more liberal regulatory practices result in a relaxation of lending constraints, in many cases being part of a pro-business policy intended to promote venturing and enterprising. That means that for the same presumptive borrower and with the same true risk profile, there are now more lenders being willing to lend more, or on cheaper terms (Mian, Sufi, and Verner, 2017: 1782).

While a variety of macroeconomic conditions may play a role in credit supply shocks, Mian and Sufi (2018: 36) suggest that bank deregulation is "the cleanest identification of credit supply shocks in recent literature." For instance, empirical evidence indicates that US states that deregulated their banking system at an earlier point saw larger increases in bank lending in the 1983–1989 period than states that deregulated at a later stage (Mian and Sufi, 2018: 36). Needless to say, deregulatory episodes do not of necessity result in financial crises, but the content and magnitude of reforms matter for finance industry activities. In a situation wherein overseas savings grow, economic inequality is on the rise (derived from, e.g., lower labor compensation; Autor et al., 2020; Covarrubias, Gutiérrez, and Philippon 2020), and the finance industry expands on the basis of the optimistic belief that a more generous credit supply would further leverage the economy, there is a risk that policy makers and regulatory agencies overemphasize the marginal benefit of cheaper credit. Furthermore, a more liberal and leniently regulated finance industry entices speculators and imprudent lenders to enter the industry, which historically has been proven to increase finance market instability and systemic risk (Agarwal, et al., 2014; McCoy, Pavlov, and Wachter, 2009; Bond, Musto, and Yilmaz, 2008).

Mian, Sufi, and Verner (2017: 1804) suggest that recent finance industry crises have been caused by a marked growth in household lending, which raises the household debt-to-GDP ratio and housing prices, which eventually results in a finance industry decline. "[T]he body of evidence suggests the chain of causality is more likely to run from credit supply shocks to house prices rather than vice versa" (Mian, Sufi, and Verner, 2017: 1804). This means that the credit supply shock of the 2003–2007 period, which resulted in global finance industry lockdown, was not exogenous but endogenous, caused by finance market actors, policy makers, and regulatory agencies (and not least the credit rating agencies that were introduced as the key control mechanism in the private ordering model, wherein allegedly independent credit raters were expected to demonstrate integrity vis-à-vis their paying clients but essentially failed to act in this way) and their joint inability to assess the emerging situation properly. Furthermore, the causal chain runs from increased mortgage loan origination to soaring housing prices, and growing levels of household debt, which ultimately may result in a contraction of the finance industry when the credit-driven household demand channel is saturated, i.e., the point where households cannot absorb more debt at current income levels. Through these mechanisms, rising levels of household debt is a solid predictor for reduced GDP growth three years after the local peak of the mortgage loan origination activities, Mian, Sufi, and Verner (2017) report.

The first driver of the decline in GDP growth is that for behavioral reasons, and because of the incentive structure in the finance sector, forecasters are commonly poor predictors, Mian, Sufi, and Verner (2017: 1758) say (see also Blanchflower, 2019: 165–171). Empirical evidence shows that the International Monetary Fund (IMF) and Organisation for Economic Co-operation and Development (OECD) "systematically overforecast GDP growth at the end of household debt booms" (Mian, Sufi, and Verner, 2017: 1758). This inability to process discordant information properly is observed in a variety of settings. First, lenders tend to mistakenly extrapolate "previously low defaults when granting new loans" (Mian and Sufi, 2018: 49), i.e., lenders inadequately assume that the future can be predicted to look basically like the documented past. Second, the creditors of mortgage lending institutions tend to underestimate "the true default risk of mortgages," and investors who hold a variety of mortgage lending-related financial assets neglect "tail risks," which leads to "aggressive lending by the financial sector via debt contracts" (Mian and Sufi, 2018: 49). On all levels, from policy makers to regulatory agencies, and all the way down to the households, overoptimistic assessments regarding both individual and not least the systemic risk were made, and this served to leverage the mortgage loan stock (Lupo-Pasini, 2017: 16) serve to leverage the mortgage loan stock to critical levels. The second effect that serves to depress the economic development, three years after the local peak in mortgage lending, is that during the expansion of the credit supply, there is little evidence of increased investment in production capital such as new machinery, R&D, workplace training and investment in human resources, i.e., there is an inadequate investment in non-financial production resources that would be able to cushion the economy once the credit supply recedes. "[P]eriods of rising household debt are associated with a rise in the consumption-to-GDP ratio, an increase in imports of consumption goods, and no change in the investment-to-GDP ratio" (Mian and Sufi, 2018: 41).

The conclusions to be made regarding the expansion of the mortgage lending activities in the 2003–2007 period, ending abruptly with the finance industry meltdown of 2008 and the Great Recession that dragged on for more than a decade in several jurisdictions, are not flattering for any participants: on balance, the evidence indicates that "market participants fail to understand the negative effects of increases in private debt" (Mian, Sufi, and Verner, 2017: 1798). Furthermore, this proposition is of key importance as the sudden and unexpected collapse of the credit supply and the finance industry crisis that followed were not some exogenous event that hit an otherwise stable economy. On the contrary, the key participants' failure to understand the economic system they either regulated, or actively operated within by, e.g., issuing credit in the form of mortgage loans, increasingly to benefit low net-worth households dominating in the so-called sub-prime market, was the true cause of the largest crisis of competitive capitalism to date, and the most significant legitimacy crisis of the capitalist economic model since the Wall Street crash of 1929. In the end, the lesson learned is that there can in fact be "too much of good thing" (e.g., credit); what Mian and Sufi (2018: 50) refer to as "financial excess" is a key term that pulls all these mechanisms, events, and decisions made together:

> [T]he most likely initial shock is one that creates an excess of savings relative to investment demand in some part of the global financial system, what we call a 'financial excess.' This initial shock can be amplified by behavioral biases, financial innovation, and even by malfeasance within the financial sector.
>
> (Mian and Sufi, 2018: 50)

Ultimately, the key insight is that housing production and the mortgage lending industry play a central role in the global finance industry as the household debt-channel that runs from the household level to the global stock of safe assets is a central mechanism in advanced financial economies, and the real economy that increasingly relies on insurances from the sovereign state to remain operational. It is within this macroeconomic and financial context that housing supply needs to be understood simultaneously as a welfare provision and a utility, and as a financial asset and a liability, which creates significant effects in the financial system beyond the mere transactions and contractual relations between mortgage loan originators and mortgage borrowers.

Fiscal policy and taxation effects on housing wealth

Goodman and Mayer (2018: 50) underline that, when all things are considered, owning a home is conductive of economic welfare on the household level:

> In fact, home equity is the principal source of savings for most American households, especially households in the bottom part of the income distribution, and ownership can serve to protect households from the financial risk of rising rents.
>
> (Goodman and Mayer, 2018: 50)

One of the key explanations for this economic welfare is that the tax code tends to exclude capital gains from real estate holdings, or, alternatively, that property owners can "deduct mortgage interest payments from their taxable income" (Floetotto, Kirker, and Stroebel, 2016: 106). In many countries, including Sweden, such tax codes are disputed as they reduce the tax burden of already economically privileged medium to high net-worth households, which increase economic inequality.[2] Furthermore, economists such as Floetotto, Kirker, and Stroebel (2016: 106) show that tax credits have "a negative welfare impact for the majority of households." This is the case because the majority of households generate tax revenue that pays for the tax credit, but these households do not benefit from "the temporary increase in house prices" (Floetotto, Kirker, and Stroebel, 2016: 106). Despite such concerns, government interventions in the housing market are considerable, and are largely intended to be supportive of home ownership through the reduction of the relative cost of owner-occupied housing (Floetotto, Kirker, and Stroebel, 2016: 107–108). For instance, in the US, tax policy prescribes the deductibility of mortgage interest payments from taxable income (Floetotto, Kirker, and Stroebel, 2016: 108), and in 1999, a total of $773 billion was deducted by 40 million homeowners, making mortgage interest payments "the second largest federal deduction after state taxes" (Floetotto, Kirker, and Stroebel, 2016: 108). While Floetotto, Kirker, and Stroebel (2016: 117) are skeptical regarding the effects on housing welfare for the majority of the households—in the long run, Floetotto, Kirker, and Stroebel (2016: 123) write, "[a]round 82% would benefit from the removal of mortgage interest deductions"—they also recognize the indirect effects of the tax policy, e.g., how it is supportive of finance industry interests and its credit formation process that supply finance capital to all sectors of the economy (Floetotto, Kirker, and Stroebel, 2016: 117). However, considered strictly in terms of housing welfare effects, in the short-run, "the immediate welfare gain from removing mortgage interest deductions is significantly smaller than the long-run gains," Floetotto, Kirker, and Stroebel (2016: 123) argue. At the same time, to avoid inconsistencies in tax policies and to reduce inefficiencies in the housing market and the housing finance industry is a thorny political affair as market actors, including the households as mortgage borrowers, are likely to respond to any changes in tax scheme in ways that are either harmful for economic stability or more widely being difficult to predict ex ante. For instance, a removal of mortgage interest deductions harms "middle-income agents," Floetotto, Kirker, and Stroebel (2016: 123) argue: when changes in the tax policy impose costs on middle-income households, they are likely to cut down on other forms of consumption, which may generate a downward economic spiral, which shifts the burden to other industries to cover the costs for reduced economic activities elsewhere. As a consequence, it oftentimes demands broad political majorities to implement new fiscal policies, not least when they affect housing finance, being of great importance on both the household level and in macroeconomic terms.

Cho and Francis (2011: 42) have designed a model that tests whether home-ownership policies are supported by the US tax system, and to what extent the tax system affects wealth inequality. The tax system is important in terms of economic inequality concerns more generally as the bottom 50 percent of the US population holds circa 3 percent of aggregate wealth, whereas the top 1 percent holds roughly 30 percent. In contrast, in terms of the distribution of housing asset wealth, the top 1 percent holds approximately 9 percent of housing assets (measured as the market value of the households' primary residence), whereas the bottom 50 percent holds approximately 12 percent of housing assets (Cho and Francis, 2011: 43), thus being a comparably smaller differential than that pertaining to the aggregated wealth distribution. From the policy makers perspective, given that policy makers seek to reduce economic inequality, housing welfare policy on the basis of tax system reforms appear to be a more effective approach to reduce a skewed distribution of wealth than other fiscal mechanisms, all things equal.

Given these conditions, the simulation model that Cho and Francis (2011) develop indicates that a reform of the tax system would affect economic inequality only modestly. If "preferential tax treatment," e.g., deducted mortgage interest payments, would be implemented, the federal state would generate additional tax revenues in the range of 0.01 to 0.95 percent of GDP (Cho and Francis, 2011: 43). Furthermore, the removal of the preferential tax treatment of housing leads to better consumption smoothing over the lifecycle, but it would also significantly reduce homeownership, which "falls to 26.4% from 64.5%" in the simulation model (Cho and Francis, 2011: 55). Tax system reforms would thus have marginal benefits regarding economic inequality reduction, at the same time as it would reduce home ownership, being one of the primary sources of household wealth and economic stability on the household level; in fact, "housing equity" makes up more than 65 percent of the average US household's wealth (Cho and Francis,

2011: 42). "Regarding inequality," Cho and Francis (2011: 43) write, "although it is clear that the preferential tax treatment of housing is a regressive policy, its impact on overall wealth inequality is negligible with no impact on reducing inequality as measured by the Gini coefficient from taxing imputed rent." Consequently, preferential tax treatment is "not a significant factor" contributing to the "extreme skewness" of the wealth distribution, Cho and Francis (2011: 43) conclude. Furthermore, a reform of the tax system is associated with a variety of dynamic effects including, e.g., the households re-allocating their assets and re-considering their expenses. For instance, "when the tax advantages of housing assets are removed, individuals re-allocate assets and pay down their mortgages faster, reducing the amount of extra revenue for the government" (Cho and Francis, 2011: 58). In the end, it appears as if tax policies that permit mortgage interest payment deductions are comparably effective to both promote home ownership and to counteract economic inequality, not least if the broader macroeconomic and monetary policy consequences are considered.

Mortgage financing in a socio-economic context

In the sections below, real life economy housing finance practices will be examined in more detail. The first section discusses the economic and social welfare implications of home ownership. The second section examines how biased, discriminatory, and excluding mortgage lending practices generate equality concerns that call for policy reform or more detailed market monitoring. With these two conditions in mind, both being indicative of far-from-perfect housing and housing finance markets, it is justifiable to critically examine the current housing policy and its connections to the finance industry, a topic examined in the third section.

The management of housing assets in the financialized economy: economic and social welfare implications

Home ownership is a political objective in many welfare states and advanced economies as it serves as a form of "self-insurance" (Ansell, 2014: 384; Conley and Gifford, 2006: 56). Ansell (2019: 173) suggests that the private housing market "has taken on a role as funder of private welfare," and as private welfare systems grow, "they may reduce the demand for public provision." In periods of economic turmoil, or economic hardship following, e.g., the loss of salaried work, families that own their homes are less vulnerable than families that rent their residence. Conley and Gifford (2006: 56) propose that home ownership "acts as a major source of income security" inasmuch as it "confers access to a valuable fungible or collateral asset." In addition, they continue, there is an "inverse relationship between the degree of economic inequality and widespread home ownership" (Conley and Gifford, 2006: 56), an empirical condition that can be interpreted as being indicative of home ownership being able to counteract other tendencies towards growing economic inequality in society. Unfortunately, empirical evidence indicates that home ownership is in decline in the US. The US Census

Bureau 2015 report reveals that the home ownership rate declined from its peak at 69 percent in 2004, to 63.7 percent in 2015 (Acolin, et al., 2016: 627; see also Judge, 2018: 329).

Even though the home ownership rate varies considerably across advanced economies for a number of reasons (being indicative of what Schwartz and Seabrooke (2008: 238) refer to as "varieties of residential capitalism"), out of the 25 most developed countries, the United States ranks 17th in homeownership rate (Richardson, Van Nieuwerburgh, and White, 2017: 29). The poor performance of home ownership policies coincides with a more general sense of reduced economic welfare among Americans. While around 95 percent of children born in 1940 in the US earned more than their parents, only 41 percent of the children born in 1984 are estimated to achieve the same absolute mobility (Atkinson, 2019: 1150). Several scholars emphasize how the mortgage lending industry and the housing market actors have been over-subsidized at the expense of households. Richardson, Van Nieuwerburgh, and White (2017) propose that current policy has encouraged overinvestment in housing, whereas other forms of investment have been neglected or postponed:

> US public policy has encouraged too much investment in housing. Concomitantly, other forms of investment—whether in physical production capital, such as plants and machinery; in community capital, such as schools, hospitals, roads, airports, etc.; or in human capital, such as more and better education and skill development for children and adults alike—have been neglected.
>
> (Richardson, Van Nieuwerburgh, and White, 2017: 37)

Given these priorities, it is perhaps not surprising that both the Obama and the preceding Bush administrations "assigned a much lower priority to solving the home foreclosure crisis" that followed the 2008 finance industry collapse, than they did to "shoring up the largest banks (which bore significant responsibility for causing the crisis in the first place)" (Wilmarth, 2013: 1359; see also Andrews, 2009). More generally, and outside of episodes of the acute resolution work, what Prasad (2012: xiv) refers to as the "mortgage Keynesianism" policy (see also Atkinson, 2019: 1099), wherein a generous supply of credit is assumed to propel economic and social welfare, but that inevitably result in considerable levels of household debt, may not be sustainable even though it is supportive of finance industry interests. Some scholars have remarked that the decline of antitrust legislation and regulation in the US has generated a deeper market power that benefits a smaller number of corporations but "without accompanying long-terms gains in consumer welfare" (Baker, 2019: 2). In this situation, the dynamics of the economic system is impaired and the productivity growth declines, as documented by, e.g., Gordon (2015).

Regardless of such concerns, more or less loosely coupled with the supply of affordable housing, some scholars call for legal and regulatory reforms that more effectively distribute economic resources. On the other hand, as Dickerson (2009: 223) notices, in the US, the mortgage industry has "opposed additional mortgage regulations," largely arguing that the government should "avoid anything that would impede the basic American 'privilege' of home ownership." Richardson, Van Nieuwerburgh, and White (2018: 28) suggest that the mortgage finance system has been protected against policies that promote the "affordability and income-redistribution goals," usually being at the center of housing policies. The current mortgage finance system, and the business practices on the housing and property ownership level it begets, is inefficient inasmuch as affordable housing is in short supply as inflated housing prices are not only in the interest of the mortgage lending industry but are a primary effect of its business operations (Richardson, Van Nieuwerburgh, and White, 2017: 28). Bubb and Prasad (2014: 1621–1622) suggest that if there is a public policy goal to expand home ownership (which is prima facie the case as such declarations have been made consistently from the highest office), then subsidies involved in this pursuit should be "explicit and transparent": "The current practice of allowing extremely high leverage mortgages to proliferate in a housing boom is an opaque and costly form of public subsidy" (Bubb and Prasad, 2014: 1621–1622). One such housing policy program that appears to play the role intended by policy makers, i.e., to preserve housing welfare for distressed households, is the First-Time Homebuyer Credit (FTHC) program passed by US Congress as a response to the financial crisis (Berger, Turner, and Zwick, 2020: 279). FTHC was a $20 billion stimulus program, "designed to support US housing markets with a temporary tax incentive for new homebuyers between 2008 and 2010" (Berger, Turner, and Zwick, 2020: 279). Berger, Turner, and Zwick (2020) point at the positive effects of the program, but it is noteworthy that this is an ex post resolution program aimed at preserving housing welfare after the event, rather than an ex ante policy supporting of, e.g., housing ownership or other forms of housing welfare. How to design subsidies so that the benefits can be claimed by households rather than the finance industry that provide mortgage lending services is no trivial matter. For instance, the current policy model has promoted finance industry expansion to increase credit supply, but rather than to push down the cost of lending (as intended by policy), the opposite trend, inflated housing and property prices, has been documented.

Biased, discriminatory, and excluding mortgage lending practices: equality and welfare implications

It is frequently emphasized in the scholarly literature that American society is constituted on the basis of its citizens accessing credit (e.g., Hurley and Adebayo, 2016), and consequently the tools, devices, and mechanisms used to calculate creditworthiness is of utmost practical importance for the individual. Given the centrality of credit supply in the American economic system, the opaqueness of this procedure is noteworthy. Even more so, accusations regarding biased and discriminatory credit-rating practices are supported by both federal and state legislation, and not least social norms regarding fairness and equality before the law. Rodriguez (2020: 1845) reports that even after controlling for several economic and social factors, mortgage lending applications from black families were "almost three times more likely than white applicants to be denied." As Rodriguez (2020: 1845) remarks, in the US, housing discrimination is not a breaking news issue as it, in fact, "has a long, sordid history in the United States." Nevertheless, discrimination can be executed on the basis of a variety of practices, assumptions and conditions, generating similar outcomes just the same, but still being possible to trace to their source as, e.g., mortgage lending practices change over time as new practices and technologies are included. Today, mortgage loan applications are processed on the basis of artificial intelligence technologies and big data applications so that landlords and lenders increasingly rely on so-called "predictive analytics" to evaluate applicants (Rodriguez, 2020: 1847–1848).

In practical terms, measures of creditworthiness are outsourced to so-called Consumer-Reporting Agencies (CRAs; Hurley and Adebayo, 2016: 154), and these CRAs do not only compile and process available market data but to a higher extent also collect a variety of data, a routine consistent with the dictum "all data is credit data." For instance, CRAs monitor social media activities and retail-spending histories, and regard them as proxies for factors indicating "how responsible an individual is" (Rodriguez, 2020: 1858). Regardless of the accuracy of such theoretical propositions, this practice may violate legislations protecting the privacy and integrity of the individual, and social norms that would prohibit such extended use of original data. Rona-Tas (2017: 53) introduces the concept of *off-label use* to denote how scores issues by credit ratings agencies are used "in new ways outside the context of credit granting." Off-label use can be exemplified by an employer hiring an applicant for a position on the basis of, *inter alia*, good credit scores, thus treating a measure of creditworthiness as reliable proxy for prudence or some other generally desirable quality projected onto the applicant. The use of social media data to generate such an original credit score would represent a form of "off-label use in reverse," or the "inversion of off-label use," as a credit score is here generated on the basis of economic and finance data, original social media data, and other data points accessed on the Internet and through data bases. Rona-Tas (2017) is concerned that the off-label use of credit scores would generate externalities, including not least discriminatory effects that penalize individuals on the basis of not only how the original parameters are operationalized (e.g., in terms of creditworthiness), but also in other contexts (e.g., in employment situations). Ultimately, such a "metrification of social life" on the basis of credit scoring (and vice versa) would push society towards a technocratic governance regime that leave little room for the individual to preserve his or her integrity in meaningful ways.

In the short-term perspective, scholars are more concerned with *algorithmic bias*, being a "serious issue" (Crawford and Schultz, 2014: 117) if it affects predictive analyses that strongly shape the distribution of resources in society, as in the case of credit supply. "An algorithm is only as good as the data it works with," Glazer (2019: 469) asserts, and therefore the "personally identifiable information" (Crawford and Schultz, 2014: 93) collected by CRAs needs to be processed in manner that is consistent with current legislation and ethical principles. That is, the dictum "all data is credit data" may be true and beneficial for the CRAs and their clients, but it may not be in the interest of other actors to be exposed to such monitoring of the personal or even private sphere, not least since substantial evidence indicates a widespread bias in the selection and processing of such data.

"One of the primary myths about Big Data is that it produces outputs that are somehow free from bias and closer to objective truth than other forms of knowledge" (Crawford and Schultz, 2014: 127).

Regarding the use of personally identifiable information in AI-based algorithmic decision making, such data are used as what Glazer (2019) refers to as *proxies*, data that serve to apprehend or stand-in for other personal qualities being of relevance for, e.g., the credit-lending institution:

> Companies use proxies, or substitute stand-in data, when they lack data for the behaviors they are most interested in. The easiest conceivable proxy can be demonstrated with the use of zip codes. For example, a company may attempt to draw statistical correlations between a person's zip code and their potential to pay back a loan or hold a job given that zip codes typically contain individuals of the same socioeconomic status. Accordingly, instead of rejecting a loan or job applicant outright based on his or her race, for example, a creditor could use an applicant's zip code as a proxy for race and thus attempt to mask their unlawful discrimination.
>
> (Glazer, 2019: 469)

Rodriguez (2020) accounts for how the algorithms now process a wider set of data, in many cases seemingly unrelated to the original business proposition but apparently being regarded as being of value for the CRA: "[e]xamples of nontraditional or alternative data that are factored into lending decisions include residential stability, criminal history, employment and address history, professional licensure, cell and landline utility bill information, balances in savings or retirement accounts, and LinkedIn profiles" (Rodriguez, 2020: 1859). It is questionable whether the access to, and the processing of such data is supported by applicants themselves, and regardless of such preferences and interests, it is a legal question to what extent the judiciary would tolerate such as infringement on the personal integrity that affects a variety of legal domains and legal statutes.

While some social groups may be monitored in great detail as they are actively participating in social media communication, or leave other digital traces for the benefit of secondary uses, other groups are suffering a predicament on the other end of the continuum, i.e., they are not deemed to be creditworthy on the basis of *absence* of such market data. Rodriguez (2020: 1854) references a report issued by the Consumer Financial Protection Bureau (CFPB) in 2015 that found that by 2010, "approximately twenty-six million Americans were 'credit invisible,'" and with an additional 19 million having "such limited credit records that they could not be scored," adding up to more than 45 million Americans not being granted a useful credit score. For this group, the question is not a matter of whether CRAs and their clients are overreaching their legal rights but rather a matter of whether they are discriminated on the basis of the inability to act in ways consistent with the design of the algorithm decision-making models.[3]

In summary, in cases where inferential statistics are indicative of model bias, resulting in discrimination, it may be still complicated for individuals to bring such cases to the court of law and to win the case (Rona-Tas, 2017: 71). Model bias in algorithmic decision making is a concern as it is difficult for outsiders to detect them as algorithms and big data applications are firm-specific assets, protected by corporate legislation from the view of outsiders. The legislation requires that the plaintiffs can prove, at the pleading stage, that "the algorithm proximately caused the injury, a seemingly insurmountable obstacle for plaintiffs who may not have all of the information on how the defendant's algorithm model functions" (Rodriguez, 2020: 1873). Furthermore, being an additional difficulty, even if the plaintiff can demonstrate discriminatory effects, the plaintiff also needs to provide evidence that the user *intentionally* discriminated, despite current legislation otherwise being based on the premise that also *unintentional* discrimination is unlawful (Rodriguez, 2020: 1873). Consequently, the chances of winning court cases appear to be slim as the "discretion by multiple decision makers at each of these steps makes it difficult to isolate the singular practice or policy that led to the disparate impact" (Rodriguez, 2020: 1874).

This leaves CRAs, their client companies, and any other corporation that use alternative and personal data to predict, e.g., creditworthiness (but potentially to assess a great variety of qualities of interest for a paying client) in the position where they can access and process public data basically as they like and as it suits their interests: "[I]t is up to data miners to decide what is 'good' for a particular business; that decision, however, may require a high degree of subjectivity and reliance on existing data" (Glazer, 2019: 469). Furthermore, there is a substantial amount of empirical evidence of bias in human cognition and decision making, and regarding what Miller and Rosenfeld (2010) refer to as "intellectual hazard"—not least in how, e.g., women and minorities are disfavored by organizational decision-making procedures, and despite the best intentions and considerable potential penalties when failing to adhere to institutionalized norms and beliefs (e.g., Rivera and Tilcsik, 2019; Castilla, 2008). There is little evidence supporting the proposition that the "data miners" (Glazer, 2019: 469) and the programmers (Davis, 2016: 511) that construct the AI applications and algorithms that generate decisions would be protected against such an all-too-human predicament. The governance concern thus remains that biased decisions and discriminatory selections are fabricated and made on an industrial basis, outside of the control of, e.g., consumers, and that this will reduce economic and social welfare if certain groups are persistently discriminated on the basis of, e.g., faulty or inadequate proxies used by the algorithms.

The question regarding whether home ownership promotes social welfare: should the conventional wisdom be questioned?

Over the last two decades, and not least after the sub-prime mortgage lending market collapse, several scholars tend to be more reserved regarding the benefits of home ownership. Mian and Sufi (2014: 30) suggest that increased household debt in fact acts as an "anti-insurance": "Instead of helping to share the risks associated with home ownership, it concentrates the risks on those least able to bear it"

(Mian and Sufi, 2014: 30). Pistor (2019) summarizes in precise terms how global finance and houses owned by residents and families are intimately connected:

> It is possible to dress up any claims by placing them into trusts or corporate entities and garnish them with alphabet soup labels, such as SVPs, MBS, CDOs and their squared, cubed, or even synthetic variants. However, at the other end of the deal, there are still the same little old houses, which their owners can barely afford and that may not hold their value once their funding machine that helps them fuel process in real estate dries up.
>
> (Pistor, 2019: 101)

As equally housing production and the finance industry are highly regulated and monitored activities, there are reason to critically question the accuracy of the current policy that appear to benefit the finance industry more than local constituencies, several empirical studies indicates (Cestau, Hollifield, Li, and Schürhoff, 2019; Schwert, 2017; Cornaggia, Cornaggia, and Israelsen, 2017).

Empirical evidence that question the current pro-home ownership policies run counter to long-standing housing policy doctrines in the US and in many other advanced economies and welfare states. "The United States has long encouraged, supported, and subsidized home ownership," Dickerson (2009: 193) argues, and Miltko (2020: 2275) proposes that "the ability to own a home is considered a fundamental part of being American." In Miltko's view (2020: 2275), "stable housing situation" is not only treated as providing "psychological benefits" but is also more widely regarded as a long-term investment in "wealth building." In such scholarly accounts, policy makers are attempting to combine two political objectives in one singular housing policy: to increase social and economic welfare on the basis of promoting home ownership, and to assist the credit formation process delegated to private financial institutions. The consequence and outcome is that US home ownership policies are "outdated, misguided, and virtually ignore the actual market realities most lower- and middle-income potential homeowners now face" (Dickerson, 2009: 189). For instance, escalating housing prices and the stagnant real wage growth experienced by a significant proportion of American households push lower and middle-income families to rely on "nontraditional mortgage products" to fulfill their dream of home ownership (Dickerson, 2009: 190). As Bohle (2014: 914) notices, such non-traditional mortgage products are not generated outside of the regulatory gaze of policy makers and other market actors but are rather the immediate consequence of the political ambition to deregulate financial market. This means that the credit supply increased under certain conditions (as in the case of the upward movement of the business cycle), but the more munificent credit supply also generates finance market uncertainties that households cannot be rationally assumed to be cognizant and/or informed about. Expressed differently, it is a considerable policy making challenge to simultaneously promote home ownership and housing welfare *tout court* as a welfare-inducing policy, and to be supportive of finance industry interests, not least as a significant proportion of households borrowing money to finance their home purchases are not financially literate, i.e., they are easily exposed to market risks and dysfunctions that are precisely the policy makers' responsibility to reduce as much as practically possible on the basis of, e.g., law enforcement and regulatory control.

Under these conditions, Miltko (2020: 2304) argues that it is irresponsible to expose households to finance market activities that imperil a sustainable household economy, whereas the lenders, say, banks and credit institutes, would simply write off defaulting borrowers as credit losses as part of the regular accounting procedures or, potentially, acting under the moral hazard of the current regulatory framework so that they are protected by the sovereign state against default if credit losses accumulate and become overwhelming.[4] Such imbalances in protection cannot be justified in a democratic political system, and therefore scholars and other commentators should "challenge the American assumption that homeownership is unequivocally better than renting," Miltko (2020: 2304) argues. Furthermore, this advocacy of new housing policy rules is not primarily based on ethical and moral convictions regarding fairness and justice, but needs to be founded on the empirical evidence that shows that "[a]ny benefits from homeownership for low-income households are limited at best" (Miltko, 2020: 2304).

Fingleton, Fuerst, and Szumilo (2019: 27), who present empirical material from the UK, suggest that policies that attempt to reduce housing prices appear to be ineffective for a variety of reasons. First, there is no proper definition of affordability, nor is there a full understanding of the market mechanisms "underlying house price formation" (Fingleton, Fuerst, and Szumilo, 2019: 27). In the UK, the government policy currently is to increase the supply of housing in order to improve affordability in the greater South East, but such policies do not sufficiently incentivize construction companies and real estate companies, which results in an output of new housing that is "lower than expected" (Fingleton, Fuerst, and Szumilo, 2019: 28). Furthermore, building new homes in the most critical areas "has little effect on affordability" (Fingleton, Fuerst, and Szumilo, 2019: 28). In this view, housing policy seems to be a fairly blunt tool to counteract soaring home prices that undermine any affordable housing campaign. Setterfield and Kim (2020: 560), two economists, demonstrate that what they refer to as the "inequality–debt–crisis nexus" is not a matter of households borrowing money to finance an extravagant life style that they would not afford under a regime with lower credit supply; on the contrary, "[p]art of the motivation for borrowing stems not from 'keeping up with the Joneses' but from what we call 'running to stand still'" (Setterfield and Kim, 2020: 560). In this situation, to add housing finance debt to already thin household budgets is unlikely to generate net social and economic welfare.

If new housing policy doctrines that more effectively distinguish between household interests and finance industry preferences are established, it may be that home ownership becomes an historical exception. Currently, the advanced finance industry and its capillary power penetrates all spheres of human lives—which is not necessarily a bad thing, if finance markets are properly regulated—but there is a need for policies that are supportive of social and economic welfare that benefit the majority of constituencies. This is at least how Forrest and Hirayama (2018: 259) anticipate the future housing market:

> [W]e argue that it is more appropriate to regard the postwar 'generation own' as the exception—a historical moment in which a propitious combination of demographic, social, political and economic factors enabled an idiosyncratic growth in mass home ownership.
>
> (Forrest and Hirayama, 2018: 259)

On the other hand, if the housing-finance nexus (Fligstein, Brundage and Schultz, 2017: 884) were to be dissolved or become more loosely integrated, it would have a considerable affect on the credit formation process as material housing assets serve a key role as collateral for safe assets. As the conventional wisdom among finance theory scholars is already today that there is a global shortage of safe assets (Caballero, Farhi, and Gourinchas 2017)—measured, e.g., as the low-price elasticity on US Treasury bonds (see Favilukis, Ludvigson, and Van Nieuwerburgh, 2017: 152)—housing policy is likely to continue to promote home ownership in one way or the other. The question is then how the costs and benefit are to be distributed between the various actors involved in housing production, consumption, and financing.

Summary and conclusion

Policy making is a complex social practice characterized by unintended consequences of purposeful action, the muddling through in a milieu that includes opposing interests and preferences, the influence of social relations and power inequality, and a variety of temporal and cognitive limitations (Battaglini and Patacchini, 2019; Campbell, 2002; Lindblom, 1959), and housing policy making cannot be assumed to reveal different qualities. Furthermore, intense lobbying and campaign donations from the FIRE (Finance, Real Estate, and Insurance) industries may add to the complexity (see, e.g., Richardson, Van Nieuwerburgh, and White, 2017: 27; Wilmarth, 2013; Mian, Sufi, and Trebbi, 2010). Regardless of such material and constitutional conditions, the policy to promote affordable housing has essentially failed as households eligible for mortgage lending encounter housing prices that have grown at a considerably faster pace than the consumer price indices in most advanced economies. For low-income households, poor housing market regulation and evidence of value extracting business practices reduce the stock of affordable housing.

Whereas much scholarly literature focuses on policy making and finance industry practices on a more aggregated level, this chapter emphasizes "on the ground" business practices in the real estate and property sector. The combination of generous credit supply, legal and deregulatory reforms, outsourcing opportunities, and novel accounting procedures enable thinly capitalized companies to quickly maximize the economic value of the housing asset portfolio that they can resell on the housing market. For free market acolytes, such business practices contribute to overall economic efficiency as they detect and repackage real estate assets to generate a return-on-equity. Ultimately, such increased market efficiency is assumed to benefit all constituencies. For more pragmatic and moderate commentators, such business practices, balancing on the thin edge of what are legitimate business practices, counteract stipulated policies regarding the supply of affordable housing as a citizenry right. By implication, commentators argue that the current affordable housing policy that oftentimes subsidizes and insures finance industry actors should be displaced by more direct subsidies that benefit the ultimate beneficiary, i.e., home owners. In the new policy regime, home owners can access finance capital at low cost and under proper contractual terms, and tenants can take advantage of housing services that do not hollow out their household budgets. How this shift in policy making is to be accomplished is a question to be answered, but there is reason to believe that further scholarly research that examines firm-level practices would shed light on the day-to-day business practices that ultimately inflate per unit housing costs in advanced economies.

Notes

1 Kohl's (2021) results are also supported by studies indicating how surplus finance capital are invested in so-called "world cities" (e.g., London, New York, Tokyo) and other metropolitan areas where housing prices are predicted to be stable, and thus provide a storage of private wealth. Fernandez, Hofman, and Aalbers (2016: 2444) study the rise of real estate prices in London and New York, a financial asset class "increasingly regarded as a mainstream investment class for the transnational wealth elite." This increasing appetite for investing in real estate in "super-prime locations" (Fernandez, Hofman, and Aalbers, 2016: 2448) derives from at least two conditions. First, on the policy-making level, there have been a number of transnational agreements that reduce the possibilities for tax evasion or that increase the costs to evade taxes when transferring income to tax havens such as Switzerland and Luxembourg. These regulatory reforms result in "the relocation of capital into real estate" (Fernandez, Hofman, and Aalbers, 2016: 2448). Second, on the structural level, what Fernandez, Hofman, and Aalbers (2016: 2448) refer to as the "endemic state of overaccumulation" in the contemporary capitalist economic system, generate surplus capital, a "wall of money" that needs to find its way into investments that generate a stipulated return and being associated with a tolerable levels of risk. This preference for high returns and low risks paves the way for growing capital flows into the real estate industry. The consequence is that today, "the transnational wealth elite" commit on average 32 percent of their investment portfolios to real estate assets. Furthermore, 81 percent of "wealth advisors" suggest that their clients are becoming even more interested in residential real estate investment, which indicates that real estate investments may remain high for a considerable period of time.

While such investment activities in, e.g., London and New York City tend to be approved by policy makers as it increases the tax-base (e.g., former New York major Michael Bloomberg stated that it would be great "If we could get all the Russian billionaires to move here," cited in Fernandez, Hofman, and Aalbers [2016: 2455]), there is also the backside of the coin. In Sidney, Australia, of all apartments, no less than 49.6 percent are currently owned by investors (Adkins, Cooper, and Konings, 2021: 558). The consequence is that the Sidney-siders and other Australians suffer a housing welfare generation gap inasmuch as home ownership is in marked decline over generations: "Whereas in 1981 61% of Australians aged 25–34 owned a home, by 2016 this had dropped to 44%; for the age group 35–44, the decline was similar, from 74% to 62%"

(Adkins, Cooper, and Konings, 2021: 560). Only the demographic category of people in the age of 55 or above have a similar home ownership rate in 2016 as they did in 1981. Such housing market conditions may easily become subject to grievances or otherwise generate unintended and undesirable effects such as lower long-term birthrates that strongly shape macroeconomic conditions on the national level. There are, in other words, good reasons for policy makers and regulatory agencies to carefully monitor the global finance capital flows, and their investment in housing and real estate assets.

2 The conventional wisdom among economists is that fiscal policy and taxation ex post is a more effective way to handle economic inequality than changes in legal rules (Grewal, 2014: 656; cf. Liscow, 2014: 2482). Fiscal policy serves to redistribute wealth in a predictable manner, whereas legal reforms open up for uncertainty and unpredictability in market actors' behavior. With this doctrine in mind, it is noteworthy that in many areas of fiscal policy, progressive taxation is applied to even out economic inequalities. In the case of deducting mortgage interest payments from households' taxable income in, e.g., Sweden, the same percentage applies *for all households*, regardless of their declared income from salaried work or finance asset holdings, up to the level of 100,000 Swedish crowns in total annual mortgage interest payment deductions. Above that point, a 21 percent (rather than 30 percent) tax deduction rate applies. At the current level of home mortgage interest rate, being in the range of a mere 1.5 percent (by June 2021), a full unpaid mortgage loan would correspond to a home worth circa 22 million Swedish crowns the underlying asset being held (22 MSEK * 0.015 * 0.3 = approx. 100,000 SEK). Very few Swedish households own real estate with this market value. In practice, the mortgage interest payments deduction is a non-progressive fiscal policy where the 30 percent deduction applies equally to households regardless of their relative wealth. A low net-worth homeowner in an inner city apartment is thus granted the same fiscal policy rights as the wealthy owner of exclusive real estate in an area with considerably higher median real estate market prices. The higher the mortgage loan (which correlates with the market price of the underlying real estate asset, and presumably also with the buyer's annual income declared, examined when, e.g., banks grant mortgage loans), the larger the tax deduction benefit. Ultimately, the mortgage interest payments deduction acts as a non-progressive fiscal policy that in nominal terms benefits high net-worth households. While some policy makers, commentators, and media pundits are concerned with the decline of progressive taxation (e.g., Hedin, Clark, Lundholm, and Malmberg, 2012), some economists argue that less progressive taxation is conducive to economic growth (Furman, 2019: 242).

3 Recent developments in the so-called fintech industry (Fuster et al., 2019), basically developed outside of the regular banking sector, serve to further pronounce these legal and regulatory challenges. Luther (2020: 1018, footnote 18) argues that the so-called P2P ("Person to Person") lending market increasingly use "alternative data," meaning "data other than that typically used by traditional lenders, such as FICO scores and debt-to-income ratios." Examples of alternative data include utility payments, rent payments, education, and "other internet footprint information" (Luther, 2020: 1018, Footnote 18). As Luther explains, the fintech market share of the US "consumer debt market" has grown substantially over the last period, and thus constitutes a major business challenge for the traditional financial institutions. In 2010, fintech companies originated less than 1 per cent of the total stock of new consumer loans in the United States; by the end of 2018, this figure stood at 38 per cent of "all loans in the $138 billion US consumer debt market" (Luther, 2020: 1020). Following these market changes, with Silicon Valley-bred high-tech companies holding larger market shares than the traditional banks that still operate on the basis of traditional lending procedures, including the honoring of fiduciary duties of care and loyalty, the use of algorithmic processing of alternative data is likely to grow in importance.

4 This scenario may sound overtly dour regarding the assumed social responsibilities of the finance industry, but these concerns are not wholly unfounded. Van Staveren (2020:

508) suggests that the Dutch population has "lost its trust in banks," following a long series of events including "the enormous diversion of public expenditures away from education and health care towards saving banks and the jobs of bankers," "a stream of scandals," and specific business deals, revealed in news media reporting, wherein "billions of euros of expensive derivative contracts sold to municipalities and social housing associations." Furthermore, insiders, finance industry staff, also have a low degree of faith in the soundness of the industry. Using a survey method targeting 7,000 union members, and finally including 617 respondents, Van Staveren (2020: 520) reports that "a large majority" (85 percent) of the bankers felt an obligation to serve the client. At the same time, this ambition was hemmed by a gradual loss of trust in the banks. Inn total, 62 percent of the respondents claimed they trusted their team, but when it came to their managers, less than half of the respondents (46 percent) argued that they trusted their boss. Even more noteworthy is that a mere 16 percent of the respondents claimed that they trusted their banks as a whole. Regarding client interest and welfare, a majority of the Dutch bankers (61 percent) said they felt a tension between "serving client interest on the one hand and the products offered by their bank on the other hand" (Van Staveren, 2020: 520). Although Van Staveren's (2020) study is limited to one jurisdiction, it is not implausible that the public in other countries would express a similar distrust in banks, and in the finance industry more widely. "Numerous polls have suggested that bankers are among the least trusted of all the professions," Gordon and Zaring (2017: 567) say, being a piece of evidence that is supportive of this proposition regarding the general validity of Van Staveren's (2020) research findings.

Part II

Empirical cases

3 The institutional setting and the design and methodology of the study

Introduction

Housing policy is part of the statecraft of the contemporary welfare state, and the welfare state is itself premised on the constitution, the legislation, and the administrative rules that set the boundaries for what activities can be initiated within the state's jurisdiction. A shorthand term for all these conditions is the institutional setup of the welfare state. North (1991: 97) defines *institutions* as "[t]he humanly devised constraints that structure political, economic, and social interaction." Furthermore, institutions consists of "[b]oth informed constraints (sanctions, taboos, customs, traditions, and code of conduct), and formal rules (constitutions, laws, property rights)" (North, 1991). Importantly, North (1991: 98) argues that both political and economic organizations are included in the "institutional matrix," and each type of organization acts to reduce production and transaction costs per exchange so that the potential gains from trade become realizable. In North's (1991) institutional perspective, the line of demarcation between politics and economic affairs remain porous.

The welfare state model is of great importance for housing policy, especially in the low end of the housing market. Korpi and Palme (2003: 428, original emphasis omitted) define the welfare state as the aggregated policies that intend to "affect outcomes of, and conditions for, distributive processes in the sphere of markets so as to decrease inequality and/or poverty." The welfare state is thus bound up with markets, but these markets are not operating freely on the basis of some private ordering mechanisms as the institutions of the welfare state influence the generation (through, e.g., subsidies) and distribution of economic wealth. What Anderson (2018: 201) refers to as "the sociology of the welfare state" is thus a scholarly project to actively examine how the welfare state was established and how it is continuously modified to better respond to changes in its milieu. In the post-World War II period, the welfare state model is characterized by three characteristics, Aghion and Roulet (2014) argue. First, it is based on a "top-down industrial policy in which the central government would make the calls, partly through the (often large) public sector and partly through subsidies directed toward national champions" (Aghion and Roulet, 2014: 914). This is the core of the industry policy that is supportive of a competitive national industry, which generates job growth, taxable income, and, in some cases, an international trade surplus. Second,

DOI: 10.4324/9781003244417-6

the welfare state, acting through the central bank and the agencies that assist its work, organizes a "Keynesian macroeconomic regulation" that serves to even out the demand over the business cycle, i.e., through increased public spending during a recession, "financed partly through public debt and partly through taxation," or through higher interest rates to cool off the economy at the height of the business cycle (Aghion and Roulet, 2014: 914). Third and finally, welfare states initiate and run a variety of social policy programs that, e.g., subsidize education and health, and supplements small wages through subsidy schemes (Aghion and Roulet, 2014: 914). For, e.g., proponents of free market theory, the welfare state is at risk to impair the alleged efficiency of non-regulated or leniently regulated markets, but despite such concerns, there is a widespread support for the welfare state model across the political spectrum, Pierson (1996: 173) argues. Primarily right-leaning governments tend to declare their skepticism towards the welfare state model, but in fact they have continued to support its operation as substantive reforms would create much uncertainty, having repercussions throughout the economic and political systems.

Regarding housing policy, which straddles economic policy, industry policy, and social policy, it is important to recognize what Schwartz and Seabrooke (2008: 238) refer to as "varieties of residential capitalism." Specific jurisdictions reveal considerable variety in how they assist the housing market and optimize housing welfare among constituencies. Independent of such local and regional variety, several commentators argue that an elaborate welfare state model generates a demand for more credit as constituencies have a firm belief in the welfare state model within which the households make their decisions: "In fact, there are good reasons to believe that generous welfare provisions can actually encourage more borrowing," Rona-Tas and Guseva (2018: 59) write. Prasad (2012: 91) advances the proposition that the credit supply of the finance industry and the welfare state model share several qualities inasmuch as they are both based on such faith in the robustness of the economic system and being premised on economic growth:

> [A]fter all, the welfare state also works [just like the finance industry] only as long as the economy is growing. Under conditions of decline and unemployment, welfare measures quickly become unaffordable, as the number of those drawing on welfare grows and the number of taxpayers shrinks. The logic of the welfare state—that productive public investment will lead to growth and therefore pay for themselves—is not so different from the logic of credit.
>
> (Prasad, 2012: 91)

There is some evidence related to housing policy that supports this proposition inasmuch as housing policy and housing finance need to move in unison to avoid housing market bubbles, which create considerable costs in the medium to long-term perspective. "Housing and more particularly housing finance was an important systemic component of the postwar welfare state by virtue of the balance-sheet connection between long-duration liabilities and long-duration assets" (Schwartz, 2012: 37). However, by design and in its implication, housing policy has largely served to protect the finance industry from risks (Schwartz (2012: 47). Unlike other welfare state provision, e.g., pension schemes, unemployment insurance, and health insurance, that all "remove market and life risks from individuals," housing policy effectively reduces the risk and uncertainty (i.e., non-parametric risk) from housing finance institutions:

> Pension funds and insurance firms have relatively stable cash inflows from contributions and premiums. This money has to go somewhere. By connecting those flows to housing finance, regulation assured a steady flow of capital to an economic sector whose interconnection with other goods-producing sectors and whose labor intensity made it macroeconomically significant.
>
> (Schwartz, 2012: 48)

This is why housing finance is premised on a welfare state model, being an important institutional condition that aligns economic policy and political policies within the welfare state's role to regulate macroeconomic conditions on the basis of a generalized Keynesian economic model (albeit commonly referred to in other, less politicized terms), wherein the oscillation of the business cycle is compressed on the basis of key mechanisms.

The Swedish society and economy and their institutional changes over time

Sweden is widely regarded as an exemplary welfare state, with a high proportion of the GDP being taxes to redistribute economic wealth, and the country hosts an innovation-led and export oriented economy that has generated a positive trade-balance over the last two decades. The Swedish economy is largely entangled with the global economy, and thus dependent on transnational trade agreement and transnational governance activities that are supportive of the liberalization of trade. Having established a specific institutional framework wherein employer organizations are negotiating compensation with a consortia of labor unions, and without the direct interference of the government or state-agencies (unless negotiations end up in a stalemate), the so-called Saltsjöbaden spirit (named after the charming seaside resort outside Stockholm where the deal was first signed in 1938), Sweden has enforced what has been referred to as a "solidaristic wage bargaining" model (Hall and Thelen, 2009: 15). In this market-based bargaining model, industry sectors compensate their co-workers equally for a similar type of work. This has resulted in a wage-compression compensation model that pushes ineffective industries into bankruptcies unless they can implement new technology or managerial practices to make operations more efficient, which uphold the productivity growth of the industry sector. Comparably more efficient industry actors can, on the other hand, reserve a larger pool of finance capital derived from the differential between salaries paid as stipulated by the industry agreement and the revenues generated on the basis of superior performance, which result in increased investments in R&D and innovations. During the economic boom of the first post-war decades, in the period 1960–1973, Sweden was in the group of OECD countries with "the highest labour productivity growth in manufacturing"

(Erixon, 2007: 282). By the late 1960s, Braunerhjelm and Henrekson (2013: 110) write, the United States and Sweden "were arguably—together with Switzerland—the wealthiest countries in the world." Over the coming decades, this competitive advantage, partially generated on the basis of the ability to remain neutral during World War II, the political stability based on Social Democratic governments holding office during the entire post-war period until 1976, and carefully crafted and implemented reforms that generated marked growth in economic and social welfare, would gradually erode.

One of the foremost consequences of the idiosyncratic compensation model is a compression of the income distribution, and comparably lower degrees of income inequality. By 1995, at the beginning of an era where market regulation reforms were initiated, the 90th percentile in the income distribution earned 2.2 times that of the 10th percentile in Sweden. In the US, essentially a free-market economy, the same ratio stood at 4.6, more than twice as high as Sweden (Rueda and Pontusson, 2000: 350). By the early 2000s, Pressman (2007: 182–186) reports, Sweden had "[t]he [proportionally] largest middle class, even though Sweden's middle class shrunk substantially, it still constituted almost half of all households." For many center-left commentators and policy makers, the distinctively Scandinavian (or Nordic, when including Finland) welfare model became an inspiration for so-called third-way politics, navigating in-between the more pure market economy of the US and the centrally planned economy of the Eastern-bloc economies. "Sweden has been seen by many on the left as the exemplary third road model of social democratic development" (Wallace, 1999: 27).

Needless to say, this model, despite its many benefits and advantages, created unintended consequences. Incentives to acquire a tertiary education degree or to participate in entrepreneurial activities were comparably weak. From the end of the 1960s until the early 1980s, the so-called educational premium, being the marginal compensation for investment in education, intended to cover wages never earned when studying, reimbursement for the cost of living during the study period, and a compensation for rewarding ambition and self-discipline, "fell dramatically" in Sweden: "The rate of return on higher education was approximately zero in [two] studies in 1981" (Henrekson and Rosenberg, 2001: 214). Similarly, the institutional structure supportive of enterprising and entrepreneurial activities was weakly developed until the mid-1990s when the state decided to invest heavily in entrepreneurship support, financing, and research. Such evidence granted Sweden an unfavorable status of being exemplary of a paternalist state outside of the centrally planned economies. Right-wing commentators such as William E. Simon, Secretary of Treasury in both the Nixon and Ford administrations, and thereafter serving as a free-market and pro-business activist, including acting as the director of the John M. Olin Foundation that supports scholarship and activism in the free-market community, portrayed Sweden in such terms in the mid-1970s: "[T]he Swedish people on the whole have willingly accepted almost suffocating bureaucratic supervision of every detail of their lives … in exchange for cradle-to-grave protection" (Simon, 1978: 35). This is arguably a knee-jerk reaction among American conservatives to dismiss any welfare state reform as evidence of a paternalist credo, but more recently, also liberal and pro-market commentators have defended the Swedish economic policy that seeks to combine market competition and the protection of labor interest and economic and social welfare:

> [T]he often used dichotomous characterizations of Sweden as a CME [Coordinated Market Economy] or a 'cuddly' form of market economy as opposed to a liberal/'cutthroat' market economy is less relevant than before and perhaps even misleading.
>
> (Braunerhjelm and Henrekson, 2013: 114)

"Indeed, it seems that there is nothing particularly cuddly about capitalists in Sweden," Kinderman (2017: 607) adds. The Swedish capitalist economy does not reveal any idiosyncrasies on closer inspection.

From the end of the 1960s, Sweden's competitive advantages waned. In the 1970s after thereafter, Sweden began to lag behind the OECD economic growth average, a decline lasting for a quarter of a century, and with Swedish purchasing power parity-adjusted growth per capita sliding down to the average among OECD countries (Braunerhjelm and Henrekson, 2013: 110):

> Between 1991 and 2005, Sweden's GDP per capita growth was equal to the average for the EU-15, but lower than that of the OECD and the USA … Sweden's loss of position in the welfare league is also 'explained' by a decline in labour force participation rates … Between 1990 and 2004, no other OECD nation, with the exception of Turkey, experienced a similar decline in participation rates to Sweden.
>
> (Erixon, 2007: 284)

For some commentators, this limited labor market participation is indicative of the welfare state expanding beyond what is supportive of a vital and dynamic economy, and in the 1990s and thereafter, several economic reforms were implemented by both social democratic and center-right governments. "[L]iberalization in Sweden has been swift and wideranging," Baccaro and Howell (2017: 144) remark. At the same time, the Swedish economy (and the Nordic economies more widely, most notably Denmark and Finland—oil-rich Norway apparently could afford to choose another path, including not to join the EU) maintained some of its central welfare state pillars and institutionalized reforms. Therefore, Baccaro and Howell (2017: 168) write, "Sweden is a difficult case for an argument about neoliberal convergence." One such institutionalized model is the bilateral labor market negotiations, wherein "almost nine out of ten Swedish workers are covered by collective agreements" (Baccaro and Howell, 2017: 168). Over the period from 1997 (when a new major industry policy agreement was implemented, sustaining the Saltsjöbaden spirit) until the end of the second decade of the new millennium, Swedish wage earners saw how negotiated real wage growth benefitted household budgets (Styhre and Bergström, 2019). Currently, the Swedish economy stands at the cross-road, having to deal with the poor labor market inclusion among immigrant and low-educated groups, and with the Covid-19 pandemic leaving several industry sectors including the hospitality and restaurant businesses in a dire state, at the same time as many economic fundamentals reveal an unbroken welfare state commitment among policy makers: "[I]t remains the case that Sweden enjoys lower level of inequality and poverty than most of its advanced capitalist counterparts, though it is also worth noting the rapid increase in inequality in the last two decades," Baccaro and Howell (2017: 170) summarize.

Other commentators are more skeptical regarding the sustainability of the current policy, being ineffective in responding to the growing economic inequality that, *inter alia*, derives from the unequal distribution of revenues from financial asset holdings, and the low inclusion of, e.g., immigrant groups in the labor market. "While there has indeed been significant aggregate wage growth in Sweden, real wages have declined sharply as a result of welfare state retrenchment … and asset price inflation since the 1990s," Belfrage and Kallifatides (2018: 877) argue. Examining a data set including OECD countries in the 2007–2016 period, Kerstenetzky and Guedes (2021: 185) found that in the period, "welfare state effort" climbed in all countries except Sweden. In the 2006–2014 period, Sweden was governed by a center-right government that actively implemented economic policies that supported economic self-sufficiency on the basis of salaried work, which generated incentives to seek employment. Sweden ended up with a higher poverty ratio, as well as "a more unequal income distribution," and in the end, "a smaller or frozen redistribution effort was to blame" (Kerstenetzky and Guedes, 2021: 185). Kerstenetzky and Guedes (2021: 185) show that postfiscal inequality increased only in the US, France, and Sweden in the 2007–2016 period.

In addition, the global expansion of the finance industry affects a small and export-oriented economy such as Sweden's, and today, the level of household debt on the basis of unprecedented levels of home mortgage lending, following long-term soaring housing prices, is a concern for both policy makers and regulatory agencies (even though the current situation is disputed in both policy making and academic quarters). By and large, this situation has created an essentially dual housing market in Sweden, wherein middle class households are heavily indebted, but can benefit from a high housing standard and can afford to live quite spaciously. In contrast, especially in urban and sub-urban milieus, low-income and low-net worth households struggle to make ends meet, but still being strongly assisted by various benefits provided by the state and/or the municipality, which pose a political challenge for two reasons: First, it means that the living standard of significant proportion of low-income households are inadequate, with more family members sharing apartment spaces originally intended for smaller families. Second, the low inclusion on the labor market and the limited ability to generate income that cover living expenses, especially for immigrant families, means that tax payers are burdened with a growing proportion of families unable to support themselves. Such transfer of economic resources to needy households can be tolerated by voters if that policy is consistent with widely endorsed social norms, but the significant growth of the voter support for nationalist and populist right-wing parties, not least among working class men, indicates that such transfers are unpopular. This creates tensions in the Swedish political systems, wherein center-left parties actively seek to marginalize the nationalist party (which results in a democratic deficit as circa 20 per cent of the Swedish voters may currently regard themselves as being actively blocked from political agreements), and center-right parties are confused regarding how well liberal or conservative ideologies, beliefs, and preferences can mingle with nationalist and populist ideas without compromising private and collective political convictions, or otherwise create undesirable social consequences (e.g., by further legitimizing heterodox political beliefs). Needless to say, by the beginning of the third decade of the new millennium, political parties grapple with a situation wherein the political landscape has been restructured, interestingly enough on the basis of long-term and multi-partisan policy commitments that generated unintended consequences.

The Swedish housing market: a mixed housing market with privately owned and rented housing units

A Terner Center for Housing Innovation (located at University of California at Berkley) report, *Housing in Sweden: An Overview*, published in 2017, provides some elementary statistics pertaining to the Swedish housing market. On average, owner-occupied tenure represents 40 per cent of the housing stock (Terner Center for Housing Innovation, 2017: 8), whereas what is named public housing accounts for "nearly 20% of the country's housing stock" (Terner Center for Housing Innovation, 2017: 6). The remaining housing stock includes "cooperative housing" (*Bostadsrätter*, in Swedish) at 23 per cent of the housing stock (Terner Center for Housing Innovation, 2017: 8), and a residual category of various ownership forms. Furthermore, the private rental market accounts for only slightly under 20 per cent of all rental units (Terner Center for Housing Innovation, 2017: 8).

In order to fully understand the Swedish housing market, some cultural traits and political traditions needs to be examined. Törnqvist (2019: 901), who studied *cohousing units* ("in which residents live in their own apartments and share communal spaces") and *small-scale communes* ("private lodging arrangement in which dwellers share an apartment or villa") in the Stockholm metropolitan area, suggests that the concept of individualism has been part of political programs and campaigns for a considerable period of time in Sweden, and therefore reflects how citizens regard and value their own housing facilities and the housing market. According to the World Values Survey, Sweden scores highest both "in regard to emancipatory self-expression and secular-rational values" and is a country with "a relatively high degree of social equality" (Törnqvist, 2019: 903). In Törnqvist's (2019: 903) view, such values and beliefs that appreciate autonomy and individualism are "not just a marker of late-modernity," but is also "historically embedded in the institutions of the welfare state." In contrast to the conventional image of Sweden as a society represented by strong social solidarity, policies and reforms have actively supported forms of individualism that are consistent with a strong state:

> [T]he logic behind policies and legislation in the areas of parental leave, taxation, union protection, children's rights and student loans aims to liberate citizens from subordinating dependencies. The state is there to unshackle

> and protect wives from their husbands, children from their parents and marginalized groups from charity, not to eviscerate these relations, but to make them more egalitarian and to assure that the individual is less vulnerable.
>
> (Törnqvist, 2019: 903)

Some commentators have used terms such as "state individualism" to denote how the protection of the individual *qua* citizen has been a political project that has been shared across the political spectrum and over time, on the one hand making the individual responsible for his or her own welfare and fortune (a form of "responsibilisation," in Shamir's, 2008, formulation), while on the other hand implementing legal and regulatory reforms that confer rights and authority to the individual. In this historical and political context, including a variety of reforms and activities, housing welfare is naturally treated both as a right, guaranteed by the sovereign state, but also as a form of expression or manifestation of the subject's autonomy and individualism. As a matter of fact, Sweden has among the highest proportion of single households in the world, a condition being further pronounced in metropolitan areas, and in Stockholm in particular.

On the other hand, the individualist credo may predict a larger proportion of single households in the housing stock, but gender equality norms act in the reverse direction, being supportive of co-habitation and the nuclear family structure. Gonalons-Pons and Gangl (2021: 493) examine the effects of what they refer to as "the gender stress mechanism," which prescribes the male in a heterosexual relationship as the primary breadwinner of the household. In the case where such gendered social norms are strongly articulated and enforced, the job loss of the male breadwinner increase the risk of divorce, which generates a higher proportion of single households. Gonalons-Pons and Gangl (2021: 473) report that out of 29 countries examined, Sweden had the lowest score in "male-breadwinner norms": only 4 percent of the population in the sample agrees with the statement, "men's primary role is breadwinning." In contrast, in Greece, having the highest score, no less than 47 percent of the population in the sample agreed with this statement. As Gonalons-Pons and Gangl (2021: 473) write, countries with low support for the "male-breadwinner model" tend to have "more generous unemployment protection policies, higher GDP, lower rates of unemployment, and higher rates of women's employment." The Swedish welfare state model thus simultaneously supports individualism and stable family structures, which generate a variety of housing market outcomes but still reveal a significant proportion of single households.

The limited role of private rental market pointed out in the 2017 Terner report is indicative of how municipality-owned real estate companies (so-called *Allmännnyttiga Bostadsbolag*, directly translating into something like "Public Utility Real Estate Companies") play a key role in providing housing units for low-income households in particular. The municipality-owned real estate companies are thus nested in a thickly textured institutional setting, and operate on the basis of a combination of more conventional market mechanisms and devices similar to any other market actor, but also respond to political interests and agendas as it is the democratically elected local political assembly that acts as the principal of these companies. As the political majority may shift, municipality-owned real estate companies need to adjust their strategies and work practices on the basis of new policies following public elections. In some municipalities the political majority changes frequently and thus generates certain disruptions (not always of necessity a bad thing), whereas other municipalities preserve a more stable political alliances over time, in many cases simply because voter preferences are stable and thus more predictable. Under all conditions, municipality-owned real estate companies are hybrid organizations (Battilana and Dorado, 2010; Oliver and Montgomery, 2000) that serve as the backbone of the Swedish low-end housing market,[1] and rent regulation policies, rules, and practices, including negotiations with the tenants' interest organization (Swedish Union of Tenants, *Hyresgästföreningen*), are all supportive of a predictable housing market:

> The Swedish housing market operates under some of the world's most pro-tenant rent control laws. Apartment rents are typically determined through once-a-year negotiations between landlords and tenant representatives, usually the Swedish Union of Tenants. Negotiations revolve around two points of emphasis: the utility value of the apartments and the changes to the cost of building management. Utility value is assessed objectively through surveys of apartments' utility values (e.g. through documentation and by means of a points system) and ascertaining the values assigned by tenants (e.g. by means of questionnaires).
>
> (Terner Center for Housing Innovation, 2017: 9)

While the regular housing market for privately owned units, primarily served by municipality-owned real estate companies, does not directly influence the low-end housing market under regular market conditions, the intermediary role of the finance industry that provides mortgage lending services to all sorts of households investing in a home, indirectly affects the supply of credit to low-income households. This condition sets the limits for how municipality-owned real estate companies can actively support the production of, e.g., affordable cooperative housing and freestanding housing units (say, smaller houses equipped with some garden facilities) owned by the resident. Through the household lending channel (discussed in Chapter 2), changes in the middle and high-end housing market segments would affect the supply of credit to less lucrative mortgage lending market niches. The literature on the Swedish housing market points at two conditions that undermine affordable housing policies. First, the level of household debt has grown substantially over the recent period, and second, the liberalization of the economy including increased finance capital supply has made the high-end housing market niches more attractive to serve, which acts to "crowd out" investment in other niches as the supply of house production capacity is limited, both regionally and nationally.

Belfrage and Kallifatides (2018: 891) address the former concern, and provide empirical evidence to substantiate the claim that household debt is now at an unprecedented level in Sweden:

> A powerful example is that prices of the common form of cooperatively owned apartments (*bostadsrätt*) increased by 250% during the period 2005–[20]15 … The rate of increase in both the rental and real estate markets, especially in the big cities, has, in other words, outpaced wage developments by a huge margin. This results in growing levels of household indebtedness, sustained only by a low interest rate environment and extremely liberal credit market regulations and tax regime.
>
> (Belfrage and Kallifatides, 2018: 891)

Soaring levels of household debt, and in metropolitan areas in particular, with the Stockholm region having the most pronounced growth in household debt levels, result in a situation wherein households cannot absorb higher levels of debt, some commentators argue. Fortunately, from the policy makers' and market regulators' perspective, Sweden has currently a comparably modest level of state debt, and can now access finance capital on the global finance market at an historically low interest rate. During the Covid-19 pandemic in 2020–2022, the state of Sweden (and many other comparable states) sharply increased its sovereign debt to be able to transfer finance capital to households (to a smaller degree, and as part of the public health care model) and to employers (having their labor compensation costs covered as employees were instructed by the authorities to stay at home to curb the spread of the virus). However, such a transfer of public resources to households and privately owned companies, tolerated under extraordinary conditions such as those during the 2020–2022 period, cannot be sustained over time as it undermines the legitimacy of the budget discipline credo, and as it more widely violates social norms regarding economic self-sufficiency. In the end, the Covid-19 pandemic would further reinforce the current trend rather than resulting in disruptions, as the finance market regulation agency Finansinspektionen granted households the right to withhold mortgage debt interest payments during the period. Thus, the household debt stock is likely to have grown during the period.

By 2018, Belfrage and Kallifatides (2018: 892) write, "a massive 25% of Swedish households with mortgages owe more than 400% of their disposable income. One in 10 owes more than six times the household disposable income." In comparison, in the UK, the number of households above the 400 percent threshold is currently at *circa* 3.5 percent (Belfrage and Kallifatides, 2018: 893). As mortgage lending is primarily serviced by a handful of stock-listed large-scale banks (unlike in the US, wherein mortgage lending is provided by so-called Government Sponsored Enterprises such as Freddie Mac and Fannie Mae; Frame, et al., 2015; Marshall and Concha, 2012), the transfer of household interest payment to the banks, reporting considerable return-on-equity levels over time, has resulted in an animated debate regarding what the adequate level of real mortgage interest rate would be. The situation with a marked growth in household debt is, however, consistent with an international trend in many OECD countries. Lower labor compensation, welfare transfer systems that are either underfinanced or substantially reduced, and less generous fringe benefits for employees (not least in the US; Hacker, Rehm, and Schlesinger, 2013), including reduced or eliminated pension fund payments, have left no other opportunity for households than to maintain budgets on the basis of increased debt, resulting in a welfare policy model at times referred to as "debtfare" (Lavinas, 2018: 515).

This brings us to the second question, pertaining to housing financing and household indebtedness. The limited capacity of medium to high-income households to absorb further debt may be interpreted as an opportunity for also low-income household to benefit from the finance industry expansion observed over more than two decades, but in fact the opposite scenario is more plausible; if medium to high-income households are in distress (as, e.g., was the case during the Covid-19 pandemic), then credit losses in the lending stock would first create higher interbank-lending costs for individual banks (Braun, 2020; Wansleben, 2020; Gabor, 2016), and second, a general concern regarding the liquidity and solvency of the finance industry and banking sector (see, e.g., Dang, Gorton, and Holmström, 2020) may result in bank runs (Bubb and Prasad, 2014; Gorton and Metrick, 2012; Diamond and Dybvig, 1983) and asset price drops (Acharya and Viswanathanm, 2011; Allen and Gale, 1994) if finance market actors collectively chase more liquid asset holdings to ward off a liquidity crisis. "[T]he 'tail risks' of mortgage loans, if held by financial institutions, can result in a run on those institutions by their short-term creditors and a breakdown in credit markets," Bubb and Prasad (2014: 1546) write. While this latter scenario is less plausible given the tighter monitoring of the finance industry after 2008, banks are still unwilling to expose themselves to risk, or to be criticized for or accused of participating in imprudent or even predatory lending. Consequently, concerns regarding levels of debt in the medium to high-income household market segment may spill over to the low-end housing market niche.

Related to housing finance, a sizeable scholarly literature, in many cases published in urban studies and other non-economic disciplines, expresses a concern regarding the limited political ambition in terms of reducing the impact of market de-regulation reforms. Hedin, Clark, Lundholm, and Malmberg (2012: 444) speak about "the neoliberalization of Swedish housing" over the last decades, beginning in the early 1990s when the new first center-right government—the first government in Sweden led by a conservative prime minister (Carl Bildt) since 1930s—decided to close down the Ministry of Housing in 1991. Thörn and Thörn (2017: 294) describe this decision as the moment when "[a] fundamental roll-back of the welfare era's urban reforms was initiated, accompanied by re-regulations supporting privatization and marketization of the public housing sector." When a social democratic government took office in 1994, following a major financial crisis that left the national finances in a poor condition (Englund, 1999), the new government effectively prolonged the existing housing market policy, relieved the state finances from a net cost of circa 30 billion Swedish crowns in the late 1980s to instead generate a net income at the same monetary level a decade later (Hedin, Clark, Lundholm, and Malmberg, 2012: 445). It should be noted that the Swedish state has maintained its generous subsidies to low-income households (*bostadsbidrag*) over the period, so the housing policy has preserved some of its welfare devices. Regardless of such provision, critical scholars have emphasized how rental costs have outpaced both the cost of living in privately owned housing units (indicating rental unit tenant disadvantages), and the rate of inflation: between 1986 and 2005, rent increased by 122 percent, while inflation grew by 49 percent (Hedin, Clark, Lundholm, and Malmberg, 2012: 446). The period was also characterized by a growth in the Gini Index, an internationally recognized standard measure of economic inequality, albeit from a low level, but nonetheless increasing from 0.226 in 1991 to 0.294 in 2000 (Hedin, Clark, Lundholm, and Malmberg, 2012: 446).

In the 2000s, legislative reforms initiated by a new center-right government elected in 2006 reduced the previous restrictions on municipal sell-outs of public housing (being effective in July 2007), which benefitted tenants living in rental units in lucrative and centrally located areas, who could both acquire a contract at a discount, and thereafter see their housing assets grow in market value. These reforms that permitted municipality-owned real-estate companies to sell off units was also accompanied by reforms in the fiscal system. In 2008, property taxation was changed from being a progressive national tax to become a "regressive municipal tax with a flat rate of 6,000 crowns per year for all properties with a taxation value above 800,000 crowns or 0.75 percent of assessed taxation value if below 800,000 crowns" (Hedin, Clark, Lundholm, and Malmberg, 2012: 458). This fiscal system reform is arguably one of the single most comprehensive economic reforms in Sweden in the recent period, not least in terms of how it benefits high-net worth households by strongly reducing their tax burden. The reason for implementing this reform was that the previous fiscal model was premised on market price evaluations that resulted, e.g., in people living in attractive locations (say, in seaside resorts increasing their population substantially during the summer) paying considerable property taxes on the basis of inflated local housing market prices (determined by documented sales), despite these residents having no intentions to themselves sell their homes and move someplace else. In its actual enforcement, the previous fiscal policy generated undesirable effects, and was widely understood to bias housing market prices, and to discredit the fiscal system more widely. In addition, it was a communication challenge for policy makers to explain why residents should pay remarkably high taxes on investments already made on an annual basis, and even being penalized when managing their housing facilities prudently (i.e., when investing in refurbishment). The previous fiscal policy was thus deeply unpopular despite contributing to the evening out economic inequality, and it included a considerable degree of information costs as the system relied on self-reported investments made in the facilities. Under all conditions, the retraction of a poorly designed fiscal policy and the replacement of the new model were widely regarded as being politically palatable in the eyes of broad political coalitions.

Free markets or regulated housing supply?

Regardless of the rationale of housing market reforms, Hedin, Clark, Lundholm, and Malmberg (2012: 460) insist that during the period from the early 1990s, "the housing sector in Sweden went from being one of the most regulated in Europe to the most liberal market governed." While "liberalization" may serve to be equally a positive and a negative marker depending on preferences and perspective, for scholars such as Hedin, Clark, Lundholm, and Malmberg (2012) and Thörn and Thörn (2017), the shift from a centrally planned and regulated housing market to a more market-based model has been detrimental to economic equality and the (relative) welfare of low-income households. As the two empirical chapters included in this second part of this volume will indicate, low-income households can hardly be accurately portrayed as being exposed to brute market forces in the same way as they are in, e.g., the US (as discussed in Chapter 1). As municipality real estate companies own a considerable share of the rental housing stock, and themselves are receptive to political objectives and agendas, these real estate companies provide affordable housing with comparably high quality, including maintenance and cleaning services to keep housing units and the local environment neat and tidy. Furthermore, actors in the political system are cognizant of the direct and indirect social costs derived from inadequate housing, such as poor schooling results in suburban city districts, and other socio-economic conditions that contribute to increased economic inequality differentials. Furthermore, rents are negotiated between the tenants' interest organization and the municipality real estate companies on the basis of a fairly detailed model wherein "tenant utility" is calculated, and where the attractiveness of the specific rental unit is estimated. These standardized procedures to determine the monthly and annual rental costs protect low-income households from being mistreated, and unlike in the case of the US, if vacancies are the case, municipality companies cannot push the additional costs onto existing tenants but need to include such costs on their balance sheets and bottom line results.

The concern is that despite all these procedures, routines, and mechanisms for negotiating rents being in place, if the demand for municipality real estate rental units raise sharply in demand, following the last ten years' of increased migration, and primarily by asylum seekers, the existing housing stock becomes saturated despite the best intentions. Therefore, when Hedin, Clark, Lundholm, and Malmberg (2012: 444) speak about the neoliberalization of Swedish housing, this is primarily true for the housing market segments that serve middle-class and high-net worth households, indicated by the level of household debt derived from mortgage lending. In the low-end of the housing market, wherein residents' degree of financial self-sufficiency on the basis of salaried work is more limited, households cannot easily access credit through the regular household lending channel. Under these conditions, housing facilities are primarily provided by municipality real estate companies, themselves being hybrid organizations combining market activities while attending to political policies and decisions.

The municipality real estate companies do generate an economic return (oftentimes determined by political decision makers), but this financial performance is plausibly generated on the basis of all the tenants' contributing differently on the basis of their varying use of resources such as heating and water, and services such as repairs and refurbishing. This means that different tenants are more or less attractive to have as clients from a financial perspective (as rents are not negotiated on how many residents each unit will host), but this "intra-subsidizing" within the tenants' community is not functionally different from wage policies in large-scale corporations, wherein less skilled, educated, and effective co-workers are subsidized by more high-performing co-workers as the employer believes the information costs demanded to negotiate absolutely fair salaries are overwhelming (Cobb and Lin, 2017: 432). This means that municipality real estate companies act consistently with other large corporations that face considerable information costs when managing clients or co-workers with diverse qualities and skills.

To speak of a neoliberalization as being a tendency in all segments or niches of the Swedish housing market thus underrates or marginalizes the key role of municipality real estate companies, and how they manage their business on the basis of rules and procedures that are partially politically determined, partially market based. Furthermore, municipality-owned real estate company executives or directors do not have the authority and discretion to make policy decisions regarding, e.g., migration, nor labor market reforms, but they are still expected to serve households with limited budgets, and in many cases with a low degree of de facto financial self-sufficiency. To indicate that these municipality real estate companies would act strictly on the basis of market conditions to maximize the return on asset holdings is incorrect. On the contrary, municipality real estate companies act as a corporate branch of the political system that is held responsible for the welfare of its constituencies. Some critics also argue that the lack of reforms and novel thinking in the low-end housing market tends to reduce social and economic welfare. It is for instance a conventional view among mainstream card-carrying economists to deplore the absence of market pricing in rental unit markets, an argument premised on the idea that lock-in effects benefit existing tenants and persistently over-subsidize such households ("the winners" of the current system), which reduces the dynamics of the rental units market. Furthermore, in dynamic business regions such as metropolitan Stockholm, the inflow of highly educated, productive, and enterprising individuals, not least younger people, is inhibited by the lack of a dynamic and flexible housing market, which results in a net loss in economic welfare that would benefit all constituencies as the use of resources cannot be optimized. In Sweden, this recurrent debate regarding "market pricing of rental units" has to date resulted in few reforms, primarily because there are few political advantages derived from acting to structurally re-organize the housing market as such reforms would be unpopular, presumably enticing voter penalties. This basically leaves a small group of economists, equipped with their economic idea that efficiency maximization is the lodestar of all legitimate economic reforms and policies, a proposition that may make sense *in abstracto* but that oftentimes ignore prevalent social norms regarding justice and fairness and the unintended consequences of purposeful action, comparably alone with their beliefs. The marginalization of the proponents of free market rental unit pricing policies in Sweden thus speaks against the neoliberalization thesis.

Taken together, the Swedish housing market can be portrayed as a form of 80/20 housing market, wherein 80 percent of the households are financially self-sufficient (even though some benefit from specific subsidies, and not least the 30 percent tax deductions on the annual interest rate cost on mortgage loans) and thus able to access credit via mortgage lending institutions. This majority of the households are exposed to a more leniently regulated housing market but with major banks acting as the primarily supplier of credit. The remaining 20 percent are low-income households that are either not financially self-sufficient on the basis of low inclusion in the labor market, or, even in the case of salaried work income, still not being eligible for mortgage loans. This group of households are dependent on the rental unit housing market, and in many cases benefit from municipality real estate companies' supply of housing units. For the top 80 percent households, the housing market looks quite different from the housing market that serves the remaining 20 per cent. Scholars who point at the reforms implemented over the last three decades tend to understate the long-term commitment made by municipalities and the government to serve the low-end housing market. Furthermore, scholars tend turn a blind eye to other economic and social reforms implemented in the period, policies that themselves are co-produced with housing market policy changes. That is, housing policy and housing market mechanisms are institutionally nested in ways that are rendered obscure by off-the-shelf catch-phrases such as "neoliberalization," unable to reach down to the level of actual business practices, and day-to-day activities that factually provide qualitative housing for also low-income households.

Study methodology

The design of the study, data collection methods, and data analysis approaches are accounted for in this section.

Design of the study

The study reported in this article is based on a case study methodology (Gillham, 2000; Stake, 1996). Gerring (2004: 342. Original emphasis omitted) defines a case study as "[a]n intensive study of a single unit for the purpose of understanding a larger class of (similar) units. A unit connotes a spatially bounded phenomenon … observed at a single point in time or over some delimited period of time." The conventional wisdom regarding interpretivist studies such as case studies is that the scholar must present a "faithful and authentic representation of people's perceptions of their lived experience" (Eisenhardt, Graebner, and Sonenshein, 2016: 114). More specifically, urbanism studies and studies of urban development oftentimes use cases study methodologies, both in the case of classic studies such as William F. Whyte's ([1943] 1993) *Street corner society*, and more recent studies of urban renewal in city districts in, e.g., London (Beswick and Penny, 2018), Berlin, New York (Fields and Uffer, 2016), and Paris (Guironnet, Attuyer, and Halbert, 2016).

The case being studied is a cross-organizational urban renewal project in an inner suburb in a Swedish metropolitan area, and the project included municipality real estate companies, private real estate developers, and city administration representatives. The current project was initiated and managed by a major municipality-owned real estate company, owning no less than 94 percent of the housing units in the city district. The city district is characterized by medium to low net-worth households (with a majority in the lower end) including *circa* 9,000 residents in total, a high proportion of immigrants including 97 different nationalities being represented among the residents, and a "blighted" urban milieu. As the municipality-owned real estate company makes significant investment in cleaning services to maintain the public spaces and the housing facilities are well kept, the first impression of the city district is far from alarming, but the local schools are underperforming, the inclusion in the labor market is markedly lower than the city average, and poverty rates are higher. Furthermore, the Swedish police authority issues reports that name city districts that are "socially vulnerable," or "particularly socially vulnerable"—districts characterized by high degrees of street crime and other social and economic risks. The city district being studied is one of five such particularly socially vulnerable districts in the local metropolitan area.

In 2017, a new project to reinvigorate the city district was initiated, and the project plan included four major pillars, whereof three related to construction management activities: (1) to refurbish the current rental units stock; (2) to create possibilities for privately owned units (e.g., rental units are transformed into privately owned apartments, so-called community housing); and (3) to build new housing units, preferably freestanding houses that could attract more affluent local residents. These three activities, essentially economic in orientation as they are associated with financial investment and thus with risk taking, were supported by (4) a campaign targeting social issues, including the perceived security of the residents, to improve the local schooling quality, and to enforce police activities to prevent, e.g., street-corner drug dealing activities. However, as the decision making authority that would affect the value of amenities (or, alternatively, reduce the cost of "negative" amenities) was in many cases located outside of the project team, e.g., in municipality agencies or in state-controlled agencies, the project team needed to continuously collaborate with such actors. This finding is consistent with the claim that the construction industry is a "loosely coupled" industry that routinely rely on cross-sector collaborations (Dubois and Gadde, 2002; Harty, 2008).

Data collection

The data collection included three sources of data. First, interviews were conducted with representatives of the companies and organizations participating in the urban renewal project. Interviews were conducted *in situ*, in most cases in the offices of the interviewees. The interviews were structured on the basis of an interview guide, were recorded, and lasted for a median duration time of approximately 1.5 hours. In total, 22 persons were interviewed, and the sample included the project leader and the project management team, business development directors in private and municipality real estate companies, CEOs of municipality real estate companies, and other expert groups.

Second, the research team participated during project meetings wherein either the contractual conditions or agreements pertaining to project activities were determined, or where specific project activities were discussed. During such participative observations, field notes were written to account for the issues being

Table 3.1 Data collected in the research project

Data collection method	*Total time*
Interviews	23h
Project meetings participation	5.5h
Informal conversation with project team members	3.5h
Total:	32h

addressed and topics being debated in the project team. Project meetings provided the research team with the opportunity to listen to how the project participants jointly addressed and defined project goals and challenges, and how certain interests were articulated at various points in time (e.g., commercial real estate companies frequently referred to the need for specific accounting information to make decisions). Third and finally, internal documents and reports issued by the participant organizations were retrieved and used as input material for understanding how large-scale urban renewal project are managed and handle a variety of interrelated project goals. For instance, the long-term strategy of the major municipality-owned real estate company indicates how economic and political (i.e., social) goals are intended to be mutually supported over the coming period). Table 3.1 summarizes the data collected.

Data analysis

The empirical data, e.g., interview transcripts, were coded according to a standardized procedure. Gioia, Corley, and Hamilton (2013: 20) distinguish between first and second-order coding, wherein first-order coding (which Strauss and Corbin, 1998, refer to as "open coding") quite broadly introduces empirical categories to label or describe interview excerpts. In the second-order coding procedure ("axial coding" in Strauss and Corbin, 1998), theoretical codes that are broader and more inclusive than the first-order codes are introduced to reduce the number of codes to "a more manageable number" (Gioia, Corley, and Hamilton, 2013: 20). Based on these second-order codes, the theorizing process is intended to formulate new theoretical categories, ultimately connected in a logically consistent and plausible manner, consistent with the empirical data, and fitting with other theoretical concepts.

The interviews were transcribed verbatim by a professional writing bureau, and each interview was coded by one senior researcher. Based on these first-order codes, interview excerpts were co-located under theoretically induced second-order categories, in the next instant subject to theorizing. By conducting this coding procedure strictly and following the credo that the research should make a "faithful and authentic" account of the empirical data, the empirical material reported below serves the two ends to demonstrate how project objectives were approached and the theoretical significance of such activities and decisions.

Summary and conclusion

The varieties of capitalism literature indicated that all national economic systems have their own features and idiosyncrasies. At the same time, studies show that housing assets are the single most important source of household wealth, over time periods and across national and regional boundaries. The observed national variety in fiscal policies, housing production, and housing policy seem to be unified in their capacity in generating economic wealth for households that owns their primary residence. The empirical material presented in the second part of this volume is collected in Sweden, and it is important to underline the specifications and traditions in this particular jurisdiction, at the same time as these differences should not be overstated. By the end of the day, housing policy, regardless of its content and combinations of tax exemptions, subsidies, regulatory rules, etc., seem to generate wealth inequality differentials that benefit households that own their homes, all things equal.

Note

1 Ambidexterity is an alternative analytical concept that denotes the capacity to handle a variety of objectives, e.g., commercial goals and goals stipulated by political agendas, simultaneously (see, e.g., Markides, 2007; Gibson and Birkinshaw, 2004; Tushman and O'Reilly, 1996). In this volume, hybrid organizations are defined as organizations that have the ambidexterity needed to serve multiple objectives.

4 Ambiguous policy objectives and their consequences

Urban development project goals, their legitimacy, and the role of professional ignorance

Introduction

Project management models are essentially structured on the basis of rationalist principles and mechanisms wherein costs and benefits are weighted against one another to optimize the return on equity investment (Lenfle and Söderlund, 2019; Hodgson, 2004). In many cases, project management devices such as time charts (Yakura, 2002) and calculative practices (Miller, 2001) serve to conceal uncertainties and ambiguities that complex projects of necessity include, to generate a sense of ontological certainty and being conducive of accountability. In a milieu where the future is uncertain and cannot be anticipated in detail, rational devices serve to stabilize and render a cognitively complex situation meaningful and manageable (Cabantous and Gond, 2011). In urban development projects, which combine construction work activities and political objectives, say, regarding increased housing quality for low-income households (see, e.g., Van Bortel et al. 2019; Metcalf, 2018), or more vague goals such as the ambitions to reduce ethnic segregation (e.g., Faber, 2020; Diamond and McQuade, 2019; Fennell, 2017), or to increase welfare more generally (Ansell, 2019; Schwartz and Seabrooke, 2008), project management practices and output are even more complicated to assess as there may be a shortage of standardized metrics regarding stipulated outcomes. For instance, how is ethnic segregation measured as a factual condition, and what are tolerable levels of ethnic segregation in a liberal and democratic society wherein individuals and families are given the decision-making authority to freely choose where to settle?

This chapter addresses whether affordable housing policies and initiatives are legitimate in the eyes of a variety of stakeholder and market participants, and second if that is the case, how can cross-organizational consortia and projects jointly generate affordable housing and housing welfare more generally under current conditions, being overdetermined by a variety of factors that are in many cases beyond the influence of market actors assigned the role to provide affordable housing? As these two issues are related to different theoretical perspectives, this chapter is divided into two parts: the first parts addresses the question of legitimacy, and the second part addresses what is referred to as *professional ignorance* in theoretical and empirical terms. Related to the second issue, which begs some explanation in this

DOI: 10.4324/9781003244417-7

context, in the case of consumer credit rating (Lauer, 2017; Kear, 2017; Polillo, 2011; Poon, 2007), wherein the creditworthiness of a presumptive loan borrower is assessed, the metrics used derive from an algorithm that legally speaking is a firm-specific asset and consequently protected from outsiders' inspection (Kroll et al., 2017; Citron and Pasquale, 2014). Under such secrecy clauses, neither the money lender (say, a mortgage loan originator) nor the borrower (e.g., a household buying a residential home) has a detailed understanding of how creditworthiness is calculated, and yet both act on the basis of such numerical information. In such situations, what is referred to as professional ignorance (Abbott, 2010), the ability to actively overlook what is in fact *not known* to be able to proceed, is a professional skill that guides the actor's work (Jeon, 2020; Schwarzkopf, 2020; Schaefer, 2019; Bakken and Wiik, 2018; Davies and McGoey, 2012).

The professional ignorance capacity is arguably closely related to the challenges that the consortia of market actors are assigned to handle. One of the key objectives with the urban development project was to get the city district off the police authority's official list over "particularly socially vulnerable city districts," an objective that was enacted by the city government and written into formal decision documents such as the project budget. Unfortunately, similar to the case of credit rating practices, the police authority's calculation of measures and the resulting assessment of socially vulnerable city district were not disclosed, which means that project team participants acted on the basis of information that was not known in detail. Consequently, project team participants were assigned the role to be held responsible for objectives whose underlying mechanisms and causes cannot be rationally assumed to be known or understood by the actors held accountable as these mechanisms were concealed to audiences. In addition, the urban development project also intended to create privately owned units in so-called community housing organizations out of the current stock of rental housing units, now owned by a major municipality-owned real estate company. In the case of this stipulated project objective, policy instructions were issued without any detailed discussions about the costs or benefits, or the wider implications of the policy if being implemented. This left project participants with two policy goals that were insufficiently detailed but nonetheless demanded actions to be taken.

The key learning from the empirical case reported is that political objectives are frequently formulated in a vocabulary that is either vague or ambiguous (Fotaki, 2010; Romano, 2005), or that leave practical issues as a secondary concern for frontline practitioners and administrators to sort out and to determine "on the ground" (Riles, 2011: 232). This political decision-making process is not of necessity faulty as policy makers oftentimes lack a detailed understanding of practical conditions and concerns, but it may unintendedly result in a loss of accountability as, e.g., project participants in the current case can make reference to imprecise performance objectives, and/or the absence of meaningful benchmarks ex post facto. Furthermore, political decision making on the basis of ambiguous goals is at risk of resulting in policy drift (Funk and Hirschman, 2014: 672) as project managers are given the authority to interpret political goals as it either suits their own (rather than the constituencies') interests (see, e.g., Westphal and Zajac, 2001), or in terms of what is deemed possible to practically accomplish under current conditions (i.e., project ambitions may be lowered in ways that are inconsistent with policy makers' expectations and/or instructions). Nevertheless, in this specific case, ignorance (here defined in theoretical terms, and not as a pejorative term in the conventional semantic meaning of the word, then denoting the individual or collective failure to cognitively process and pay attention to available data and information) on the part of both policy makers and project participants plays a key and oftentimes underappreciated role in large-scale and politically shaped urban development projects. Taken together, the empirical material demonstrates how ambiguously or poorly operationalized goals do not leave large-scale urban development projects in a state of paralysis as project team participants use professional ignorance to construct an action plan regardless of incomplete policy instructions. Finally, the empirical material indicates that policy making should preferably balance quite precise goals, if possible accompanied by accurate and standardized performance metrics, and broader social-economic ambitions, potentially not always easy to measure with great precision, and still render the question of accountability ex post a primary concern in policy making and governance activities.

The municipality-owned real estate company model: the question of legitimacy

Suchman (1995) distinguishes between *strategic legitimacy* and *institutional legitimacy*. Strategic legitimacy is based on an instrumental view of legitimacy wherein insiders, e.g., CEOs or the board of directors can maintain a high degree of control over how the organization is perceived by market actors or audiences. In contrast, the institutional legitimacy concept does not assume such agential capacities or authority. Rather, external institutions provide "cultural definitions" that "determine how the organization is built, how it is run, and, simultaneously, how it is understood and evaluated," Suchman (1995: 576) proposes. In this view, legitimacy is not a species of an organizational asset that can be built, modified, and subjected to decision making discretion but is derived from the organization's factual activities in a social field or a specific market; in the institutional legitimacy view, Suchman (1995: 576. Emphasis in the original) writes, "*legitimacy* and *institutionalization* are virtually synonymous."

To further substantiate the concept of institutional legitimacy, Suchman (1995: 578) introduces three types of legitimacy: (1) *pragmatic legitimacy*, which "rests on the self-interested calculations of an organization's most immediate audiences" (Suchman, 1995: 578); (2) *moral legitimacy*, which reflects "a positive normative evaluation of the organization and its activities" (Suchman, 1995: 579); and (3) *cognitive legitimacy*, being a concept that underlines that legitimacy does not always only derive from interests and evaluations but is cognitively constructed as being an indispensable component of, e.g., governance systems or markets. In Suchman's (1995) account, legitimacy is derived from the location of focal organization in nested institutional and governance structures, and, more specifically, in order to be perceived as legitimate, an organization (say, a municipality-owned real estate company, as in the specific case discussed shortly) needs to provide some benefits for market actors (pragmatic legitimacy), be regarded as acting consistently with stipulated moral and ethical principles (moral legitimacy), and more widely be perceived as contributing to social and economic welfare among stakeholders and audiences (cognitive legitimacy). Based on Suchman's (1995) concept of institutional legitimacy, in the following, the role of municipality real estate companies in the Swedish housing market is examined as being a hybrid organization that in the eyes of market actors effectively combine the political objective to provide affordable housing with a more regular market actor and market maker role. In the end, the hybridity of the municipality-owned real estate company device, a specific organization form in the Swedish housing policy model, generates benefits for a variety of constituencies, and not least for low net-worth households that rely on these organizations.

In the sections below, three issues in the empirical material are discussed: (1) the role of the municipality real estate companies in the housing market; (2) the legitimacy of the municipality-owned real estate company model; (3) the unintended consequences of the municipality-owned real estate company model.

The role of the municipality real estate companies in the housing market

In the Swedish housing market governance model, the municipality-owned real estate company (referred to with the acronym MREC in the following) is a somewhat odd legal entity. On the one hand, the MREC is assigned the role to provide affordable housing while operating on the basis of market rules and sound business practices; on the other hand, the MREC is responsive to the political interests expressed by the local government in the City Hall. In Sweden, this role is regulated on the basis of the Municipality Real Estate Company Act (*Lagen om allmännyttiga kommunala bostadsaktiebolag*, Swedish law number 2010: 879).

The CFO of a major MREC accounted for this dual governance model: "We act in a situation with two governance structures: The political governance and the executive governance." The CFO continued by emphasizing the operative autonomy of the MREC regardless of political interests: "We are not the City Hall. We're *owned* by the City Hall, but our assignment is something completely different. City Hall mustn't believe they can shovel money back and forth. That cannot be done" (CFO, Municipality-owned real estate company, male). Under all conditions, MREC plays a key role in the Swedish housing market, especially in terms of providing affordable housing for less affluent households. In suburban city districts characterized by lower purchasing power and various socio-economic challenges, MRECs have been given an even more pronounced role in the being the contact point between tenants and the municipality and, by default, the state and its defined agencies. In addition to provide qualitative affordable housing, activities organized by MRECs include social activities for elderly tenants, support to homework assistance initiatives for school children, the creation of internships and certain employment in, e.g., maintenance and cleaning work, support for local labor market agencies helping, e.g., women to find salaried work, the sponsoring of a variety of so-called "yard clubs" (i.e., tenants sharing the same yard jointly run a club of interest) including agriculture activities, chess clubs, or book reading clubs, and participation in a variety of corporate social responsibility activities, including collaborations with local sports clubs to provide post-curricular activities for school children.

The CEO of a major MREC recognized the role of serving as a "frontline organization," and emphasized that there was great expectation laid on MREC to handle a variety of issues:

> We need to be skilled facility management providers. In these [socially vulnerable] neighbourhoods, we need to be *super-skilled* facility management providers. That includes a variety of activities, including keeping the city districts neat and tidy, safe, and such things.
>
> (CEO, Municipality-owned real estate company, female)

The CEO referred to one of her predecessors who frequently referred to the MREC as "a form of government agency," being in the position to act as an agent representing the municipality and, by implication, state administration (CEO, Municipality-owned Real Estate Company, Female). According to the CEO, it is only possible to maintain such a role as long as the tenants have full confidence in their landlord: "There is a great confidence in the real estate company's role in the local community … That is a reputational capital that we can make use of" (CEO, Municipality-owned Real Estate Company, Female). In addition, other actors being involved in local urban development projects shared this affirmative view of the role of the MREC. One interviewee, representing a city agency, referred to the "social responsibilities" of the MREC: "A municipality-owned real estate company have [a certain role to play] that is part of its responsibilities … Its social responsibility, I'd call it" (Urban Development Officer, City Agency, Female).

Even though MRECs have the resources and the skills needed to provide qualitative affordable housing, it could not act on its own to alter the precarious situation in some of the suburban city districts, several interviewees argued. The project leader in the major urban development project argued that in order to improve the welfare of socially vulnerable city districts, the MREC needed to be assisted by a variety of private companies and municipality agencies, at the same time as the MREC was expected to take responsibility for the situation and was held accountable for outcomes:

> It is oftentimes remarked that the real estate companies must lead the way because they are closest to the residents. But also the schooling department needs to carry its responsibilities, and the local authorities, and the sport clubs need to take theirs, because they all need to be involved to make this happen. But it is probably correct to say that we need to coordinate and take responsibility. We need to be held accountable.
>
> (Project leader, Municipality-owned real estate company, male)

In these accounts, MRECs are legitimate and centrally located agents in the housing market, being the bridge between political entities and local residents, and consequently having the authority to accomplish many politically stated objectives but in many cases in close collaboration with a variety of market actors and other organizations.

The legitimacy of the municipality-owned real estate company model

MRECs are by design and by implication part of a governance model that is intended to increase economic and social welfare by supplying affordable housing as a welfare provision. At the same time, this dual role as a market actor and political device is far from uncontroversial, especially when political objectives are introduced and affect the regular housing market. The CEO of one of the MRECs addressed the question of what services and support that benefits the tenants could be included in the rent-income based activities as a "grey zone," an area that was subject to constant deliberation, reflection, and bargaining (CEO, Municipality-owned real estate company, female):

> This discussion has been ongoing for as long as I can remember: How far do our responsibilities extend after all? What are sound business activities, and what can we justify or not? The policy makers have no clear benchmarks. Say, when the budget prescribes that the municipality real estate companies 'should have security hosts guarding the tram stops'—is that even legally justifiable? ... These activities are funded by the tenants' rents, not by tax-money; these are the tenants' money [paying for social services].
>
> (CEO, Municipality-owned Real Estate Company, Female)

The CFO of another MREC was equally concerned with the lack of demarcation lines regarding what social responsibilities should be carried by municipality-owned companies:

> We have some activities in the borderlands. What are our core business, and what are the key responsibilities of the City Hall? It's a grey zone. I am not so concerned with acting in that grey zone, but we mustn't cross the line. At times, I believe we're at risk to do so.
>
> (CFO, Municipality-owned real estate company, male)

The CFO referred to another city district that has been subject to considerable reforms over more than two decades, and argued that the local MREC, owning the majority of the rental units, was today "run like a small municipality," and with the CEO acting in the role of a local politician, or even landowner. According to the CFO, this is an unfortunate situation as it extends the authority of the owner of the housing stock in ways that potentially violate administrative law and municipality law, governance standards, and social norms.

In practice, the line of demarcation between "just right," and "too much" social responsibility taking is far from easily determined. Several interviewees argued that if the choice is between taking responsibility for the economic and social welfare of low net-worth households but under the risk to generate externalities, and taking no such responsibilities at all, the former alternative is preferred. That is, social norms justified current market activities, given the complexity of the housing and housing financing market, one of the interviewees argued: "To just wait around and to hope that some organization would come forward and declare that they are willing to do something, I believe that is a disastrous position. You need to take responsibility yourself" (Business developer, Municipality-owned housing development company, male). He continued:

> I believe the dominant municipality real estate companies have the incentives. For starters, they want to raise the market value of their own real estate stock. Furthermore, they want to reduce the cost of vandalism, and to raise the satisfaction of tenants ... There are many things you can do, and a lot of money to save.
>
> (Business developer, Municipality-owned housing development company, Male)

The business developer added that at present, there is a shortage of market actors that have the authority, the skills, and the financial resources needed to act the way MRECs do to provide affordable housing and increase housing welfare. In this view, MRECs can legitimately act on the basis of a policy makers' instructions if net economic and social welfare are generated. Needless to say, to prove that such welfare is actually generated is a far from trivial affair, which results in extended discussions regarding the MRECs' legitimate role in both legal and practical terms.

The unintended consequences of the municipality-owned real estate company model

Even though many of the interviewees argued that MRECs would assume social responsibilities that extend outside of merely being a conventional market actor and landlord, the dual governance structure of the MRECs resulted in situations that were debated. The CFO of one MREC argued that there was a "considerable degree of goal incongruence" in the political objectives articulated by policy makers: the MREC should build new housing units (primarily serviced through the new housing production division), maintain the housing stock, and handle a variety of social responsibilities, but strictly on the basis of rental revenues and with no additional funding provided by the City Hall or the government, that is, within the stipulated budget. Furthermore, several interviewees representing either private market actors or municipality agencies accounted for how the "political process" imposed complications for all actors. One business developer in a cooperative building society argued that the general election cycles, lasting four years in Sweden, tended to disrupt the process as new political agendas were formulated after each new election, which oftentimes rendered previous agendas and agreements obsolete:

> It is a political process, also in the municipality real estate companies. So it's important that there is an ambition that can last over time. But the political

> majority changes. Only since we started this project, a new political coalition has presented new policies. This thing with privately owned units was not part of the first draft.
>
> (Business developer, Cooperative building society, female)

Another interviewee, a project pre-study coordinator representing a private construction engineering company, argued that politicians too often had unfounded expectations regarding what could be accomplished within stipulated budgets and within short time horizons. This resulted in a less than steadfast support for projects being initiated if, e.g., limited progress in projects was criticized in news reporting: "It's one thing that the politicians wish for something, but it is quite another to actually stand up to respond to criticism when there are experiments or work being done," the project pre-study coordinator argued. Another concern was that policy makers were too engaged in "visionary thinking," a tendency that came at the expense of more robust instructions and credible calculations regarding how resources should be allocated to specific projects (Project pre-study coordinator, female). These two concerns resulted in delays and additional costs in also ongoing construction projects, which caused much frustration among various project participants.

Several of the private company representatives were concerned that policy makers failed to pay sufficient attention to the fact that private companies are managed on the basis of a market logic and business principles, and the capacity to generate a bottom line result, and therefore cannot rely on tax-money to cover up for unprofitable urban development or construction projects. The business developer in the cooperative building society said:

> It is important to take responsibility for the social issues and how our city is planned, and to take social responsibilities. But investments also needs to generate a return, because we have no treasury department to extract resources from: there are no other money than the project finances.
>
> (Business developer, Cooperative building society, Female)

Furthermore, in the MRECs, the profit motive was also understated at times, some interviewees argued. The CFO of one of the major MRECs, with extensive experience from private industry, praised his colleagues' commitment to their tenants' welfare but also called for a better understanding of how such projects were financed and what the limitations of "activism" were: "There is much commitment, and much ambition. But the imminent risk is that you [become an activist] rather than to primarily run a business. We need to consider what is best for the corporation" (CFO, Municipality-owned real estate company, male). Referring to himself as a person who "care for what's best for the corporation," while still hoping that he had his "heart in the right place" even though he rejected activist commitments, the CFO were concerned about political objectives gaining the upper hand vis-à-vis business interests, not least because it would, he argued, harm the tenants in the end.

In summary, MRECs were regarded as a resource for the City Hall inasmuch as these corporations have the skills, experience, and the trust needed, and the formal legitimacy to actually provide qualitative affordable housing. On balance, the municipality-owned real estate company model was seen as a legitimate actor, or at worst a "necessary evil" in a housing market situation wherein low net-worth households have few alternatives than to rely on municipality-controlled housing providers. At the same time, there is always the risk of overreaching political objectives, especially when intentions are declared to be good, which generate externalities that befall a variety of market actors and ultimate the benefactors, the tenants that access affordable housing via municipality-owned real estate companies.

The limits of the legitimacy of municipality-owned real estate company initiatives

Interviewees, representing a variety of housing market actors, suggest that the municipality-owned real estate company model is tolerable given the difficulties to provide affordable housing for low net-worth households. In this view, the MRECs serve as the extended arm of the municipality, but this role needs to be honored by promoting transparency in the managerial decision making process, and by encouraging a critical discussion of what are in fact legitimate initiatives for MRECs to finance and to sponsor. All of the interviewees were aware of this delicate balancing of interests in the municipality-owned real estate company model, and the maintenance of regular market activities, but the line of demarcation is not necessarily perfectly clear to all actors.

The concept of legitimacy may not per se prescribe any strict line of demarcation between initiatives being "just right," and activities overreaching formal policies or expectations. What are particularly cumbersome in the specific case is the distinction between activities financed by rental revenues and by tax-money, i.e., activities financed by the municipality-owned real estate company, vis-à-vis the municipality or the state. As recognized by the CEO of one of the municipality real estate companies, much managerial decisions pertaining to tenants' welfare are located in a "grey zone"; there is always the risk that tenants are paying for services via their rent that otherwise are regarded as the responsibility of the municipality and/or the region (e.g., health care activities) or the state (e.g., police work). Furthermore, one of the weaknesses of the municipality-owned real estate company model, unless being carefully monitored by, e.g., policy makers or their defined regulatory agencies, is that it trends toward expansionism, i.e., previous successful initiatives are interpreted in favorable terms, and are therefore complemented by new projects that allegedly make an additional net contribution to the welfare of tenants. Under such conditions, the diminishing marginal utility of the *n*th initiative is easily obscured by the stated ambition to maximize (rather than to optimize) the tenants' welfare.

Instead of being conventional market actors, MRECs respond to policy makers' objectives, at the same time as they are expected to act on the basis of, and to be supportive of regular market practices. This dual governance structure imposes complications in the managerial decision-making process, as in the case to determine how much "social responsibility" should legitimately be carried by MRECs. Yet the municipality-owned real estate company model is widely recognized as being legitimate and perhaps even necessary by a variety of market actors. A skeptical attitude towards state or municipality-controlled housing market activities needs to be recognized, but in the domain of housing policy, low net-worth households will inevitably be disadvantaged, or excluded in the housing market, which leaves municipalities and the state with few alternatives than to provide affordable housing on the basis of other means.

As discussed in Chapter 1, Metcalf (2018: 61) suggests that policy makers promoting affordable housing have four classes of policy tools: (1) direct provision of social housing; (2) vouchers to increase the purchasing power of households; (3) price controls on rents; and (4) regulations on development of new housing supply. In Metcalf's account, speaking about the national US housing market, the two first policy tools have a limited impact as the demand for such financial support is widely overshadowing the supply, and as in the current political climate, increased budgets in this area is an unlikely scenario. In contrast, rent control is commonly discredited by economists, but Metcalf (2018: 66) proposes that once rent control is established (as it is in, e.g., New York City), it is "generally not very damaging in its impacts on the housing market." Fourth and finally, to modify the regulatory framework for housing production, e.g., reduce the fees paid by real estate development companies and other costs would possibly increase the supply of housing, but such reforms take time and demand political bargaining. As cities and municipalities can extract considerable costs when selling land, regulatory reform supportive of housing production is not a very promising scenario either. That is, under current conditions, Metcalf (2018) suggests, rent control appears to provide the shortest route and less costly approach to secure a stock of affordable housing units. In the light of the efficacy of the four policy tools examined by Metcalf (2018), the municipality-owned real estate model arguably has benefits over other, complementary or competing models. Furthermore, in the current housing policy model, municipality real estate companies are also held responsible for the production of new housing, and the close ties between municipality-owned real estate companies and policy makers in collaboration with private real estate developers and construction companies, are potentially supportive of new housing production in the low-end of the housing market.

Speaking in theoretical terms, in the current case, affordable housing is provided outside of the social housing/council housing model, widely used in, e.g., the UK and the Netherlands. The concept of legitimacy has been introduced to address the porous line of demarcation between an adequate level of ambition regarding the responsibilities of the municipality real estate companies, and the overreaching of such authority. Suchman (1995: 579) suggests that in the institutional legitimacy perspective, legitimacy is grounded in, and justified by institutional conditions, further specified in terms of pragmatic, moral, and cognitive legitimacy, i.e., housing market actors, including not least municipality-owned real estate companies need to consider a variety of conditions when making decisions regarding how to provide affordable housing but without generating externalities whose costs befalls other market actors or social groups, i.e., in the form of market disruptions.

The social production of professional ignorance: acting under uncertainty and ambiguities

Governance systems are oftentimes separated into principals and agents (in the agency theory vocabulary, see, e.g., Shapiro, 2005), wherein the principals are, e.g., the owners of stock in a public corporation, or politically assigned agents who are granted the authority to enact and issue policies that agents are expected to implement, or otherwise recognize when making decisions. In many cases, policy making is made in abstract and vague terms, oftentimes being the outcome from political deliberation and bargaining as a variety of concerns and interests are considered (Battaglini and Patacchini, 2019; Funk and Hirschman, 2014), yet intended to instruct first-level agents on how to proceed in their domain of expertise. In such contexts, professional ignorance is a trained skill to selectively pay attention to information and instructions that are operable within a current horizon of meaning, and on the basis of stipulated budgets and project timeframes. Ignorance is associated with negative connotations in everyday semantics, and denotes the failure to properly recognize, e.g., available information or other conditions of relevance for the situation (McGoey, 2012; Westphal and Bednar, 2005). At the same time, ignorance is a matter of fact in human lives as cognitive limitations makes ignorance more of a necessity than a vice. "[P]ervasive ignorance is an intrinsic and irredeemable aspect of all individual and collective decision-making processes," Davies and McGoey (2012: 67) propose. McGoey (2012: 3) argues that despite ignorance being a widespread phenomenon, it has essentially been overlooked in scholarly research: "[A]ttention to ignorance has been viewed as too obvious or banal to warrant much scrutiny"; "As an organizational phenomenon in its own right, ignorance is rarely problematized," Schwarzkopf (2020: 198) adds.

In the management studies literature, there is a renewed recognition of ignorance as a form of trained skill (Schaefer, 2019; Souleles, 2019). Jeon (2020: 842) refers to the "social production of ignorance," which is "orchestrated by the power inequalities at the structural level." For instance, the concept of *strategic ignorance* denotes how, e.g., institutions and organizations are capable of "deploying societal ignorance for the service of their own interest" (Jeon, 2020: 842). On a more practical level, on the level of the "interaction order" (Goffman, 1983), individuals "construct, justify and secure a common perception of their world via interactions" (Jeon, 2020: 843) so that certain conditions are downplayed or overlooked, while others are foregrounded. Consequently, the social production of ignorance on the group level should be seen as "a relational product of collaborative efforts," in turn being "embedded within various positions at the organizational field, with taken-for-granted routine and habitual mode of thoughts and practices" (Jeon, 2020: 844). To provide two practical examples, McGoey (2012) suggests that judges who make legal decisions in the court of law actively ignore emotional conditions in their pursuit for justice based on factual evidence. In scientific practices, to ignore certain ambiguities to enhance the "generalizability of scientific findings and to attain consensus about the merits of a new discovery" is conducive of the individual scholars' reputation for "scientific sobriety" (McGoey, 2012: 4). In the case of scientists' professional ignorance, "scientists value ignorance as much as the knowledge they produce—it is a means of survival and professional development" (Jeon, 2020: 857).

Also in day-to-day occupational work, professional ignorance serves a variety of interests and maintains the day-to-day business operations. For instance, Fine's (1996: 36) ethnography of restaurant chefs somewhat surprisingly reveals that individual cases of food poisoning—understandably a disastrous event for a restaurant if it is deemed culpable for the event—are ignored by "cooks, inspectors and journalists" as such events are regarded as being part of the business and dining out, and can rarely be traced in any meaningful way. The credo that "The show must go on," shared by a variety of market actors, may abhor food poisoning victims and sensitive audiences, but this ignorance arguably enables the operations to continue at the same time as a number of actors recognize the need to learn from these unfortunate but ultimately understated cases. Importantly, in this context, "being ignorant" does not denote a situation wherein the agent has incomplete knowledge or lack knowledge altogether, but rather ignorance denotes "deliberate inattention" (Schaefer, 2019: 1389). For instance, when intendedly being inattentive to details, an agent can protect him or herself against accusations of culpability ex post facto, Souleles (2019) argues, which indicates that professional ignorance is a learned skill in its own right. This skill is of particular value in situations wherein agents operate in a milieu characterized by overwhelming complexity (as in the case of finance trade; Souleles, 2019), or wherein either objectives, or the means to achieve declared objectives are obscure or concealed to the actor. This latter situation will be examined in more detail below.

To cope with incomplete or concealed performance metrics: a consumer-lending industry example

In the US, wherein the access to credit markets is part of a full economic citizenship and conducive of economic welfare (Lauer, 2017; Polillo, 2011), the so-called FICO score is the credit market industry standard measure of a presumptive borrower's creditworthiness. In the American consumer lending market, the "big three" consumer rating agencies of Experian, Equifax, and TransUnion account for over 90 percent of the market (Rona-Tas and Hiss, 2010: 118), and currently, FICO scores are used "in ninety percent of lending decisions in the United States" (Fourcade and Healy, 2013: 561). The acronym FICO denotes Fair & Isaac Co., a privately owned corporation that uses an algorithm to calculate a credit score on the basis of a number of parameters (Poon, 2007), but whose details are not disclosed to market actors—neither lenders nor borrowers. By design, the FICO measure calculates the "probability of a negative credit event over a two-year horizon" (Keys et al., 2009: 316), which means that, e.g., mortgage lenders, who frequently originate loans with a 30-year maturation period (as in the case of mortgage lending), can only assess the short-term solidity of the client. Furthermore, it is known that the FICO score includes parameters such as (1) payment history, (2) amounts owed, (3) length of credit history, (4) new credit, and (5) types of credit used (Karger, 2005: 46–47), but otherwise the three-digit credit score being issued remains "a process that cannot be fully understood, challenged, or audited by the individuals scored or even by the regulators charged with protecting them" (Citron and Pasquale, 2014: 10). Credit bureaus "routinely deny requests for details on their scoring systems," and consequently "no one outside the scoring entity can conduct an audit of the underlying predictive algorithms" (Citron and Pasquale, 2014: 10). Presumptive borrowers therefore act in the dark regarding how to "work the credit score" (Kear, 2017: 358) as the scoring systems that provide the access to credit markets "are shrouded in secrecy ... [and] the algorithms are zealously guarded trade secrets" (Citron and Pasquale, 2014: 5). While this secrecy protects the consumer credit rating agencies from critical scrutiny, the inability to demonstrate how what Kiviat (2019) refers to as "actuarial fairness"—fairness in terms of each individual being assessed individually and not as a representative of a larger socio-economic or even ethnic group—is ensured, result in a legitimacy problem for credit rating agencies. This legitimacy problem is derived from the inability to rule out that the calculated FICO scores are not biased in any measure.

In analogy with the FICO score and the consumer credit rating business, in the urban development project being examined, the police authority's rating of the degree of socially vulnerable city districts, presented to audiences as a taxonomy including three levels of perceived social vulnerability (but with no internal ranking within categories) are based on police authority metrics and field work reporting, yet concealed to other authorities and agencies and to the wider public. Despite the opaqueness of the taxonomy—which largely runs counter to the overall reverence of transparency in all corners of the governance system (Mehrpouya and Salles-Djelic, 2019; Pozen, 2018; Kosack and Fung, 2014)—policy makers in the local city government were anxious to reduce the number of city district in the highest taxonomy class (being labeled as "particularly socially vulnerable city districts"). Consequently, one of the primary performance metrics in the urban development project was to ensure investments and other activities that would increase the socio-economic welfare of residents so that that the targeted city district would eventually be excluded from this category. As indicated by the empirical material, the reference to the police authority's taxonomy resulted in much deliberation in the project team regarding how to achieve a stipulated and politically defined goal, whose empirical substantiation is concealed to audiences, including the project workers themselves. However, professional and trained ignorance in the form of "deliberate inattention" was needed to operate on the basis of political objectives while at the same time accomplishing project goals that potentially would result in the stipulated goals. In the end, the empirical case demonstrates how professional ignorance is a vital skill when operating in milieus shaped by political objectives that only insufficiently take into account practical conditions and what are in facts doable within stipulated project budgets and time frames.

The value of professional ignorance in urban development projects

In the following, two cases of political objectives shaping an urban development program will be examined. First, an urban development project was initiated with the explicit political objective to eliminate the targeted city district from the police authority's national list over "particularly socially vulnerable" city districts. Second, in order to create possibilities for a "housing career" among the residents, policy makers wanted to support an increase in "mixed housing," as recommended by the United Nation's committee for affordable housing. This second goal demanded that rental units were transformed into privately owned so-called community housing units, wherein each apartment is owned by the resident while the resident pays a monthly fee to the community housing board of directors (recruited from the residents in the building), which is held responsible for the maintenance and the running costs of the housing unit. To own one's apartment is commonly portrayed as an upward movement in the "housing market career," which in turn is associated with positive socio-economic consequences. Both these objectives were politically justifiable on the basis of the current governance model, yet the details and the practical implications derived from such political objectives were understated. Consequently, to be able to act on the basis of vague and/or incomplete policy decisions, professional ignorance served to eliminate a proportion of issues and questions that would block joint action for a considerable period of time. Similar to the scientists who ignore what they do in fact *not know* for the time being, to be able to extract meaningful information from the data generated in an experimental system, the project team professionally ignored that they did not had a complete understanding of the conditions influencing their work, but nonetheless they initiated and participated in the urban development program. In the following, conditions included in the policy, yet being poorly mapped and known in substantive terms, but consequently guiding project decisions are examined on the basis of the empirical material.

How to achieve political goals when the data is concealed to decision makers

The CEO of the municipality-owned real estate company that owned no less than 94 percent of the rental units in the city district argued that her organization was in the position to simultaneously handle "a complex political process," and "a physical reality" (i.e., the day-to-day housing activities in the capacity of the landlord). That is, on the one hand, policy makers regarded the municipality-owned real estate company as a tool for the realization of policy objectives, ranging from abstract visions to concrete goals; on the other hand, the municipality-owned real estate company handled a great variety of "on the ground" activities, of great importance for the welfare and quality of life of the tenants, by and large separated from political deliberations. When policy makers express their ambition to create a more mixed housing market in the city district, the municipality-owned real estate company needs to balance the political objectives implied, embedded in international guidelines and instituted by academic research work, against how this will affect the welfare of current and future residents. For instance, if new privately owned housing units are constructed in the city district, will this generate a net welfare effects for all residents (as stipulated by the theory of positive externalities that guide international policy recommendations; see, e.g., Chetty, Hendren, and Katz, 2016) or does it further stratify the residents into discrete groups and housing welfare differentials? For the private companies being involved in the urban development project, it is not so much political objectives as the actual purchasing power of presumptive home buyers that matters. "The land slots are not worth very much for the time being," one business developer said (#1, Private company, Male): "Today, you wouldn't be able to build anything there [with a positive return]." At the same time, having extensive experience from the industry, the business developer understood the value of maintaining a long-term perspective:

> If we are part of this, we need to take a long-term view. I'd say it takes at least ten years, possibly twenty [to turn things around]. And the City Hall needs to be part of the process. During the first five years, there may be no black bottom line figures.
>
> (Business developer #1, Private company, male)

The main concern regarding the valuation of new housing units, and the transformation of rental units into community housing units was that visible street crime and covert criminal activity would suppress the willingness of presumptive buyers to make an investment in the city district. One of the principal targets for the urban development project was therefore to be eliminated from the policy authority's list of particularly socially vulnerable city districts. The project participants largely regarded this as a reasonable goal, at the same time as they emphasized that this list did not reveal to audiences what parameters were included, which imposed a fair share of uncertainty regarding what actions to take to accomplish the stipulated goal. A project pre-study coordinator (#2, Female) argued that the list included qualitative and "subjective" assessments, and therefore the project team should determine whether getting off the list was a "relevant measure to use or not?"

In addition, the police authority listing was inconsistent with other available metrics. Tenant satisfaction surveys revealed that most of the tenants were "fairly pleased" with their housing situation, the urban development project leader said. The city district was not on the top of the list of all the municipality-owned real estate company's neighborhoods, but the survey data revealed no particularly worrying conditions. Regarding perceived safety, little indicated that tenants regarded their city district as being unsafe, despite the police authority assessment. In addition to the ambiguities pertaining to the policy authority assessment, and its accuracy regarding perceived safety among residents, several of the interviewees argued that the policy makers' ambition to get the city district off the list was a most difficult goal to accomplish within the stipulated short-term time horizon of five years. The project pre-study coordinator said: "There's nothing right now that indicates that the political goal that there would be no particularly socially vulnerable city districts by 2025 will be met. There is nothing that even moves in that direction" (Project pre-study coordinator #2, female).

If policy makers fail to prescribe project goals that are clearly defined, nor achievable within stipulated time frames and budgets, there is a need for alternative performance measures to coordinate project activities. Such performance measures could be allocated "upstream" (as in the case of local schooling quality and schooling results), serving as predictors of problems surfacing in the future unless being properly handled, or "downstream" (as in the case of the valuation of the housing stock, and the market prices and positive market price differentials in newly produced housing). All project participants and informants agreed that schooling quality was of great importance for reducing the individual's risk of inclusion in criminal activities later on, especially for boys and younger men as indicated by official statistics. A school agency representative was included in the project team, but unfortunately the agency had few possibilities for allocating additional resources to specific school districts on the basis of urban development initiatives; the school agency operates on the basis of legislation, regulatory rules, and protocols that emphasize the needs of *individual pupils*, not to be supportive of the market pricing of housing facilities in specific city districts, or any other policy objectives. At the same time, school agency representatives understood that their cooperation was key to the policy makers' stated objective to increase the overall welfare in low-income city districts. Regarding the second performance metrics, representatives of private companies who participated in the project emphasized how sales and market prices were credible indicators of project performance but only in a long-term perspective: "The ultimate evidence of a successful project is if newly build housing is being sold. That would indicate a market interest, and a faith in the city district. Otherwise, there would be no sales," a business developer argued (Cooperative building society, female).

Regardless of the metrics being used, all interviewees argued that some kind of measurement to monitor project performance was needed, especially given the vague instructions from policy makers. Furthermore, to actually increase the welfare of residents and to support a market for new housing and cooperative housing units, a variety of activities and initiatives had to be mutually supportive. For instance, building new housing without paying attention to perceived safety and schooling quality concerns is unsustainable, while on the other hand, to merely focus on social issues without making actual investments is at risk of rendering such social initiatives merely symbolic in the eyes of residents and other audiences. In this view, to make the project team take action on the basis of the policy makers' instruction to eliminate the city district from the list of particularly socially vulnerable urban areas demands professional ignorance in terms of overlooking the opaque nature of stated objectives, and the absence of details regarding the substance of the assessments underlying such objectives.

Prior to examining the theoretical implications, the second case of policy makers' instructions, in this case regarding the transformation of rental units into cooperative housing units, is discussed. Similar to the case regarding police authority assessments, policy makers' instructions are vague to the point where "on the ground activities" need to include a considerable degree of informed guesswork regarding how to implement the policies enacted by democratically elected entities. In other words, to proceed on the basis of such instructions, professional ignorance is supportive of practical activities despite considerable ambiguities regarding assumptions made, the process to be managed, and desirable outcomes being the case.

The increase of community housing supply in the low end of the housing market

According to the United Nation's housing agency, which several of the interviewees referred to during the interviews as being the basis for the current housing policy, mixed housing is both an indication of and a pathway toward increased socio-economic welfare in a city district. If rental units are combined with the possibilities for privately owned housing, local residents and incoming residents can make a "housing career," and positive externalities are stipulated to follow from the increased degree of residents included in the labor market settling in the city district. Based on these premises, anchored in both theoretical models and empirical evidence, local policy makers argued that the proportion of rental units was too high, and that community housing units should be provided to create a more dynamic housing market in the city district. While the project leader argued that few of the residents were moving out of the city district, and that a significant proportion of the residents had "moderate" purchasing power, many of the interviewees were skeptical regarding the efficacy of the policy makers' ambition to transform rental units into community housing corporations.

By and large, there were three principal concerns regarding the projected welfare of such initiatives. First, the limited purchasing power and the lower degree of market inclusion of the residents would make it difficult for them to make the long-term commitment and investment in a community housing unit would entail. Second, as a response to the financial crisis of 2008, regulatory agencies that monitor the mortgage-lending industry have imposed stricter lending rules that make it more difficult for medium to low-income households (which also include young people and younger families) to access mortgage loans. As the state by tradition does not meddle with market-based mortgage lending activities, nor provide direct subsidies at the mortgage loan origination stage, presumptive low net-worth community housing buyers are therefore likely to encounter difficulties when financing their purchase. Third and finally, the community housing ownership model demands a certain degree of expertise regarding how community housing facilities and resources are managed and financed, e.g., how the cooperative housing unit is governed on the basis of a board of directors, selected from the pool of residents. Individuals who have spent most of their lives in rental units must learn that the costs and responsibilities previously being carried by the landlord are now being a responsibility of the community housing corporation, i.e., the residents themselves. A business developer in a private company, specializing in producing privately owned of community housing units, emphasized the "educational demand" and the role of private companies in instructing prospect cooperative housing residents how to handle a series of responsibilities that the community housing corporation carries:

> There is an educational demand here as few have owned their homes and have limited know-how regarding what that means. So we provide a fair share of support to newly created community housing corporations … What is ownership of an apartment in a community housing corporation? The board of directors, the residents, how does all that work? What are individual and communal responsibilities?
>
> (Business developer, Private real estate developer, male)

Regardless of such support and help from both municipality real estate companies, and private companies active in the low-end housing market, many of the interviewees regarded the market for community housing units as being thin. Given these conditions (low purchasing power among the low net-worth households being the presumptive buyers, stricter mortgage-lending regulation, and an estimated shortage of know-how needed to successfully manage a community housing corporation), several of the interviewees regarded the policy makers' instructions as being overoptimistic. The CFO of a municipality-owned real estate company expressed his concern regarding the efficacy of the stated policy:

> To merely declare that 'Start creating community housing units, and so forth, because that would lead to improvements' [is insufficient]. I don't believe in that. I think the difficulties in making [the tenants] understand how this works and what it takes are gigantic.
>
> (CFO, Municipality-owned real estate company)

Policy makers may have the full faith and confidence in market actors' ability to generate a local cooperative housing market, but the cost and effects on long-term welfare for the residents are concerns that are left in the dark in the current policy formulation. The CEO of the municipality-owned real estate company that owned the absolute majority of the housing stock said the community housing units would be created on the basis of the available rental housing stock:

> In the first place, this is a matter of being able to offer new possibilities that does not make the step to buy a newly produced apartment appear as an insurmountable achievement. We believe that transforming rental units into community housing units may speed up this process more than in the case of building entirely new [community] housing units.
>
> (CEO, Municipality-owned real estate company, female)

At the same time, the tenants' national interest organization, Hyresgästföreningen, has repeatedly emphasized that every time a cooperative housing unit is created on the basis of one rental housing unit being transformed into privately owned apartments, the dynamics of the housing market may increase in theoretical terms, but it also reduces the total stock of rental units that are available for, e.g., new entrants on the housing market. In this view, the tenants' interest organization objects to the privatization of the current housing stock (but, importantly, still being supportive of newly built cooperative housing) as this policy is deemed to reduce the overall welfare. In the case of the policy making preceding the specific urban development project, it was more general and consequently more abstract housing policy guidelines that was mirrored in the policy instructions. Furthermore, the center-right political majority of City Hall, established after the general election of 2018, was generally more positive toward the idea of home ownership as a welfare generating device than the social democratic political majority ruling prior to 2018. The new policy was thus part of a more comprehensive shift in governance practice that also involved municipality real estate companies.

Under all conditions, policies tend to be enacted in general terms, and thereafter delegated to defined agencies and assigned private companies and market actors to implement (Riles, 2011). Policy ideas that appear to be theoretically consistent, embedded in robust evidence, and harmonized with international agreements and directives, but nevertheless being enacted *in abstracto*, may impose considerable difficulties when being interpreted and translated into proper action by "frontline" actors (see, e.g., Edelman, Fuller, and Mara-Drita, 2001; Edelman, 1992). In the specific case of the urban development project, the ambition to get the city district off the police authority's list is reasonable but only if agents' assigned decision making is consistent with, and supportive of, stipulated policy goals and objectives. In the current situation, that was not evidently the case. In the case of the policy to increase the proportion of cooperative housing units in the city district, formally enacted policies were passed on and further pronounced on the basis of the belief in the value of privately owned housing being conducive of net social and economic welfare, but there were few instructions regarding how to accomplish such goals given the current housing and mortgage-lending market conditions. Neither were there any extensive deliberations or assessments made regarding the risks, unintended consequences, or externalities generated in the transformation of rental units into cooperative housing facilities, neither for the local community, nor more broadly on the regional or national level. Under such conditions, to be able to navigate in housing markets that are shaped by policy making, yet instituted as bone fide market activities "on the ground" (as in the case of mortgage lending), professional ignorance is a mechanism or learned skill that serve to create possibilities for meaningful practice in the shadow of perceived policy making inconsistencies, and/or uncertainty regarding the future more largely.

The value of professional ignorance in policy implementation

In order to act, humans and, as in this case, project teams, need proper know-how and information to act upon. In the absence of favorable conditions in such terms, assumptions are commonly made to "fill in the blanks" and to create a shared ground for, e.g., project activities (Weick, 1995; Daft and Weick, 1984). Being in the position to act on the basis of incomplete, ambiguous, or contradictory information or instructions is a regular condition in governance systems (Mehrpouya and Salles-Djelic, 2019; Kosack and Fung, 2014), and professional actors must learn to cope with this predicament (Lifshitz-Assaf, 2018; Hayward and Boeker, 1998; Gerrity et al., 1992). Professionalism is based on the capacity to act individually and collectively on the basis of a combination of available information, assumptions made on the basis of previous experience, extrapolations made on the basis of existing data, and qualified guess-work (Freidson, 2001; Abbott, 1988). In governance systems characterized by political decision making, wherein preferences, priorities, and agendas tend to change over time, and where policy makers rely on qualified professional agents to handle the practical work to implement and to materialize policy (Riles, 2011), policy instructions are frequently vague or incomplete, which oftentimes results in policy implementation being a mere afterthought—an issue for lower-tier functionaries and market actors to practically handle (see, e.g., Kellogg, 2014; Edelman, Fuller, and Mara-Drita, 2001). Under such conditions, professional ignorance is supportive of policy implementation as it both recognizes the policy makers' stated intentions, and mindfully neglects the incompleteness of the instructions.

Scholars argue that ignorance is "rarely problematized" (Schwarzkopf, 2020: 198) despite being an "an intrinsic and irredeemable aspect" (Davies and McGoey, 2012: 67) of decision making processes. In the urban development project case reported in this chapter, the "strategic ignorance" (Jeon, 2020: 842) and the "deliberate inattention" (Schaefer, 2019: 1389) of the project participants, representing a variety of market actors and agencies including both private companies and municipality real estate companies, played a key role. In the specific case, stipulated (negative) performance metrics was concealed to project co-workers, which potentially prevented informed decisions regarding how to achieve project goals, and the ambition to create a market for mixed housing was to a considerable extent based on ideological preferences and external policy inspirations (as in the case of the UN report on mixed housing) than based on substance regarding, e.g., actual purchasing power in the local housing market. Despite policy makers' broad-sweeping decisions and instructions regarding desirable outcomes and preferred future conditions, the project participant acted on the basis of stipulated project goals, formulated on the basis of policy objectives. In this context, professional ignorance denotes the capacity to create an alignment between factual conditions, available resources, and declared or assumed goals, to generate an action plan that is plausible in the eyes of relevant actors. If successfully handled, such action plans generate material consequences within existing budgets and time frames, regardless of inconsistencies in problem definitions, the resources assigned to their solutions, and projected outcomes.

Urban development projects, especially in low-end housing markets where the purchasing power of targeted buyers is modest, are in many cases surrounded by uncertainty (e.g., regarding labor market conditions that immediately affect the purchasing power of households with limited savings) and include risk-taking (e.g., in terms of assessing presumptive home buyers' access to credit). To better assess risks and uncertainties, a variety of market actors and agencies are represented in the urban development project team to collectively cover a larger number of joint concerns of practical relevance for the project. Such complex urban development projects demand communication skills and the capacity to recognize the role and interests of all participants. At the same time, different participating actors need to ensure that they can benefit in ways that are consistent with individual goals or else the output may be meagre. That is, urban development projects include a considerable amount of bargaining so that all participants are better off in the end. In the ideal case, policy makers make decisions that are supportive of such team-based and cross-organizational bargaining activities and the activities that are decided in this process, with decisions being sufficiently precise to generate an action plan for the participants, yet flexible and open to interpretation so that a variety of interests can be recognized and contained in one single instruction. In many cases, such qualified policy instructions are not provided, which puts pressure on project participants to jointly formulate how activities should unfold over time, and to what end they are introduced. Professional ignorance here denotes the trained and learned capacity to overlook the fact that data and information may be missing, and to circumvent incomplete instructions on the basis of joint assumptions and/or extrapolated data so that the decisions needed can be made, and the project work can proceed. In this view, professional ignorance is a thoughtful response to a governance situation that is far from optimal but wherein project actors nonetheless remain capable of formulating action plans under conditions including competing goals, shifting preferences, and struggles over the authority to define problems. Seen in this view, professional ignorance is the capacity to "meet the policy makers halfway," i.e., to recognize the difficulty of providing complete policy instructions given cognitive and temporal limitations, etc., while at the same time also making vague or incomplete policy decisions actionable in the domain where they are implemented.

To formulate a more general theoretical contribution to the professional ignorance literature (e.g., Jeon, 2020; Schaefer, 2019; Souleles, 2019; McGoey, 2012), it is first noteworthy that the semantic meaning of the term *ignorance* is loaded with negative associations. Still, ignorance can be helpful as it protects the individual or the project team from ending up in a stalemate wherein the lack of detailed information would otherwise prevent further action. In this view, professional ignorance is tangential to what Daston (2019) refers to as *intuition*, being a key term in cognition science studies, but also in the management studies literature (see, e.g., Dane and Pratt, 2007; Khatri and Ng, 2000; Simon, 1987), denoting the capacity to apprehend social reality as a "distinctive form of understanding" that grasps the whole and "reveals interconnections" but on the basis of cognitive fragments of the totality of the social reality (Daston, 2019: 331). "Ideally," Daston (2019: 331) continues, intuition "seizes upon essentials" and "forges a whole out of disparate parts or steps." In the intuitive understanding of social reality, the sum is always of necessity larger than the parts, and also inconclusive data and incomplete information can be used to generate an image of social reality that is sufficiently coherent to be supportive of individual or concerted action. The deliberate inattention (professional ignorance) or intuition-based comprehension of professional communities is consequently less of a vice than it is a mode of understanding, a quality of an epistemic community that is trained to act on the basis of data and information that is oftentimes far from complete but that demands that action is to be taken just the same. Future scholarly research on the role of professional ignorance "in the wild" and "on the ground" is therefore welcome, not least in management studies, wherein many policies and decisions are dependent on professional groups' joint capacity to ignore the incompleteness of available data or information. Also in the domain of urban studies research, the concept of professional ignorance may inform scholarly research that increase the understanding of how complex urban development projects are organized.

Summary and conclusion

The study of an urban development project demonstrates that policy makers' stipulated goals are vague (as in the case of the objective to eliminate the city district from the police authority's list), or inconsistent with factual conditions (as in the case of the ambition to create mixed housing despite low net-worth households being the intended primary residents), but that condition is mediated by the project teams' capacity to make decisions and take action also on the basis of incomplete policy instructions. The downside risk is that in lieu of more precise policy instructions and prescribed activities, urban development teams tend to reproduce off-the-shelf solutions, i.e., as in the current case, generate additional new housing, but without necessarily grappling with the broader set of socio-economic challenges that is arguably part of a more sustainable urban development policy. Professional ignorance has primarily been recognized in scientific communities (McGoey, 2012), but the current study indicates that professional ignorance also has a role to play in governance systems, in project management, and in urban development projects.

5 Housing welfare and the value of amenities

Introduction

This chapter examines how the economic worth of the real estate stock in a city district cannot be calculated strictly on the basis of projected rental income and other cost-covering contributions from, e.g., authorities. Instead, the economic valuation of the real estate stock is dependent on what housing market studies scholars refer to as *amenities* (Banzhaf and Farooque, 2013; Rappaport, 2008; Tyrväinen and Miettinen, 2000), that is, tangible (e.g., the presence of shops or restaurants in the neighbourhood) or intangible (e.g., the reputation or "mood" of the neighbourhood) qualities that are not specified in the rent to be paid or the price paid to purchase a house or an apartment in a neighborhood, but that still affect the attractivity of the neighborhood so that the valuation of the housing unit (made by the presumptive tenant or owner) or the real estate stock which it is included in (made by the real estate company, the market actor, or financial trader) is raised. Amenities include, e.g., access to natural reserves such as parks and recreational areas, the perceived safety and security of the local neighborhood or city district, the supply of local businesses and cafés and restaurants, the quality of public transportation, and similar perceived benefits in the close geographical area (Diamond, 2016; Brueckner, Thisse, and Zenou, 1999). In this view, the economic valuation of the real estate stock is blending with the social valuation of a series of amenities so that the calculative practices used to determine a book value of asset holdings in, e.g., the real estate company cannot only recognize objectively true and undisputed accounted book values but also need to include the (perceived) value of amenities.

In theoretical terms, amenities are subject to economic valuation and thereafter included in the pricing of housing. In advanced capitalist economies, the pricing of commodities and services remains dependent on what has been referred to as economic valuation (Fourcade, 2011), or social valuation practices (Zuckerman, 2012), oftentimes based on professional expertise and the authority to determine the economic and social value of, e.g., a commodity. On the basis of such assessments, the pricing of the commodity can be completed (Beckert and Aspers, 2011). Studies of valuation practices include a variety of assets and resources including natural reserves (Fourcade, 2011), human lives (Hood, 2017), labor (Ruef, 2012), children's life and work effort contributions to the household

DOI: 10.4324/9781003244417-8

economy (Zelizer, 1985), human gametes such as ova or sperm used in reproductive medicine (Almeling, 2011), and what Fourcade (2011) more broadly speaks of as "peculiar objects"—singular objects (Karpik, 2010) such as art objects (Coslor, 2016), or more mundane objects such as thrift shop items (Degenshein, 2017). In real estate markets, housing is a peculiar good inasmuch as its value is derived from both its practical use (e.g., as a family residence), as a storage of wealth for the family, and an asset holding for finance market traders (Ansell, 2019; Pattillo, 2013; Hui, Ng and Lau, 2011; Punwani, 1997). Consequently, as discussed in Part I of this volume, the access to housing is simultaneously subject to policy making and plays a key role in the broader credit formation process as housing is the near-perfect collateral in the credit formation process in the finance industry (Fernandez and Aalbers, 2016; Favara and Imbs, 2015).

This chapter contributes to the urban studies and construction management literature as it presents an empirical case that shows that economic valuation is inextricably bound up with social valuations of conditions that are oftentimes excluded from more strictly calculative practices, including, e.g., the valuation of amenities, either in positive (as in the case of the access to natural reserves) or negative terms (as in the case of the absence of visible street crime or a perceived insecurity in the neighborhood). The study calls for more research on the role of valuation in a variety of economic projects and policy activities that formally rely on the ideal of "disinterested valuation," but de facto considers a broader variety of factors when pricing commodities or services.

The role of valuation in pricing

As most people intuitively recognize, there is a difference between the price and the value of, e.g., a commodity. Some people may value an artifact very highly, and yet the market price could be fairly low, or *vice versa*. In the scholarly literature, valuation precedes pricing inasmuch as the valuation is concerned with people's preferences, whereas pricing is a matter of defining the nominal monetary worth of the item in the light of such preferences, and the supply and demand in the market (Karpik, 2010). Aspers (2018: 140) defines valuation as the process wherein "values are ascribed to actors or things based on peoples' views (preferences)." Furthermore, there is a difference between *valuation* and *evaluation* inasmuch as evaluation is based on "standards that exist and are in use independent of individuals' views or preferences," whereas valuation is based on non-standardized information; "valuation is about differentiation and evaluation is about uniformity" (Aspers, 2018: 140). As a consequence, an individual is able to make an evaluation on the basis of standards, whereas a valuation process is a result of "mutual adjustment in a process in which many actors take part" (Aspers, 2018: 140). In practical terms, valuation is oftentimes based on verification by expertise, and expertise is primarily granted to professional communities or groups.

Gourevitch (2011: 88) remarks that there are many fields wherein verification is of key importance, including "efficacy in medicine, safety in cars, or energy use in appliances." More generally, Kornberger (2017: 1759) speaks about intermediaries such as "experts, critics, consultants, matchmakers and others," who all play "an important role in valuation practices." The proposition that valuation is a matter of a professional assessment of economic worth on the basis of preferences and beliefs is consistent with John Dewey's ([1939] 1991) view of processes of valuation as a form of "criticism": objective value arises from the active criticism of human valuations, being a self-reflexive assessment of not only the artifact being valued per se, but also the wider social context wherein the artifact is located and appreciated (Putnam, 2002: 103). Kornberger (2017: 1759) recognizes this self-reflexivity, and emphasizes the performative nature of valuation, wherein "[v]aluation practices do not merely mirror or bring to the fore pre-existing values, but that valuation practices are actively involved in the constitution of values." The process of valuation also includes a number of heuristics and devices such as commensuration, categorizing, and visualizations that are all constitutive of value (Kornberger, 2017: 1760). Seen in this view, valuation is an epistemologically embedded process wherein a broader number of conditions are recognized and taken into account. Once the valuation is completed, the price of an artifact needs to be determined to render it tradable on a market. Prices are in many cases quite unstable and/or negotiable as they include a large variety of concerns and information: "Prices are never the result of purely mechanistic market forces, but are instead shaped by complex social processes" (Hood, 2017: 444).

Taken together, the concept of valuation underlines that economic activities are inextricably bound up with the broader social context associated with the object or artifact being valued and priced. This proposition applies to the housing and real estate market, wherein so-called amenities, the proximity of natural, social, or historical resources that local residents can benefit from but pay for only indirectly, are included in the valuation process and in the pricing, even as the access to amenities are not included in the contract written between, e.g., buyer and seller, or tenant and landlord. In this view, amenities may not only be additional or complementary to the housing facility but may in fact serve to determine the value of the real estate stock, especially if amenities are defined in negative terms, as the absence of, e.g., low-quality schooling or street crime.

Urban renewal programs, housing prices, and the role of amenities

The term amenity is defined as a desirable or useful feature or facility of a building or place. Diamond (2016: 484) identifies "six broad categories": "retail amenities, transportation amenities, crime amenities, environmental amenities, schooling amenities, and job quality amenities." Brueckner, Thisse, and Zenou (1999: 94) define three types of amenities, including *natural amenities*, which are generated by an area's "topographical features, including rivers, hills, coastline, etc," *historical amenities*, which include "monuments, buildings, parks, and other urban infrastructure from past eras that are aesthetically pleasing to current residents of the city," and *modern amenities*, which include, e.g., access to shops, cafés and restaurants, and other services being appreciated by residents. While natural and historical amenities are exogenous conditions, given by conditions that are complicated and costly to modify or amend, modern amenities are endogenous, i.e., this class of amenities can be attracted to a neighborhood if the conditions are favorable. For instance, the process of gentrification, highly controversial among some urban studies scholars (e.g., Stein, 2019; Zukin, 2010) as it is seen as the process wherein poor neighborhoods are gradually overtaken by more affluent socio-economic groups, and consequently pushes former residents to the margin, is a primary example of how modern amenities are introduced in formerly blighted neighborhoods (as in the case of former working class neighborhood being sites where urban culture thrives, marked by the presence of boutiques, coffee shops, microbreweries, etc.). Furthermore, even though natural and historical amenities are exogenous, it does not imply that they are protected from erosion. For instance, Brueckner, Thisse, and Zenou (1999: 105) argue that one of the reasons for Paris being widely regarded as a livable and charming city is that high net-worth households have decided to stay in the city center rather than to move to the suburbs, and the net value invested in maintaining historical buildings has in fact preserved historical amenities. Seen in this way, historical amenities are a public good that generates positive externalities such as tourism. Similarly, natural amenities such as parks and recreation areas need to be protected from economic exploitation to uphold the amenities benefitting the existing housing units.

It is noteworthy that the concept of amenities is mostly defined in positive terms, i.e., the presence of amenities is associated with higher official real estate valuations and prices, but it is also possible to consider an amenity as the absence of undesirable qualities in a neighborhood or city district, including, e.g., the *absence* of street crime, polluting manufacturing facilities, the lack of noise or undesirable disturbances, and so forth (Diamond, 2016). Consequently, the decision to invest in new housing production in a city district is not based strictly on projected revenue streams and the return on investment or equity, but is also bound up with broader initiatives pertaining to schooling quality, local labor market inclusion projects, and activities that reduce both visible and covert street crime (Bernhardt, 2012; Colic-Peisek and Tilbury, 2006). This valuation of, e.g., new housing production projects is particularly important when investing in neighborhoods and city districts with primarily low net-worth residents insofar as the profit margin is already thin as the stipulated buyer of, e.g., newly produced housing have limited purchasing power, not least on the basis of lower access to financial capital serviced through the mortgage-lending channel (Ansell, 2019; Hsu, Matsa, and Melzer, 2018). Furthermore, undesirable local conditions would reduce both the interest for investing in such city districts, and, as a second-order effect, dampen the market valuation of the new housing stock, which would make it more difficult for prospect buyers to be granted a mortgage loan, which potentially further suppresses housing prices in the new neighborhood.

The valuation and pricing of amenities

There is a considerable literature that estimates the value or price of amenities, and the conventional wisdom is that amenities are reflected in housing prices, even though households self-reporting the value of their housing unit may not recognize their full value. Rappaport (2008) examines the correlation between population growth and "quality of life," operationalized as the access to "consumption amenities" (being similar to what Diamond, 2016, refers to as "retail amenities"), and finds that population growth is "strongly positively correlated" with "several exogenous consumption amenities." This results is indicative of how households value "quality of life," which drives urban population density and results in higher housing financing costs Rappaport (2008) argues.

> Under the baseline parameterization, wages fall slightly with density, house prices rise moderately, and land prices rise steeply. Compensation for high quality of life is primarily capitalized into land and house prices rather than into wages. In return for enjoying high quality of life, individuals sacrifice small amounts of traded-good and leisure consumption and a large amount of housing consumption.
>
> (Rappaport, 2008: 551)

Expressed differently, the production of a variety of amenities makes a region or city district more attractive and increases the population growth, which is associated with a positive spiral as, e.g., the local tax-base grows, which may justify further investment in amenities. On the household level, Tyrväinen and Miettinen (2000) have calculated the economic value of natural amenities (operationalized as the distance to a forest) is reflected in housing prices in Finland. Tyrväinen and Miettinen (2000: 206) calculate that the value of "a forest view" represents 4.9 percent of the total value of the housing unit. In addition, an increase in distance of 1 kilometer to a forest "reduced the average price of a dwelling by 5.9 percent" (Tyrväinen and Miettinen, 2000: 220). Economists refer to calculations that measure how "housing values" are associated with differences in "public goods and taxes" as "hedonic prices," i.e., housing prices are regarded as a proxy for how much households are willing to pay for public goods (Banzhaf and Farooque, 2013: 635). At the same time, Banzhaf and Farooque, 2013: 644), who examine community housing price indices for 99 communities in the Los Angeles area, find that households have difficulties when assessing the economic value of amenities, i.e., households fail to recognize "components of their property values capitalizing local amenities" (Banzhaf and Farooque, 2013: 636). Consequently, Banzhaf and Farooque (2013: 644) propose that "actual transaction prices appear to better capture local amenities than do self-reports, perhaps because households do not consider these factors."

For policy makers, Banzhaf and Farooque's (2013) study indicates that households may not accurately or sufficiently value local amenities, at the same time as substantial evidence indicates that housing unit market prices are premised on such amenities. Under all conditions, the dominant doctrine is that local housing markets, especially in markets dominated by low net-worth households, need to be supported by at least the absence of negative amenities, and preferably by investment in schooling and retail amenities. Consequently, real estate developers need to act on a broad basis of concerns to ensure that their new production projects include both amenities and eliminate or exclude undesirable local conditions. This means in practice that real estate developers investing in low net-worth city districts need to join hands with municipality agencies and NGOs to collectively "let the tide lift all boats" (as the economic policy jargon puts it) to render such investment plans plausible and attractive in the eyes of executive decision makers and investors. In theoretical terms, this means that the *pricing* of renovated rental units and newly produced housing is co-dependent on the *valuation* of amenities in the city district, at the same time as such amenities are determined by the work of, e.g., the city schooling agency, or the local or regional police department. In the end, urban development projects are premised on the capacity to combine valuation and pricing in ways that circumvent the risk of social dilemma, wherein individual real estate owners would benefit from collective action to raise the valuation of communal amenities, yet accessing few mechanisms that propel such initiatives.

The valuation of housing in low-amenity and low purchasing power city districts

In the sections below, the project activities to develop a suburban city district are examined. In order to change a precarious situation, the urban development project team were convinced the city needed to invest in amenities in addition to the new housing production and renovation activities. If combined in a meaningful way so that it changes the local residents' expectations regarding the value of the local housing market, and encourages them to take pride in their city district, the combined investment in housing and amenities has several benefits, including a higher valuation of the real estate stock and increased risk-taking in terms of new housing purchases among old and new residents, which is stipulated to jointly generate a virtuous social circle that increases the quality of life and welfare of residents in the target city district.

Urban development in low-net worth city districts

All of the interviewees were committed to urban development activities and regarded the current initiative highly socially relevant and urgent, especially given the recurrent negative media coverage regarding soaring street crime and gang-based organized crime in Swedish metropolitan suburbs. At the same time as the project participants called for new initiatives, they were aware of the difficulties involved in transforming the city district into a more attractive neighborhood wherein current and future residents would be willing to invest in newly built housing facilities, or in community housing units. One of the municipality-owned real estate company project participants argued that the ambition should be within what is actually "doable" given the current conditions:

> The project can raise the city district to level three on a five item scale, and make it stay there. It will never be high status [to live in the suburbs]. We mustn't hope for that. People from [more affluent city districts] would never think this is a superior place for settling.
>
> (Business developer, Municipality-owned real estate company, male)

Another project participant, a business developer in a private real estate development company, argued that the city district had many benefits and amenities, not least the short distance to the city center, but argues that the suburban milieu was widely regarded as a markedly different milieu for many Swedes with no prior experience of living in metropolitan suburbs. The city district has "a great location," the business developer argued, "only a few minutes to the city center," but "the mental distance is considerable," he added (Business developer, Private real estate developer, male). The project team members also emphasized the natural reserves and recreational areas in close proximity as a significant amenity. Important project goals were to invest in renovation activities in the rental units, to create possibilities for apartment ownership in so-called community housing units, and to build new housing facilities, preferably both rental housing units and private homes to increase the degree of "mixed housing" (a widely endorsed urban development policy objective, derived from a United Nations report) in the city district. There were also ideas that student housing facilities could be built in the city district to better blend individuals with different background. Such economic activities would demand both financial investments in amenities, and in the socio-economic infrastructure, and cross-organizational collaborations, the project participants argued.

Investing in amenities

The project participants were confident in their joint capacity to organize and manage a variety of renovation and new housing project activities, but they were concerned that the socio-economic problems defined in the particularly socially vulnerable city districts could not be eliminated on the basis of such initiatives alone. A business developer in a municipality-owned housing development company, specializing in building affordable private homes, claimed that what is oftentimes portrayed as the "sideshow" (i.e., what is additional or complementary in housing production activities) is now better located at the center of the project activities: "If you examine the project team, the focus is on the production of new housing … Most [participants] are real estate developers … But the sideshow is actually the main act," the business developer said (Municipality-owned housing development company, male). The business developer listed a number of activities pertaining to schooling quality, the reduction of street crime and perceived insecurity, labor market inclusion initiatives, and after school curriculum activities as being important conditions to handle to support project goals:

> These additional projects with job market initiatives, and the social work and schooling quality, and the police including all security and criminality issues need to be the main concern to get all these things straight. Then we can make investments in new housing over time.
>
> (Business manager, Municipality-owned housing development company, male)

A project pre-study coordinator argued that "the broader perspective" is very important for the project outcomes, and consequently called for a variety of actors to be involved in the process: "You cannot bury [these social issues] under new constructions … There is a need for investments in social activities: listen to the residents! A number of collaborating parties need to move in lockstep," the project pre-study coordinator said (#2, Female), making a reference to a long-standing tradition in municipality-owned real estate companies to actively engage the tenants when making changes in the local built environment. Formally speaking, negative amenities such as substandard schooling and criminal activities were the responsibilities of the city schooling agency and the national police authority, respectively. That is, the project team could only create collaborative relationships with such agencies and authorities to jointly alter the situation for the better over time.

In the original planning documents, the project team defined three principal amenities to improve: (1) schooling quality; (2) the perceived safety of the city district; (3) commercial amenities including local shops, stores, cafés and restaurants. Of these three amenities, the two first were regarded as being critical to the urban development project. One project participant, representing a science park organization specializing in urban development and new housing facility technologies, argued that a local "housing career" in the city district demanded qualitative schooling services, which foregrounds the role of the local schooling agency: "If the school quality increases, the residents would like to stay and make a 'housing career' by investing in an ownership unit or in a house. Unless the school works, that is not going to happen," he argued (Science park representative #1). The CFO of the municipality-owned real estate company having the overall financial responsibility for the project, agreed on these terms, that schooling quality was critical to all other project goals:

> The key to the problem, that is the schooling quality, for sure … It's all about engaging actors with the competence to run the school in a good way. We can act as some kind of facilitator for all this … but we definitely cannot accomplish these things on our own. So we need to enroll the City Hall and the schooling agency, and so forth. That is of key importance.
>
> (CFO, Municipality-owned real estate company)

The concern is that the schooling agency is managed on the basis of administrative legislation and rules, professional expertise, and political objectives, which all create limited incentives or leeway for agency officials to commit specific resources to certain school districts, even in the case where, e.g., an urban development project in a disadvantaged city district would benefit from such concessions, and would serve as exemplary cases for all city districts if being successful. The project pre-study coordinator remarked that the schooling agency adheres to an "individualized perspective" (i.e., administrative rules and professional norms prioritize individual student welfare over broader socio-economic interests), and would presumably respond that, "We mustn't treat individual students differently because we serve individuals, not geographical areas," if being asked to reallocate additional resources to certain school districts. "There are a variety of equal rights policies, and so forth, involved," she clarified (Project pre-study coordinator #1, female).

Also the science park representative accounted for these conditions: "The new schooling agency director, he manages 178 school leaders and schools. Why would he invest extra money in this particular school? That is the challenge. How can we incentivize the city administration to prioritize *this* city district?" (Science park participant #1).

Second, regarding the perceived safety in the city district among the residents, largely premised on the level of street crime and gang-related criminal activities, the regional and local police authorities were informed about the project activities but maintained its jurisdictional authority to make decisions regardless of such project goals and activities. The city district was not particularly hard hit by criminal activities, but the project participants were concerned that housing prices, especially in newly produced units, would be suppressed by the presence of street crime such as drug dealing. Discussions were maintained between the project leader and the local police office regarding how to handle the situation. Third and finally, the relatively low degree of commercial amenities was targeted as a concern for the urban development project. A local shopping galleria was in a bad condition, and had gradually become a location where local groups of boys and younger men were hanging out, and this was perceived as a safety concern by several of the project team members. Being closer to the regular day-to-day activities of the project participants than schooling affairs and police work, the city district's commercial center was widely regarded as being underdeveloped, but was within the domain of the decision-making authority of municipality-controlled real estate companies. Unfortunately, the outbreak of the coronavirus epidemic in the spring of 2020 did not improve the local business climate, and the project team was concerned about how to amend the situation. By and large, the question of how to reduce negative amenities and to further support, e.g., commercial amenities was of key importance for the urban development program.

The value of amenities: higher real estate stock valuation, increased risk-taking among residents, and the virtuous spiral

Urban development projects are rooted in economic and financial interests, and amenities are part of the housing-related assets being valued and priced. Improved amenities, including qualified schooling services, perceived safety, and an attractive supply of commercial services, are expected to raise the valuation of real estate, which benefits all agents. Representatives of the municipality real estate companies, e.g., the chief financial officer, argued that the standard methods for the valuation of the housing stock was a key concern as it largely determined the bottom line result and the solidity of the corporations:

> The [housing stock] evaluation is very important. It affects all of our key performance indicators, and how we perceive risks, and so forth. What is our leverage, how much can we borrow in relation to the value of the housing stock, and so forth?
>
> (CFO, Municipality-owned real estate company, male)

Also the project leader, representing the municipality-owned real estate company that owned roughly 94 percent of the rental units in the city district, underlined this financial accounting model as being the main rationale for the urban development initiative:

> In terms of real estate valuations, if we can move [the city district] up a few steps on the ranking scale, then we can increase the market value of the housing stock. Historically, we have done a few of these transitions … Automatically, the value of the real estate stock is appreciated.
>
> (Project leader, Municipality-owned real estate company, male)

The centrality of amenities, both in term of "positive" amenities (e.g., parks and recreation areas, public transportation quality, etc.) and the absence of "negative" amenities, are particularly pronounced in city districts dominated by low net-worth households with limited purchasing power, not least because the risk aversion can be expected to be considerable in such market segments. The joint creation of new housing and renovated housing units and the amenities that affect the market valuation of the housing stock favorably is thus a form of market making activity, one of the project representatives argued, here cited at length:

> If I examine the economic potential of the project, it is quite meagre. That is fairly obvious. During the start-up meeting, the [municipality agency representative] addressed what performance metric we would regard as the most important. For [the municipality agency] it is the quality [of housing]. But for us and [other private real estate developers] it is clearly the financing. Everything that is included in the building plan risk to drive costs and thus undermine the whole project. The financial headroom is quite low: in the best case scenario, there would be a small return. In principle, this is a break-even project for us.
>
> (Business developer, Municipality-owned housing development company, male)

Municipality real estate companies partially respond to political objectives, while at the same time being managed on the basis of the business goals to generate a net economic return. In contrast, for private companies, each construction project needs to cover its own costs. "Since quite a number of years, there are no subsidies in new housing production—a few remains, though. It is basically a market [today]," one private company business developer said (Business developer #1, Private company, male). Consequently, new construction projects need to be developed on the basis of actual market demand and the purchasing power of presumptive buyers, not on the basis of some fictive ideal case situation, stipulated by policy makers. Another private company developer, representing a cooperative building society in operation since the 1920s, argued that to make a return on new housing projects is beset by substantial challenges, a concern that was particularly accentuated in weakly developed "micro-markets" characterized by low-purchasing power, as in the case of the specific city district:

> You may think there are considerable returns in new housing production projects. But things change this quickly [makes a gesture with the hand] … If you have been part of a few downturns in the business cycle … [you know that] it does not take a long time before these revenues are consumed.
>
> (Cooperative building society representative, female)

At the same time, urban development project participants are aware of the need to take a long-term perspective, i.e., to act as "market makers" also in city districts where the market demand is currently predicted to be weak or even non-existent: "We have been given this assignment to help creating a market," one business developer said (Municipality-owned housing development company, male).

Taken together, the Swedish housing market and market making model is based on the collaborative efforts of municipality real estate companies and private developers, all being subject to the legal rules regarding the allocation of land slots and being managed by the local Real Estate Development Bureau, the municipality agency assigned the role to service all contracts and legal agreements pertaining to land sales, new housing projects, and urban development activities. In this specific model, real estate valuation cannot be functionally separated from the amenities related to a specific housing stock in a meaningful way. Urban development projects in city districts dominated by low net-worth households are consequently more complicated to manage as project participants cannot assume that presumptive buyers of new housing facilities can afford to cover the costs for amenities that collectively raise the attractiveness and the market valuation of the housing stock. Under such conditions, costs have to be covered either by other actors (i.e., the City Hall re-allocating resources, or municipality real estate companies negotiating rents in ways that de facto transfers financial capital from more affluent to less affluent city districts), or as direct funding from state agencies or philanthropy donors. In the end, housing stock valuation is intimately entangled with amenities that oftentimes fall to the side of conventional calculative practices, especially if negative amenities such as the presence of street crime are expected to be handled by state-controlled agencies and financed by tax money. Despite these conditions, urban development projects need to be managed as if amenities matter for both short-term housing stock valuations and medium to long-term housing market making activities.

Creating better amenities to improve housing welfare

The project team, composed of a consortium including representatives of municipality real estate companies, private companies, and city agencies, regarded the urban development project not only as a matter of new housing production, the creation of cooperative housing units, and the renovation of the housing stock, but anchored such activities in the broader project ambition to improve the social and housing welfare of the city district residents. Of particular interest is the presence of "negative amenities" such as "crime amenities" and "substandard schooling amenities" (see Diamond, 2016: 484). In this view, hard economic calculation and the more "soft side" of economic affairs are entangled in ways so that they are complicated to fully separate. Valuation theory is supportive of breaking down the barrier between economic calculation and the valuation of resources as valuation processes are premised on actors' preferences. Valuations are consequently collective and social processes, being the "mutual adjustment" of several actors' preferences and interests (Aspers, 2018: 140). Furthermore, the valuation that precedes, say, the pricing of an artifact has "performative" qualities inasmuch as valuation practices do not reflect stable and immutable individual preferences but actively shape how values are constituted, Kornberger (2017: 1759) proposes. For instance, if newly built housing facilities are marketed vis-à-vis presumptive buyers and prospect residents on the basis of the access to "high quality schooling" in the city district, this valuation of schooling quality, already made by the construction company marketing its newly developed housing stock, may affect how buyers assess the price of the housing units. Fourcade (2011) stresses how valuation theory underlines how "economic concerns" can never stand "outside of society"—a condition particularly pronounced in urban development projects in low-income city districts:

> Economic valuation is so revealing precisely because it is so much more than a process of monetary commensuration: it is, much more powerfully, a process of 'definition' or social construction in a substantive sense … which incorporates all kinds of assumptions about social order and socially constructed imaginaries about worth. Economic valuation, in other words, does not stand outside of society: it incorporates in its very making evaluative frames and judgments that can all be traced back to specific politico-institutional configurations and conflicts.
>
> (Fourcade, 2011: 1769)

Furthermore, the valuation theory perspective recognizes that not every single project activity can be fully recognized in a strict accounting vocabulary only, but instead some decisions need to be based on professional experience and an intuitive understanding of the situation and its needs. Much of the urban development literature emphasizes the "hard" calculative side of housing investment, and the financing of the real estate industry (see, e.g., Ghent, Torous, and Valkanov, 2019), but the current case, which draws on valuation studies literature, emphasizes that strict metrics only cover a subset of all conditions that are included when, e.g., pricing a commodity such as a rental unit.

In the specific project objective examined in this chapter, the project participants represent a variety of interests and perspectives, which incentivizes them to combine a variety of activities so that economic, financial, and social objectives are met. At the same time, a challenge for the project organization was that not all interests were represented in the project team (e.g., the city police department), and that existing project representatives (e.g., the schooling agency representative) do not always have decision-making discretion but need to negotiate project-specific issues at their home organizations. In practical terms, when investing in housing markets dominated by low net-worth households, market prices are pushed down and the profit margins become thin, which creates incentives for market actors to promote investment in public goods such as amenities. For policy makers, the externalization of production costs, to generate local markets with mixed housing, which is stipulated to generate positive effects as, e.g., the tax-base in the city district is broadened, is tolerable under certain conditions if such public investment generate net economic and social welfare. Seen in this view, valuation theory provides a theoretical perspective that disentangles market pricing from the valuation of assets (e.g., amenities) in the form of being a collective activity. If market actors, including not least low net-worth presumptive buyers of newly produced housing units, value amenities but cannot afford to pay a premium price to access them, then the cost to produce such amenities can be transferred to taxpayers. To what extent and on what scale this "subsidizing" of amenities can be justified vis-à-vis taxpayers is a political issue, the empirical case indicates, but it is beyond the scope of this chapter to outline a model or rules for how to make such policy decisions.

Summary and conclusion

Housing is a social provision in the welfare state model, but real estate assets and mortgage lending are also a key component in the financialized global economy (e.g., Pattillo, 2013). This dual nature of housing, being both a stipulated "citizenry right" and a financial asset class, put pressure on the state, cities and municipalities, and municipality-owned real estate companies to provide qualified, yet affordable housing, but in the shadow of housing market conditions. These challenges are particularly pronounced in city districts that primarily host low net-worth households with more limited possibilities for borrowing money to purchase a home. To handle such challenges, the current urban development project was constructed around a consortium that, among other project activities, assesses how local amenities can be supported and further developed. Valuation theory, being an authoritative and practically useful analytical framework when studying such activities, underlines how urban development project goals are premised on the capacity to make investment in amenities, i.e., local public goods.

The empirical material presented in this chapter enables a more detailed understanding of how low-end local housing markets are contingent on investment in public good, especially in the case where negative amenities tend to suppress housing prices and reduce the economic and social welfare of the local community.

6 What needs to be done?

The institutional challenge to provide affordable housing

Introduction

In the wake of sector-wide financialization of the economy, taking off by the turn of the millennium (Carruthers, 2015; Davis and Kim, 2015; Dore, 2008), the supply of affordable housing is increasingly becoming a policy concern in many jurisdictions. On the one hand, affordable and qualitative housing is widely recognized as a foremost welfare state provision (Pattillo, 2013); on the other hand, the financialization of the housing market has resulted in an unprecedented level of household debt (Mian, Sufi, and Verner, 2017; Kumhof, Rancière, and Winant, 2015; Zinman, 2015). During the 1983–2007 period, the ratio of household debt to gross domestic product (GDP) doubled in the US (Kumhof, Rancière and Winant, 2015: 1220), and by 2009, about 60 percent of all "outstanding residential mortgages by dollar amount" was securitized (Gelpern and Levitin, 2009: 1081). In the subprime mortgage lending market niche that essentially propelled the housing market bubble in the 2003–2006 period, this figure was even higher, with *circa* 80 percent of all loans issued being securitized (Gorton and Metrick, 2012: 430). More broadly, mortgage debt, securitized or not, generally constitutes "one of the largest or the largest asset in many OECD countries" (Schwartz, 2012: 38). While the abundance of comparably cheap finance capital, accomplished on the basis of central bank interest rates at the zero lower bound (see, e.g., Eggertsson, Mehrotra, and Robbins, 2019; Blanchard, 2019; Benigno and Fornaro, 2017; Rogoff, 2017), has benefitted some constituencies, including not least some housing market speculators, it has also tended, counter-intuitively, to exclude low net worth and low-income households from the regular housing market (Metcalf, 2018; Bubb and Prasad, 2014). To amend the situation, various forms of social housing policies and initiatives are implemented, but the scholarly literature indicates that the financing of such projects tends to generate externalities such as comparably higher costs for tenants, or taxpayers, or both (Cestau, Hollifield, Li, and Schürhoff, 2019; Schwert, 2017; Cornaggia, Cornaggia, and Israelsen, 2017). In the low end of the housing market, the sovereign state, city, or municipality administrations need to actively participate in the production of affordable housing, and to create livable city districts to satisfy the housing demand in urban areas in particular. Whereas affordable housing is a policy widely recognized across the political spectrum, it appears to be remarkably complicated to provide such

DOI: 10.4324/9781003244417-9

housing facilities for particularly vulnerable groups, for the most part excluded from the regular credit market and the mortgage lending circuit. In order to both provide affordable housing and to comply with policy makers' objective to create "mixed housing districts," which purportedly have positive externalities according to dominant urban development doctrines, the current production of suburban space combines community housing, new privately owned housing units, and the creation of more attractive commercial spaces, including grocery stores and cafés and restaurants. Drawing on the scholarly literature on the production of space as a socio-economic practice that needs to balance interests and to recognize trade-offs between competing, or mutually excluding goals, the suburban space is hybridized in several ways. Scholarly studies of the supply of affordable housing needs to recognize how "affordability" is premised on a variety of conditions that extend outside of the mere production of housing facilities, but also include the creation of city districts with a diversity of residents, mutually supporting one another and generating a housing market that benefit also low-income households and residents.

Learnings made from the affordable housing policy implementation activities

If housing welfare is defined, following the definition of affordable housing being formalized in the literature, as the household's capacity to pay no more than 30 percent of its post-taxation income on housing, then housing welfare can be measured in practical terms and thus guide policy making and policy implementation activities. In addition, housing welfare can more widely be understood in financial terms, as the total economic value stored in housing units owned by the household, in many cases difficult to render liquid prior to the sale of the housing unit (even though so-called "reversed mortgage" contracts, primarily targeting senior citizen homeowners, are now available in the market). In this latter meaning of the term, housing welfare is unevenly distributed in most societies, with households owning their primary residences benefitting the most. The empirical studies reported in Part II of this volume indicate that municipality-owned real estate companies play an active role in providing affordable housing to low net-worth households. They do so on the basis of their capacity to both pay attention to market conditions, including their capacity to monitor how much the households are able to pay in monthly and annual rents, and to act as market markers so that private companies and other market actors such as building societies can contribute with their expertise and know-how. Furthermore, municipality-owned real estate companies maintain close ties with policy makers, in turn conducting decisions (in the ideal case) that are consistent with constituencies' needs and expectations. Municipality-owned real estate companies thus play an important role, widely regarded as being legitimate by a variety of collaborating organizations and companies, in both preserving functional housing markets, and in paying attention to the needs of households in the low-end housing market niche.

The hybridity needed to maintain such ambidextrous capacities renders municipality-owned real estate companies as corporate entities that neither sit well with free market theory doctrines (as their activities are informed by political objectives), nor with the social housing model description (as they are run and managed like regular companies, with an annual stipulated return on investment to be reported and returned to the principals, the local municipality or city). Furthermore, the empirical material indicates that housing markets and the supply of affordable housing are premised on conditions that fall to the side of the market price or the monthly rent determined in Sweden on the basis of standard pricing models and negotiations. Amenities such as the access to "positive amenities" such as parks and recreational areas, restaurants and shops, but also the absence of "negative amenities," including poorly performing schools and visible and covert street crime, matters greatly for perceived housing welfare. In order to finance and generate such amenities, municipality-owned real estate companies need to collaborate with, e.g., municipality agencies (e.g., the schooling agency) or state-governed authorities (such as the police authority), which further underlines the hybridity of affordable housing production activities. Such agencies and authorities are governed on the basis of other legal frameworks and regulatory rules than, e.g., municipality-owned real estate companies are (e.g., the schooling agency are considering each pupils' individual needs and demands, and thus cannot consider a wider number of socio-economic interests without violating administrative legislation rules). Consequently, there are intense deliberations and negotiations whenever certain city districts are considered to be in need of specific reforms and resource allocations. This reform process calls for not only delicate managerial skills and competencies in all participating organizations but also a great deal of patience and prescience to be able to anticipate issues before they become overwhelming to handle.

Taken together, affordable housing policy is shaped by the nested institutional conditions that cross the boundaries between economic and financial interests, and social and welfare concerns. The central role of housing assets, both as being an important motor in the economy as they provide collateral and safe assets in the credit formation process, makes affordable housing policies a most difficult policy domain in liberal market economies, combining straightforward market valuation and pricing devices, social welfare policies, and extensive collaborations between state and municipality-controlled entities such as agencies and authorities, and privately owned firms such as listed and closely held construction companies and real estate companies. Based on such empirical conditions, some more elaborate theoretical contributions can be discussed.

Theorizing the production of hybrid suburban space: The case of urban development projects in low-end housing markets

Social theory portray social space as inherently fluid and changeable, and analytical concepts such as *space* or *spatiality* are consequently highly sophisticated in terms of being associated with a series of mechanisms and devices that define and render these concepts operable in analytical work (see, e.g., Lefebvre, 1991). This inherent dynamic of space makes it interesting to study from a social theory perspective, especially if a social space has specific economic, social, or cultural significance for its users or other audiences. Boundaries and boundary-making and boundary-protection been subject to much scholarly attention (Lamont and Molnár, 2002), as in organizations (see, e.g., Santos and Eisenhardt, 2005) wherein lines of demarcation between, e.g., front and back office, public and private spaces, personal offices and collective lunchrooms, are surrounded by norms, obligations, penalties, and so forth, all serving to carefully maintain social spaces as they are intended to serve local activities.

Town and cities have historically served as commercial centers and are consequently associated with affluence and economic welfare (Braudel, 1992). At the same time, urbanization, and especially quick urbanization processes, like in the mid-nineteenth century, are oftentimes associated with social challenges including growing poverty, poor housing standards, and sanitary issues. In the modern era, cities have been positively associated with modernity and with new social attitudes and norms. As an American sociologist argued in the late 1930s, the social interaction among a variety of "personality types" in the urban milieu, tends to "break down the rigidity of caste lines and to complicate the class structure, and thus induces a more ramified and differentiated framework of social stratification than is found in more integrated societies" (Wirth, 1938: 16). However, over time, it has become increasingly evident that cities are stratified into income groups that tend to self-segregate on the basis of their ability to acquire credit to finance house purchases. From a mainstream neoclassical economic theory perspective, such stratification is associated with economic dynamics and the market pricing of, e.g., investment made in human resources and education. That is, differentials in compensation mirror a diversity in human society that is otherwise encouraged, or at least tolerated. From a social perspective, though, the segregation of the housing market results in externalities as in the case of the risk that more talented or ambitious school children, a capacity that correlates with the parents' educational attainment, studies show, cease to serve as a positive inspiration for children with less educated parents when such families chose to move elsewhere. Furthermore, the concentration of individuals with a lower inclusion in the labor market tends to generate negative externalities, including an increased demand for social benefits, and is also associated with higher levels of criminal activity. The dominance of low-income households also limits the commercial space that can be sustained on the basis of local purchasing power.

In addition to economic trends and social tendencies, doctrines also regarding governance, and what is now referred to as "city management," explain how urban development projects are designed. Schragger (2010: 328) proposes that the policy prescription for cities has "long emphasized attracting the 'right kind' of people." That is, by providing a blend of subsidies, tax exemptions, and other benefits, city administrations may attract both investors and middle to high-income groups to invest in urban assets. In Peck and Whiteside's (2016: 239) account, "[c]ities, urban governance, and interurban relations have been comprehensively entrepreneurialized." That is, rather than being based on traditional policy-making goals, targeting net welfare benefits for residents, policy makers and their assigned agencies and collaborators regard land, buildings, and other urban resources owned by the city or municipality as a portfolio of assets whose value should be maximized.

In practice, this means that the low-end of the housing market, where affordable housing is needed the most, is underinvested as the return on equity is lower than in the middle to high-end segments of the market. Kohl (2021: 429) emphasizes the decline of the "social housing sector" as being particularly alarming for households in the low-end housing market:

> The demise of the social housing sector and its associations particularly in the European countries with a strong public-provision sector left a void in new construction because these associations had been a disproportionately important construction sector for new housing units, both in the private and the social stock … Public housing associations had established collaborations with local authorities for the provision of land for construction and the necessary local infrastructure, with state investment banks for short-term construction loans, and with state agencies for subsidized mortgages.
>
> (Kohl, 2021: 429)

Furthermore, Kohl (2021: 429) emphasizes that the social housing sector organizations also have the know-how, expertise, and credentials needed to act as "government instruments" when orchestrating a new housing supply. If these organizations recede, shortages in their primary market segment, i.e., affordable housing units in suburban city districts, are much more likely to be observed. At the same time, in countries with a developed welfare state and entrenched democratic institutions such as the Scandinavian countries, the housing market governance model effectively recognizes both the need for affordable housing and to maintain a functional market that includes private companies. In this setting, urban development projects are oftentimes designed on the basis of the collaborative efforts of a variety of actors, both public and private. This condition calls for some theoretical elaborations in terms of separating individual and organizational "rights" in housing policy and housing market governance.

The importance of organizational rights in affordable housing policy implementation

The history of affordable housing policy implementation reveals many difficulties and disappointing outcomes, in many cases despite the best stated intentions and coalitions across both party lines and in private–public relations. Linos (2021) argues that organizations are comparably more effective in protecting "organizational rights" than individuals defending "individual rights," either on their own or in collaborations with others, are. These insights may be of general relevance for the analysis of both the supply and demand side of affordable housing production. Linos (2021: 729) proposes that organizations are "[p]otential defenders of rights in challenging times," simply because the rights of organizations are protected by the "built-in advocates" of, e.g., religious groups, trade unions, and political parties, ready to enforce such rights. In contrast, Linos continues, "individual rights," which include both civil rights such as "freedom from torture," and social rights such as "the right to education," have no comparable built-in organizational advocates, and are therefore "harder to protect." "States can crush individuals however precisely their rights are enumerated—the power asymmetry is too large" (Linos, 2021: 736). In contrast, organizations that advocate certain rights, procedures, or protocols on the basis of a civic role in society have much better prospects for successfully facilitating coordination and collective action, and thus to protect the organizational rights that they have negotiated and institutionalized at some earlier stage (Linos, 2021: 736).

Linos's (2021) argument is of great relevance for affordable housing production as the housing market is commonly construed as a bilateral relation between buyer and seller in a market transaction setting. This transaction is heavily structured on the basis of a variety of legislations, regulatory rules, and established business practices so that the interests of either party is considered, and their rights are enforceable in the court system. At this level, the *already available* stock of housing can be handled on the basis of individual rights. The concern is that the housing stock and the affordable housing stock is an issue that matters for not only individual households and families but is a social concern that remains also after the *n*th family are able to purchase their home, and thus no longer are actively engaged in shaping the housing market. Expressed differently, how to ensure housing supply, not least affordable housing supply, is a social dilemma: all want to have the issue handled, but few are committed to alter the situation as they are only weakly incentivized to do so. In Linos's (2021) view, the question of how to provide an adequate level of housing supply is thus essentially a matter of being an *individual*, not an *organizational* right. Again, despite individual rights may be widely recognized and respected, they are much more difficult to enforce than organizational rights.

As has been argued by a number of scholars, the supply of affordable housing is unlikely to increase merely on the basis of, e.g., increased production (Fingleton, Fuerst, and Szumilo, 2019) or a more equal access to finance capital through the household lending channel (Atkinson, 2019): these policies are only further reinforcing individual rights that benefit medium to high net worth households that can already access the resources needed to primarily access qualitative housing. In contrast, in the low-end housing market, organizations that also actively support housing welfare for low net-worth households need to be established. As indicated in this volume, in the Swedish welfare state model, the municipality-owned real estate company plays this role on the supply-side, being assisted by, e.g., the tenants' interest organization on the demand-side. The municipality-owned real estate company plays a civic role to protect a steady and preferably growing stock of rental or privately owned housing units that are accessible for tenants with smaller budgets.

The supply-side view: the role of municipality-controlled real estate companies

Housing policy needs to consider that medium to high net worth households have the financial strength to navigate in the housing market but that such capacities do not of necessity trickle down to low net-worth households in the way that housing policy architects may hope it would. A standing critique of housing policy is that it is geared towards increasing the supply of finance capital to households with limited income, either as mortgage loans or subsidies, and that such policies fuel rather than dampen housing market prices (see, e.g., Atkinson, 2019). In the Swedish welfare model, the municipality real estate company is a specific organizational form that operates on the housing market, both in the role of being a major supplier of rental units and privately owned housing, and in the role of market maker in certain segments of the housing markets so that it benefits private real estate developers and construction companies. In the latter role, municipality real estate companies act as an intermediary between municipality agencies and private companies as new development projects are initiated. Municipality real estate companies are legally speaking chartered business entities, but they are fully owned by the municipality wherein their operate, and the board of directors include, *inter alia*, political party representatives from across the political spectrum. Municipality real estate companies deliver a net return to their owners, but the reported return on assets is stipulated to be at the level where the long-term survival of the corporation can be ensured. At the same time as sound business principles serve as guidelines for municipality real estate companies, they act on the basis of the political ambition to provide affordable and qualitative housing for all tenants, which means that certain neighborhoods with an overrepresentation of households with specific socio-economic challenges may be subsidized by the rental income acquired within the total rental unit stock managed by the real estate companies. In this way, municipality real estate companies can, in the ideal situation, bridge and blend market practices and political ambitions so that the aggregated housing welfare is optimized. In this model, housing welfare become not only an individual right that is advocated vis-à-vis a variety of actors and institutions, but it is granted the status of being an "organizational right" (as proposed by Linos, 2021)—a right that the municipality-owned real estate company consistently act to protect and advocate in communication with both market actors and policy makers and political bodies, e.g., political parties.

Critics of the municipality-owned real estate company point at number of challenges and difficulties associated with this housing market model. First, there is a general concern that any corporation can honor both good business principles and a political will at the same time without any direct or indirect costs. In the principal-agent governance model, the executives and directors of the municipality-owned real estate company, being the agents, are thus expected to act on the basis of the dual objective to run a business at a profit and to respond to shifting, at times even ambiguous political agendas and goals, and this results in outcomes that may be suboptimal. In addition, critics argue that the structural power of municipality real estate companies may impose costs on other market actors, including not least private real estate developers and construction companies that serve the housing market. While these critiques needs to be taken seriously—to serve several rather than one objective may for instance create tensions between, e.g., short-term interests and long-term returns in the executive decision making process—there seem, on balance, to be net socio-economic benefits generated within the current housing market model. Rather than having net-worth households living in rental units that are poorly maintained, and paying up to 70 percent of their monthly income for housing (Desmond and Bell, 2015: 16), and having their rights, even when being subject to court ruling, neglected (as being reported from the US; Summers, 2020), the current model provides affordable housing on the basis of the municipality-owned real estate company protecting affordable housing as an organizational rather than an individual right. Furthermore, this model is based on fiscal discipline and the social norms that paying one's taxes is not only a duty of all citizens; it is also a socio-economic imperative if one wants to preserve the welfare state model. As, e.g., the Swedish fiscal authority maintains a sophisticated tax collection apparatus, and because there is a considerable degree of transparency throughout this housing market model, the key role of municipality real estate companies is widely recognized across the political spectrum and in the wider public, and rarely subject to animated debates in news reporting media. Also political representatives who have a firm belief in the value of free markets and market transactions tend to believe that there is currently no competitive model that would provide affordable housing with a similar degree of quality and precision.

Despite this model having many benefits, the difficulties involved in preserving the affordable housing stock, not least during episodes of increased migration flows, should not be underestimated. As housing costs are considerable on the average family's account (and commonly falling in proportion with higher income, not least correlating with proportionally higher returns from financial asset holdings; Ivanova, 2019: 716–717), the capacity to increase the stock of affordable housing units on short-term notice remains limited. This which means that migration policies and labor market conditions are two main factors strongly shaping the performance of municipality real estate companies, two issues that are beyond the influence of the executives and directors of these public companies.

The demand-size view: the need for a new political organization of tenants

One question that may be considered regarding the possibility to access affordable housing is to what extent civil society organizations can play a new and more important role in advocating the interests of the primary beneficiaries of affordable housing policies (e.g., low net-worth households). In the US, Andrias and Sachs (2021: 566) report, the membership in the organizations that served such civic roles during the Progressive and New Deal eras dropped by 60 percent between 1974 and 1994. Today, "less than a third" of the organizational advocates that operates in Washington are "membership associations of any kind," and only about one eighth are "membership associations of individuals" (Andrias and Sachs, 2021: 566). This means that in the cases where the 1960s' social movements organizations have survived, they are no longer the democratically governed mass-membership organizations they were originally designed to be; today, they are best described as "professionally managed advocacy groups," organized as charitable nonprofits and "funded mainly by wealthy donors" (Andrias and Sachs, 2021: 566). Such data and conditions indicate that civic organizations no longer play an active role in advocating the interests of members or citizens more widely. Instead, these organizations are part of the political system that has essentially failed in its ambition to provide affordable housing. Wealthy donors may have the best intentions regarding how to be supportive of social and economic welfare, but these individuals are unlikely to have first-hand experiences from the low-end housing market, and therefore cannot plausibly fully apprehend the hardship that the exposure to unregulated housing markets implies. Furthermore, Andrias and Sachs (2021: 549) add, "[w]ealthy individuals are spending record sums on electoral politics and that elected officials are at best only weakly accountable to non-wealthy constituents." The decline of mass-membership organizations is a concern as democratic societies are premised on their capacity to ensure "social inclusion," i.e., to engage citizens in a variety of activities that purportedly indicates their active role in society in day-to-day life. Such parameters include "voting participation," "political participation" (e.g., membership in political parties and similar political organizations), "civic participation" (e.g., membership in civic organizations of the kind discussed by Andrias and Sachs, 2021), and the "degree of engagement" (a parameter that include a variety of measures indicative of the individual's interest in social conditions; Bruch, Ferree, and Ferree, 2010: 213).

This decline in the role of democratic membership associations, wherein individuals can have their concerns addressed and their interests advocated vis-à-vis policy makers, imposes costs and risks to reduce social and economic welfare. Andrias and Sachs (2021: 560) propose that one legal reform that would counteract this tendency is to grant, e.g., tenants the right to "form and join tenant unions." Andrias and Sachs (2021: 560–561) point at some of the rights conferred to such tenant unions:

> [New legislation] would grant such unions the right to access information and landlord property for organizational purposes. It would vest the organization with authority to collect dues payments through deductions from rent payments. It would mandate that landlords negotiate with tenants' organizations over rent and housing conditions. It would ensure that organizations have special rights of participation in administrative processes related to housing policy. And it would provide for the right of tenants to engage in rent strikes and protests, free from retaliation.
>
> (Andrias and Sachs, 2021: 560–561)

Legal reforms are called for in this area because it would provide a common frame for addressing the current housing market situation and define a legal framework wherein a larger number of stakeholders' interests are considered. Needless to say, such legal reforms would at best assist current market practices but could still potentially play an active role in putting pressure on policy makers and their close allies to pay closer attention to the housing conditions in low-end markets in particular. Andrias and Sachs (2021) thus advocate a rehabilitated civic organization, supported by legal reforms, as one means to re-frame housing policies and housing market conditions.

Taken together, there may be good reason to consider Linos' (2021) proposition that organizational rights are more easily protected than individual rights. As Levitin and Wachter, 2020: xvii) remark, housing is a peculiar good inasmuch as it a form of "communitarian asset," an asset that is not entirely private as it serves as collateral in the credit formation process, and is subject to taxation during both ownership and when being sold, etc. Based on these premises, housing welfare can, on the one hand, be strictly treated as a private property concern (as it is in the segments of the housing market that serve medium to high net worth households), while, on the other hand, it may be fruitfully recognized as an "organizational right" that is part of the jurisdictional domain of, e.g., municipality real estate companies and similar corporate entities that act to supply affordable housing in the low-end housing market segment. Under all conditions, there are good reasons for policy makers and market actors to consider the implications from taking a new perspective on the housing market, and to implement policies and solutions that assist specific niches of that market.

Contributions to housing policy

One of the policy implications from the review of the relevant literature and the empirical material is that the housing market is best considered as what can be divided into tranches or segments. In the middle to high-end housing market segments, regular market incentives and market devices such as contracting in combination with limited or some subsidies to either real estate developers or households, or to both, depending on local policy preferences, appear to be highly effective. Middle to high net worth households have incomes that translate into a purchasing power that makes them qualified for making individual decisions on the basis of available market information and market practices. Excessive price rises on the housing markets are still preferably monitored by, e.g., finance market regulation agencies and the central bank, but otherwise, the scholarly literature suggests that few if any subsidies or tax exemptions contributes in any sustainable way to housing market efficiency and the optimal allocation of housing welfare.

In the low-end housing market, the situation is radically different, as households have either a low degree of self-financing capacity (e.g., households are not included in the labor market and benefit from transfers in the welfare system) or have limited budgets more widely. As new housing production is costly and associated with uncertainty, few regular market actors are specializing in serving this niche of the market. Municipality-owned real estate companies are thus actively supportive of affordable housing policies inasmuch as they act as a vehicle for the implementation of policy makers' decisions. At the same time, the corporate structure of municipality-owned real estate companies in Sweden serves as a warrant against a more comprehensive politicization of the housing market; municipality-owned real estate companies act to provide affordable housing for low-income households under a profit motive, but they are also assigned the role to act as market makers inasmuch as they actively collaborate with private companies that build new housing units in city districts with thin housing assets markets (i.e., the choice of housing units is limited). While there may be political debates in the city hall regarding the best use of municipality-owned real estate companies, especially during periods of turbulence, including economic recession periods (like in the early 1990s in Sweden), or towards the end of the public election cycle, the governance of municipality-owned real estate companies has been fairly consistent over time. The literature review and empirical material thus indicate that municipality-owned real estate companies have a key role to play in providing affordable housing in an otherwise market-based housing sector.

The critique of social housing initiatives is centered on the difficulties in drawing the line of demarcation between households that are eligible for tax-financed housing services and those that are not, and the externalities generated when the state absorbs a certain proportion of the housing market. While such discussions are important, not least from an ideological perspective regarding how to set the boundaries for the paternalist state and how tax payers' money is committed to various activities, in many cases, municipalities have no choice but to abide by the legislation that stipulates certain minimal welfare rights, including access to housing facilities. At the end of the day, academic debates and "what-if" scenario discussions are important for developing new and better housing supply and housing financing models, but the social costs of not providing affordable (or even free) housing for certain groups are plausibly higher than the overall benefits. That is, if low-income households are provided with affordable housing, family members can make other contributions to the joint economic welfare that are in excess of the aggregated costs for such services. This renders the wholly unregulated and unsubsidized housing market, freed from political interests and pressures, a piece of theoretical fiction, difficult to materialize without overwhelming social costs, and easily migrating outside of the housing market. At the same time, to commit tax money to affordable housing projects without any detailed monitoring of the process and the outcomes (preferably to be defined and eventually measured in metric terms prior to the implementation of the project activities) is likely to make social housing activities appear once again as a value-destroying policy, as it was perceived in the 1980s and beyond in, e.g., the UK (Boughton, 2018). As the housing stock is costly and time-consuming to change, a capricious experimental attitude in these quarters is unlikely to hold water for a considerable period of time. On the contrary, cross-sectional collaborations and the hybridity they generate are presumably the only way forward to provide at least a minimal level of housing welfare for the largest possible proportion of the population. This means that there are few prospects of "quick fixes" or "silver bullets" being ready to hand; the work needed demands time, effort, financial resources, and a fair share of patience and tenacity, not very different from many other welfare state responsibilities that the sovereign state and its collaborators handle on an everyday basis.

Contributions to management studies and related social science disciplines

Social and economic welfare tends to be unevenly distributed, but economic policy including fiscal policy and the taxation system serves to transfer economic resources so that it benefits disadvantaged groups in welfare states. At the same time as the state can actively be supportive of dynamic, yet efficient housing markets, the state and its defined agencies are still dependent on the corporate system to provide affordable and qualitative housing. Construction companies, real estate companies, finance institutions, including mortgage lending institutions, are all of key importance for the materialization of affordable housing. A key question is then whether more regulations or targeted subsidies to either companies and industries or specific households is the better approach than to leave to market actors to provide affordable housing on the basis of current and projected market demand? It is reasonable to assume that hybrid markets are more effective in providing affordable housing. On the one hand, as in the case of Sweden, there has been an endemic shortage of affordable housing in metropolitan areas over the entire Post-World War II period if alarmist journalistic and popular accounts are taken as prima facie evidence of poorly functional housing markets. On the other hand, Stockholm has reputedly one of the highest proportion of single households in the Western world (in one study estimated to be in the range of 63 percent of all households), which is indicative of its inhabitants still having the economic resources to pay for their very own individual homes. In Sweden, on average, roughly 40 percent of the households are single person households (SCB, 2021). In many other parts of the world, such housing welfare are simply unattainable, even inconceivable. Similar to health care services or in the culture sector, there is an almost insatiable demand for more resources that would allegedly generate better, cheaper, and more qualitative housing, and in the case where the primary homestead is secured, many middle class and more wealthy households are considering investing in also a secondary home outside of their residence areas. This makes the question of how to handle housing policy issues a thorny policy affair, and when it comes to disadvantaged groups, including migrants with limited possibilities for supporting themselves, housing policy indubitably makes a significant difference in terms of housing welfare. One managerial implication is that private companies contribute to functional housing markets, but that the profit motive that is the basis for chartered business ventures incentivize managers to avoid low-end housing markets with slim or close to non-existent profit margins, which means that there are comparably fewer companies that are actively involved in servicing affordable housing in this market niche. However, as indicated in Part II of this volume, if municipality real estate companies, acting on the basis of political objectives, act to be supportive of such markets and to buffer some of the risks, there are incentives for private companies to create low-end market niches where affordable housing production is maintained. It is important to notice that the alignment of political interests and economic incentives demand considerable work "on the ground" to avoid that, e.g., private companies fail to generate a return on their investment, which would reduce their appetite for further construction projects in market niches with slim margins. To supply affordable housing to low-end housing market clients is thus best characterized as a form of public-private partnership, forged on the basis of conventional business practices and political ambitions and agendas, in turn being fueled by tax money.

Summary and conclusion

Housing is an interesting economic asset as it is, as opposed to a variety of increasingly exotic derivative asset classes introduced in the finance industry trade, intuitively understandable for most people. A family's residential home has many immediately recognizable benefits, and from an historical perspective, the house was a short-hand term (as in Thomas Mann's novel *The Buddenbrooks*) denoting the full socio-economic situation and the legality of the resident's household. Furthermore, access to housing is also subject to what French historian René Girard spoke of as "memetic desire" or "memetic rivalry": the house you want, I want too, simply because you wanted it in the first place. The uneven distribution of housing welfare (in its theoretical re-description) is thus likely to cause grievances in a population, and to remain a matter of joint concerns under all conditions. Even in countries with a low income inequality such as Sweden and Norway, the wealth inequality that is primarily derived from differentials in housing welfare and equity asset holdings is considerable (Pfeffer and Waitkus, 2021). In practical terms, policy makers need to first cope with the issue to provide affordable housing here and now for low net-worth households, and thereafter, if successful with these policy ambitions, address the wealth inequality caused by, e.g., housing asset ownership more widely. As policy makers frequently attend to the most acute issues, the growth in wealth inequality measures is likely to be left unnoticed by the majority. In the long run, it may be that wealth inequality is not a major political issue (see, e.g., Mijs, 2019), at least not in a liberal political program, as middle to high net worth households may be permitted to use their economic surplus as they wish after all taxes and fees are paid to tax collecting agencies. It is thus advisable that policies are directed towards low-end housing markets wherein the marginal effect of each tax dollar (or in the currency of choice) invested makes the highest contribution. When considering such policies, this volume has sought to demonstrate, decisions made are far from trivial and they can have lasting percussions through the local and regional—at times even the global, as in the fall of 2008—economic system. This means that policy makers need to pay close attention to a variety of arguments and objections to be able to finally determine how affordable housing is optimally provided in the specific housing market being served.

Bibliography

Abbott, A. (1988), *The system of professions: An essay on the division of expert labor*, Chicago and London: Chicago University Press.

Abbott, A. (2010), Varieties of ignorance, *American Sociologist*, 41(2): 174–189.

Acharya, V. and Viswanathanm, S. (2011), Leverage, moral hazard, and liquidity, *Journal of Finance*, 66: 99–138.

Acolin, A., Bricker, J., Calem, P., and Wachter, S. (2016), Borrowing constraints and home-ownership, *American Economic Review*, 106(5): 625–629.

Adkins, L., Cooper, M. and Konings, M. (2021), Class in the 21st century: Asset inflation and the new logic of inequality, *Environment and Planning A: Economy and Space*, 53(3): 548–572.

Agarwal, S., Amromin, G., Ben-David, I., Chomsisengphet, S., and Evanoff, D.D. (2014), Predatory lending and the subprime crisis, *Journal of Financial. Economics*, 113(1): 29–52.

Aghion, P. and Roulet, A. (2014), Growth and the smart state, *Annual Review of Economics*, 6: 913–926.

Ailon, G. (2012), The discursive management of financial risk scandals: The case of Wall Street journal commentaries on LTCM and Enron, *Qualitative Sociology*, 35(3): 251–270.

Ailon, G. (2014), Financial risk-taking as a sociological gamble: Notes on the development of a new social perspective, *Sociology*, 48(3): 606–621.

Aizenman, J., and Glick, R. (2009), Sovereign wealth funds: Stylized facts about their determinants and governance, *International Finance*, 12(3): 351–386.

Akers, J. and Seymour, E. (2018), Instrumental exploitation: Predatory property relations at city's end. *Geoforum*, 91: 127–140.

Alexander, C., Bruun, M.H., and Koch, I. (2018) Political economy comes home: On the moral economies of housing. *Critique of Anthropology*, 38(2): 121–139.

Alexander, J.C. (2018), The societalization of social problems: Church pedophilia, phone hacking, and the financial crisis, *American Sociological Review*, 83(6): 1049–1078.

Alhashel, B. (2015), Sovereign wealth funds: A literature review, *Journal of Economics and Business*, 78: 1–13.

Allen, F., and Gale, D. (1994), Liquidity preference, market participation and asset price volatility, *American Economic Review*, 84(4): 933–955.

Allen, M.P., and Lincoln, A.E. (2004), Critical discourse and the cultural consecration of American films, *Social Forces*, 82(3): 871–894.

Almeling, R. (2011), *Sex cells: The medical market for eggs and sperm*, Berkeley, Los Angeles, and London: University of California Press.

Anderson, E. (2018), Policy entrepreneurs and the origins of the regulatory welfare state: Child labor reform in Nineteenth-century Europe, *American Sociological Review*, 83(1):173–211.

Andrews, E.L. (2009), *Busted: Life inside the great mortgage meltdown*, New York: W.W. Norton.

Andrias, K., and Sachs, B. (2021), Constructing countervailing power: Law and organizing in an era of political inequality, *Yale Law Journal*, 130(3): 546–635.

Ansell, B.W. (2014). The political economy of ownership: Housing markets and the welfare state, *American Political Science Review*, 108(2): 383–402.

Ansell, B.W. (2019), The politics of housing, *Annual Review of Political Science*, 22: 165–185.

Ansell, B.W., Broz, J.L., and Flaherty, T. (2018), Global capital markets, housing prices, and partisan fiscal policies, *Economics & Politics*, 30(3): 307–339.

Anteby, M. (2008), *Moral gray zones: Side production, identity, and regulation in an aeronautics plant*, Princeton: Princeton University Press.

Apgar, W.C. (1990), Which housing policy is best? *Housing Policy Debate*, 1(1): 1–32.

Ashton, P. and Christophers, B. (2015), On arbitration, arbitrage and arbitrariness in financial markets and their governance: Unpacking LIBOR and the LIBOR scandal, *Economy and Society*, 44(2): 188–217.

Aspers, P. (2018), Forms of uncertainty reduction: Decision, valuation, and contest, *Theory and Society*, 47(2), 133–149.

Atkinson, A. (2019), Rethinking credit as social provision, *Stanford Law Review*, 71(5): 1093–1162.

Autor, D., Dorn, D., Katz, L.F., Patterson, C., and Van Reenen, J. (2020), The fall of the labor share and the rise of superstar firms, *Quarterly Journal of Economics*, 135(2): 645–709.

Baccaro, L. and Howell, C. (2017), *Trajectories of neoliberal transformation: European industrial relations since the 1970s*, Cambridge: Cambridge University Press.

Baker, J.B. (2019), *The Antitrust paradigm: Restoring a competitive economy*, Cambridge: Harvard University Press.

Baker, T. (1996), On the genealogy of moral hazard, *Texas Law Review*, 75(2): 237–292.

Bakken, T. and Wiik, E.L. (2018), Ignorance and organization studies, *Organization Studies*, 39: 1109–1120.

Banzhaf, H.S. and Farooque, O. (2013), Interjurisdictional housing prices and spatial amenities: Which measures of housing prices reflect local public goods? *Regional Science and Urban Economics*, 43(4): 635–648.

Barker, R. and Schulte, S. (2016), Representing the market perspective: Fair value measurement for non-financial assets, *Accounting, Organizations, and Society*, 56: 55–67.

Bartram, R. (2021), Cracks in broken windows: How objects shape professional evaluation, *American Journal of Sociology*, 126(4): 759–794.

Battilana, J. and Dorado, S. (2010), Building sustainable hybrid organizations: The case of commercial microfinance organizations, *Academy of Management Journal*, 53(6): 1419–1440.

Battaglini, M. and Patacchini, E. (2019), Social networks in policy making, *Annual Review of Economics*, 11: 473–494.

Baumer, E.P., Ranson, J. W.A., Arnio, A.N., Fulmer, A., and, De Zilwa, S. (2017), Illuminating a dark side of the American dream: Assessing the prevalence and predictors of mortgage fraud across US counties, *American Journal of Sociology*, 123(2): 549–603.

Bayer, P., Mangum, K., and Roberts, J.W. (2021), Speculative fever: Investor contagion in the housing bubble, *American Economic Review*, 111(2): 609–651.

Beckert, J. and Aspers, P., eds. (2011), *The worth of goods: Valuation and pricing in the economy*, Princeton: Princeton University Press.

Belfrage, C. and Kallifatides, M. (2018), Financialisation and the new Swedish model, *Cambridge Journal of Economics*, 42(4): 875–900.

Benigno, G. and Fornaro, L. (2017), Stagnation traps, *Review of Economic Studies*, 85(3): 1425–1470.

Benton, R.A. and Cobb, J.A. (2019), Eyes on the horizon? Fragmented elites and the short-term focus of the American corporation, *American Journal of Sociology*, 124(6): 1631–1684.

Berger, D., Turner, N., and Zwick, E. (2020), Stimulating housing markets, *Journal of Finance*, 75(1): 277–321.

Bernhardt, A. (2012), The role of labor market regulation in rebuilding economic opportunity in the United States, *Work and Occupations*, 39(4): 354–375,

Besbris, M., and Faber, J.W. (2017), Investigating the relationship between real estate agents, segregation, and house prices, *Sociological Forum*, 32: 805–873.

Beswick, J. and Penny, J. (2018), Demolishing the present to sell off the future? The emergence of 'financialized municipal entrepreneurialism' in London, *International Journal of Urban and Regional Research*, 42(4): 612–632.

Biven, Josh and Shierholz, Heidi (2013), The great recession's impact on jobs, wages, and incomes, in Wolfson, Martin H. and Epstein, Gerald A., eds., *Handbook of the political economy of financial crises*, New York and Oxford: Oxford University Press, pp. 61–94.

Blackwell, Timothy, and Kohl, Sebastian (2018), The origins of national housing finance systems: A comparative investigation into historical variations in mortgage finance regimes, *Review of International Political Economy*, 25(1): 49–74.

Blanchard, Olivier (2019), Public debt and low interest rates, *American Economic Review*, 109(4): 1197–1229.

Blancheton, Bertrand (2016), Central bank independence in a historical perspective: Myth, lessons and a new model, *Economic Modelling*, 52: 101–107.

Blanchflower, D.G. (2019), *Not working: Where have all the good jobs gone?*, Princeton: Princeton University Press.

Bohle, Dorothee, (2014), Post-socialist housing meets transnational finance: Foreign banks, mortgage lending, and the privatization of welfare in Hungary and Estonia, *Review of International Political Economy*, 21(4): 913–948.

Boiral, Olivier (2012), ISO certificates as organizational degrees? Beyond the rational myths of the certification process, *Organization Studies*, 33(5–6): 633–654.

Bond, Philip, Musto, David K., and Yilmaz, Bilge (2008), Predatory mortgage lending, *Journal of Financial Economics*, 94: 412–427.

Borio, Claudio (2011), Rediscovering the macroeconomic roots of financial stability policy: Journey, challenges, and a way forward, *Annual Review of Financial Economics*, 3:87–117.

Botzem, S. and Dobusch, L. (2017), Financialization as strategy: Accounting for inter-organizational value creation in the European real estate industry, *Accounting, Organizations, and Society*, 59: 31–43.

Boughton, John (2018), *Municipal dreams: The rise and fall of council housing*, London: Verso.

Bourdieu, Pierre (2005), *The economic structures of society*, Cambridge: Polity Press.

Bourdieu, Pierre (2020), *On the state: Lectures at Collège de France, 1989–1991*, Trans. by David Fernbach, Cambridge: Polity.

Boy, N. and Gabor, D. (2019), Collateral times, *Economy and Society*, 48(3): 295–314.

Bratton, W.W. (2017), The separation of corporate law and social welfare, *Washington & Lee Law Review*, (74): 767–790.

Braudel, Fernand (1992), *The wheels of commerce: Civilization & capitalism 15th–18th century*, Vol. 2, Berkeley and Los Angeles: The University of California Press.

Braun, Benjamin (2016), Speaking to the people? Money, trust, and central bank legitimacy in the age of quantitative easing, *Review of International Political Economy*, 23(6): 1064–1092.

Braun, Benjamin (2020), Central banking and the infrastructural power of finance: The case of ECB support for repo and securitization markets, *Socio-Economic Review*, 18(2): 395–418.

Braunerhjelm, Pontus and Henrekson, Magnus (2013), Entrepreneurship, institutions, and economic dynamism: Lessons from a comparison of the United States and Sweden, *Industrial and Corporate Change*, 22(1): 107–130.

Brecht, Bertholt (2003), *Brecht on art and politics*, ed. by Tom Kuhn and Steve Giles, trans by Laura Bradley, Steve Giles, and Tom Kuhn, London: Methuen.

Bruch, Sarah K., Ferree, Myra Marx, and Ferree, Joe (2010), From policy to polity: Democracy, paternalism, and the incorporation of disadvantaged citizens, *American Sociological Review*, 75(2): 205–226.

Browning, Christopher R., Calder, Catherine A., Boettner, Bethany, Tarrence, Jake, Khan, Kori, Soller, Brian, and Ford, Jodi L. (2021), Neighborhoods, activity spaces, and the span of adolescent exposures, *American Sociological Review*, 86(2): 201–233.

Brueckner, Jan K., Thisse, Jacques-Francois, and Zenou, Yves (1999), Why is central Paris rich and downtown Detroit poor? An amenity-based theory. *European Economic Review*, 43(1): 91–107.

Brummer, Chris and Yadav, Yesha (2019), Fintech and the innovation trilemma, *Georgetown Law Journal*, 107: 235–307.

Bryan, R. and Rafferty, M. (2014), Political economy and housing in the twenty-first century – From mobile homes to liquid housing? *Housing, Theory and Society*, 31(4): 404–412.

Bryan, D., Rafferty, M., Toner, P., and Wright, S. (2017), Financialisation and labour in the Australian commercial construction industry, *Economic and Labour Relations Review*, 28(4): 500–518.

Bubb, Ryan and Prasad, Krishnamurthy (2014), Regulating against bubbles: How mortgage regulation can keep main street and Wall Street safe-from themselves, *University of Pennsylvania Law Review*, 163: 1539–1630.

Budd, Kate, Kelsey, Darren, Mueller, Frank, and Whittle, Andrea (2019), Metaphor, morality and legitimacy: A critical discourse analysis of the media framing of the payday loan industry, *Organization*, 26(6): 802–829.

Burnside, Craig, Eichenbaum, Martin, and Rebelo, Sergio (2016), Understanding booms and busts in housing markets, *Journal of Political Economy*, 124(4): 1088–1147.

Caballero, Ricardo J., Farhi, Emmanuel, and Gourinchas, Pierre-Olivier (2017), The safe assets shortage conundrum, *Journal of Economic Perspectives*, 31(3): 29–46.

Cabantous, Laure, and Gond, Jean-Pascal (2011), Rational decision making as performative praxis: Explaining rationality's *Éternel Retour*, *Organization Science*, 22(3): 573–586.

Calomiris, Charles W. and Haber, Stephen H. (2014), *Fragile by design: The political origins of banking crises and scarce credit*, Princeton and Oxford: Princeton University Press.

Campbell, John L. (2002), Ideas, politics, and public policy, *Annual Review of Sociology*, 28: 21–38.

Carruthers, Bruce G. (2015), Financialization and the institutional foundations of the new capitalism, *Socio-Economic Review*, 13(2): 379–398.

Cary, W.L. (1974), Federalism and corporate law: Reflections upon Delaware, *Yale Law Journal*, 83(4): 663–705.

Case, Anne and Deaton, Angus (2020), *Deaths of despair and the future of capitalism*, Princeton: Princeton University Press.

Castilla, Emilio J. (2008), Gender, race and meritocracy in organizational careers, *American Journal of Sociology*, 113(6): 1479–1526.

Cestau, Dario, Hollifield, Burton, Li, Dan, and Schürhoff, Norman (2019), Municipal bond markets, *Annual Review of Financial Economics*, 11: 65–84.

Charles, Kerwin Kofi, Hurst, Erik, and Notowidigdo, Matthew J. (2016), The masking of the decline in manufacturing employment by the housing bubble, *Journal of Economic Perspectives*, 30(2): 179–200.

Cheng, Ing-Haw, Raina, Sahil, and Xiong, Wei (2014), Wall Street and the housing bubble, *American Economic Review*, 104(9): 2797–2829.

Chetty, Raj, Hendren, Nathaniel, and Katz, Lawrence F. (2016), The effects of exposure to better neighborhoods on children: New evidence from the moving to opportunity experiment, *American Economic Review*, 106(4): 855–902.

Cho, Sang-Wook (Stanley) and Francis, Johanna L. (2011), Tax treatment of owner occupied housing and wealth inequality, *Journal of Macroeconomics*. 33(1): 42–60.

Christophers, Brett (2015), *The great leveler: Capitalism and competition in the court of law*, Cambridge: Harvard University Press.

Christophers, Brett (2018), *The new enclosure: The appropriation of public land in neoliberal Britain*, London and New York: Verso.

Citron, D.K. and Pasquale, F.A. (2014), The scored society: Due process for automated predictions, *Washington Law Review*, 89(1): 1–33.

Clegg, Stewart R., Rhodes, Carl, and Kornberger, Martin (2007), Desperately seeking legitimacy: Organizational identity and emerging industries, *Organization Studies*, 28(4): 495–513.

Cobb, Adam and Lin, Ken-Hou (2017), Growing apart: The changing firm-size wage premium and its inequality consequences, *Organization Science*, 28(3): 429–446.

Cohney, Shaanan, Hofman, David, Sklarof, Jeremy, and Wishnick, David (2019), Coin-operated capitalism, *Columbia Law Review*, 119(3): 591–676.

Colic-Peisek, V. and Tilbury, F. (2006), Employment niches for recent refugees: Segmented labour markets in Twenty-first century Australia, *Journal of Refugee Studies*, 19(2): 203–229.

Conley, D. and Gifford, B. (2006), Home ownership, social insurance, and the welfare state, *Sociological Forum*, 21: 55–82.

Conti, Joseph A. (2010), Producing legitimacy at the World Trade Organization: The role of expertise and legal capacity, *Socio-Economic Review*, 8(1): 131–155.

Conti-Brown, Peter, and Wishnick, David A. (2021), Technocratic pragmatism, bureaucratic expertise, and the federal reserve, *Yale Law Journal*, 130(3): 636–706.

Conti-Brown, Peter and Zaring, David (2019), The foreign affairs of the federal reserve, *Journal of Corporation Law*, 44: 665–712.

Corley, K.G.. and Gioia, D.A. (2011), Building theory about theory building: What constitutes a theoretical contribution?, *Academy of Management Review*, 36(1): 12–32.

Cornaggia, Jess, Cornaggia, Kimberly J., and Israelsen, Ryan D. (2017), Credit ratings and the cost of municipal financing, *Review of Financial Studies*, 31(6): 2038–2079.

Coslor, E. (2016) Transparency in an opaque market: Evaluative frictions between "thick" valuation and "thin" price data in the art market, *Accounting, Organizations and Society*, 50(1): 13–26.

Covarrubias, Matias, Gutiérrez, Germán, and Philippon, Thomas (2020), From good to bad concentration? US industries over the past 30 years, *NBER Macroeconomics Annual*, 34(1): 1–46.

Crawford, Joe and McKee, Kim (2018), Hysteresis: Understanding the housing aspirations gap, *Sociology*, 52(1) 182–197.

Crawford, Kate and Schultz, Jason (2014), Big data and due process: Toward a framework to redress predictive privacy harms, *Boston College Law Review*, 55: 93–128.

Daft, R.L. and Weick, K.E. (1984), Toward a model of organizations as interpretation systems, *Academy of Management Review*, 9(2): 284–295.

Dane, E. and Pratt, M.G. (2007), Exploring intuition and its role in managerial decision making, *Academy of Management Review*, 32(1): 33–54.

Dang, Tri Vi, Gorton, Gary, and Holmström, Bengt (2020), The information view of financial crises, *Annual Review of Financial Economics*, 12: 39–65.

Daston, L. (2019), The coup d'oeil: On a mode of understanding, *Critical Inquiry*, 45(2): 307–331.

Davies, W. and McGoey, L. (2012), Rationalities of ignorance: On financial crisis and the ambivalence of neo-liberal epistemology, *Economy and Society*, 41(1): 64–83.

Davis, Gerald F. (2010), After the ownership society: Another world is possible, *Research in the Sociology of Organizations*, 30B: 331–356.

Davis, Gerald F. (2016), What might replace the modern corporation? Uberization and the web page enterprise, *Seattle University Law Review*, 39: 501–515.

Davis, Gerald F. and Kim, Suntae (2015), Financialization of the economy, *Annual Review of Sociology*, 41: 203–221.

Deaton, Angus (2013), *The great escape: Health, wealth and the origins of inequality*, Princeton: Princeton University Press.

De Goede, M. (2005), *Virtue, fortune, and faith: A genealogy of finance*, Minneapolis and London: Minnesota University Press.

Degenshein, A. (2017), Strategies of valuation: Repertoires of worth at the financial margins, *Theory & Society*, 46: 387–409.

Dequech, David (2017), Some institutions (social norms and conventions) of contemporary mainstream economics, macroeconomics and financial economics, *Cambridge Journal of Economics*, 41(6): 1627–1652.

Desmond, Matthew and Bell, Monica (2015), Housing, poverty, and the law, *Annual Review of Law and Social Science*, 11:15–35.

Desmond, M. and Wilmers, N. (2019), Do the poor pay more for housing? Exploitation, profit, and risk in rental markets, *American Journal of Sociology*, 124(4): 1090–1124.

Devers, Cynthia E., Dewett, Todd, Mishina, Yuri, and Belsito, Carrie A. (2009), A general theory of organizational stigma, *Organization Science*, 20(1): 154–171.

Dewey, John ([1939] 1991), *The theory of valuation*, in *John Dewey: The later works, 1925–1953, Vol. 13: 1938–1939*, ed. by J.A. Boydston, Carbondale and Edwardsville: Southern Illinois University Press.

Diamond, Douglas W. and Dybvig, Philip H. (1983), Bank runs, deposit insurance, and liquidity, *Journal of Political Economy*, 91: 401–419.

Diamond, Rebecca (2016), The determinants and welfare implications of US workers' diverging location Choices by skill: 1980–2000, *American Economic Review*, 106(3): 479–524.

Diamond, Rebecca and McQuade, Tim (2019), Who wants affordable housing in their backyard? An equilibrium analysis of low-income property development, *Journal of Political Economy*, 127(3): 1063–1117.

Dickerson, A. Mechele (2009), The myth of home ownership and why home ownership is not always a good thing, *Indiana Law Journal*, 84: 189–237.

Dore, Ronald (2008), Financialization of the global economy, *Industrial and Corporate Change*, 17(6): 1097–1112.

Dworkin, Ronald (1981), What is equality? Part 1: Equality of welfare, *Philosophy and Public Affairs*, 10(3): 185–246.

Dubois, A. and Gadde, L.-E. (2002), The construction industry as a loosely coupled system: Implications for productivity and innovation, *Construction Management and Economics*, 20: 621–631.

Edelman, Benjamin G. and Geradin, Damien (2016), Efficiencies and regulatory shortcuts: How should we regulate companies like Airbnb and Uber, *Stanford Techology Law Review*, 19: 293–328.

Edelman, L. (1992), Legal ambiguity and symbolic structures: Organizational meditation of civil rights law, *American Journal of Sociology*, 97(6): 1531–1576.

Edelman, L.B., Fuller, S.R., and Mara-Drita, I. (2001), Diversity rhetoric and the managerialization of law, *American Journal of Sociology*, 106(6): 1589–1641.

Eggertsson, Gauti B., Mehrotra, Neil R., and Robbins, Jacob A. (2019), A model of secular stagnation: Theory and quantitative evaluation, *American Economic Journal: Macroeconomics*, 11(1): 1–48.

Eisenhardt, K.M., Graebner, M.E., and Sonenshein, S. (2016), Grand challenges and inductive methods: Rigor without rigor mortis, *Academy of Management Journal*, 59(4): 1113–1123.

Englund, Peter (1999), The Swedish banking crisis: Roots and consequences, *Oxford Review of Economic Policy*, 15(3): 80–97.

Erixon, Lennart (2007), The Swedish third way: An assessment of the performance and validity of the Rehn–Meidner model, *Cambridge Journal of Economics*, 32(3): 367–393.

Faber, J.W. (2020), We built this: Consequences of New Deal era intervention in America's racial geography, *American Sociological Review*, 85(5): 739–775.

Favara, G. and Imbs, J. (2015), Credit supply and the price of housing, *American Economic Review*, 105(3): 958–992.

Favilukis, Jack, Ludvigson, Sydney C., and Van Nieuwerburgh, Stijn (2017), The macroeconomic effects of housing wealth, housing finance, and limited risk sharing in general equilibrium, *Journal of Political Economy*, 125(1): 140–223.

Fennell, L.A. (2017), Searching for fair housing, *Boston University Law Review*, 97: 349–424.

Ferguson, Frances (2019), Bitcoin: A reader's guide (the beauty of the very idea), *Critical Inquiry*, 46(1): 140–166.

Fernandez, R. and Aalbers, M.B. (2016), Financialization and housing: Between globalization and varieties of capitalism, *Competition & Change*, 20(2): 71–88.

Fernandez, Rodrigo, Hofman, Annelore, and Aalbers, Manuel (2016), London and New York as a safe deposit box for the transnational wealth elite, *Environment and Planning A: Economy and Space*, 48(12): 2443–2461.

Fernández-Albertos, José (2015), The politics of central bank independence, *Annual Review of Political Science*, 18: 217–237.

Fields, Desiree (2017), Urban struggles with financialization, *Geography Compass*, 11: 1–13.

Fields, D. and Uffer, S. (2016), The financialisation of rental housing: A comparative analysis of New York City and Berlin, *Urban Studies*, 53(7): 1486–1502.

Fine, Gary Alan (1996), *Kitchens: The culture of restaurant work*, Berkeley, Los Angeles and London: University of California Press.

Fingleton, B., Fuerst, F., and Szumilo, N.N. (2019), Housing affordability: Is new local supply the key? *Environment and Planning A: Economy and Space*, 51(1): 25–50.

Fisher, Lynn M., Pollakowski, Henry O., and Zabel, Jeffrey (2009), Amenity-based housing affordability indexes, *Real Estate Economics*, 37(4): 705–746.

Fligstein, N. (2005), The end of (shareholder value) ideology, *Political Power and Social Theory*, 17: 223–228.

Fligstein, Neil, Brundage, Jonah Stuart, and Schultz, Michael (2017), Seeing like the Fed: Culture, cognition, and framing in the failure to anticipate the financial crisis of 2008, *American Sociological Review*, 82(5): 879–909.

Fligstein, Neil and Roehrkasse, Alexander F. (2016), The causes of fraud in the financial crisis of 2007 to 2009: Evidence from the mortgage-backed securities industry, *American Sociological Review*, 81(4): 617–643.

Floetotto, Max, Kirker, Michael, and Stroebel, J. (2016), Government intervention in the housing market: Who wins, who loses? *Journal of Monetary Economics*, 80: 106–123.

Florida, Richard L. (2017), *The new urban crisis: How our cities are increasing inequality, deepening segregation, and failing the middle class—and what we can do about it*, New York: Basic Books.

Forrest, R. and Hirayama, Y. (2018), Late home ownership and social restratification, *Economy and Society*, 47(2): 257–279.

Fotaki, M. (2010), Why do public policies fail so often? Exploring health policy-making as an imaginary and symbolic construction, *Organization*, 17(6): 703–720.

Fourcade, M. (2011), Cents and sensibility: Economic valuation and the nature of "nature", *American Journal of Sociology*, 116(6): 1721–1777.

Fourcade, M. and Healy, K. (2013), Classification situations: Life-chances in the neoliberal era, *Accounting, Organizations and Society*, 38(8): 559–572.

Frame, W. Scott, Fuster, Andreas, Tracy, Joseph, and Vickery, James (2015), The rescue of Fannie Mae and Freddie Mac, *Journal of Economic Perspectives*, 29(2): 25–52.

Freidson, Eliot (2001), *Professionalism: The third logic*, Chicago: The University of Chicago Press.

Friedman, Rachel and Rosen, Gillad (2020), The face of affordable housing in a neoliberal paradigm, *Urban Studies*, 57(5): 959–975.

Fuller, Gregory W. (2015), Who's borrowing? Credit encouragement vs. credit mitigation in national financial systems, *Politics & Society*, 43(2): 241–268.

Funk, Russell J. and Hirschman, Daniel (2014), Derivatives and deregulation: Financial innovation and the demise of Glass–Steagall, *Administrative Science Quarterly*, 59(4): 669–704.

Furman, Jason (2019), Should policymakers care whether inequality is helpful or harmful in growth? In Blanchard, Olivier J. and Summers, Lawrence H., *Evolution or revolution: Rethinking macroeconomics after the Great Recession*, Cambridge: MIT Press, pp. 229–252.

Fuster, Andreas, Plosser, Matthew, Schnabl, Philipp, and Vickery, James (2019), The role of technology in mortgage lending, *The Review of Financial Studies*, 32(5): 1854–1899.

Gabor, Daniela (2016), The (impossible) repo trinity: The political economy of repo markets, *Review of International Political Economy*, 23(6): 967–1000.

Gabor, Daniela, and Ban, Cornel (2016), Banking on bonds: The new links between states and markets, *JCMS: Journal of Common Market Studies*, 54(3), 617–635.

Garud, Raghu, Schildt, Henri A. and Lant, Theresa K. (2014), Entrepreneurial storytelling, future expectations, and the paradox of legitimacy, *Organization Science*, 25(5): 1479–1492.

Gelpern, Anna and Gerding, Erik F. (2016), Inside safe assets. *Yale Journal on Regulation*, 33: 363–421.

Gelpern, Anna and Levitin, Adam J. (2009), Rewriting Frankenstein contracts: The workout prohibition in residential mortgage-backed securities, *Southern California Law Review*, 82: 1077–1152.

Gerring, J. (2004), What is a case study and what is it good for? *American Political Science Review*, 98(2): 241–354.

Gerrity, M.S., Earp, J.A.L., DeVellis, R.F. and Light, D.W. (1992), Uncertainty and professional work: Perceptions of physicians in clinical practice, *American Journal of Sociology*, 97(4): 1022–1051.

Ghent, A.C., Torous, W.N., and Valkanov, R.I. (2019), Commercial real estate as an asset class, *Annual Review of Financial Economics*, 11: 153–171.

Gibson, Christina B. and Birkinshaw, Julian (2004), The antecedents, consequences, and mediating role of ambidexterity, *Academy of Management Journal*, 47(2): 209–226.

Gillham, B. (2000), *Case Study Methods*, London and New York: Continuum.

Gilson, Ronald J. and Milhaupt, Curtis J. (2008). Sovereign wealth funds and corporate governance: a minimalist response to the new mercantilism, *Stanford Law Review*, 60(5): 1345–1370.

Gioia, D.A., Corley, K.G., and Hamilton, A.L. (2013), Seeking qualitative rigor in inductive research: Notes on the Gioia methodology, *Organizational Research Methods*, 16(1): 15–31.

Glaeser, E. and Gyourko, J. (2018), The economic implications of housing supply, *Journal of Economic Perspectives*, 32(1): 3–30.

Glazer, Kodyl (2019), Fair housing act at 50: Challenging the disparate impact of predictive analytics, *Florida State University Law Review*, 46(2): 457–484.

Goda, Thomas, Stewart, Chris and García, Alejandro Torres (2020), Absolute income inequality and rising house prices, *Socio-Economic Review*, 18(4): 941–976.

Goffman, E. (1983), The interaction order: American Sociological Association, 1982 Presidential Address, *American Sociological Review*, 48(1): 1–17.

Goldstein, Adam (2018), The social ecology of speculation: Community organization and nonoccupancy investment in the US housing bubble, *American Sociological Review*, 83(6): 1108–1143.

Golub, Stephen, Kaya, Ayse, and Reay, Michael (2015), What were they thinking? The Federal Reserve in the run-up to the 2008 financial crisis, *Review of International Political Economy*, 22(4), 657–692.

Gonalons-Pons, Pilar and Gangl, Markus (2021), Marriage and masculinity: Male-breadwinner culture, unemployment, and separation risk in 29 countries, *American Sociological Review*, 86(3): 465–502.

Gond, Jean-Pascal, Cabantous, Laure, Harding, Nancy, and Learmonth, Mark (2016), What do we mean by performativity in organizational and management theory? The uses and abuses of performativity, *International Journal of Management Reviews*, 18: 440–463.

Goodman, Laurie S. and Mayer, Christopher (2018), Homeownership and the American Dream, *Journal of Economic Perspectives*, 32(1): 31–58.

Goodrick, Elizabeth and Reay, Trish (2010), Florence Nightingale endures: Legitimizing a new professional role identity, *Journal of Management Studies*, 47(1): 55–84.

Gordon, Gwendolyn and Zaring, David (2017), Ethical bankers, *Journal of Corporation Law*, 42: 559–596.

Gordon, Robert J. (2015), *The rise and fall of American growth: The US standard of living since the Civil War*, Princeton: Princeton University Press.

Gorton, Gary (2017), The history and economics of safe assets, *Annual Review of Economics*, 9: 547–586.

Gorton, Gary, Lewellen, Stefan, and Metrick, Andrew (2012), The safe-asset share, *American Economic Review*, 102(3): 101–106.

Gorton, Gary and Metrick, Andrew (2012), Securitized banking and the run on repo, *Journal of Financial Economics*, 104: 425–451.

Gourevitch, P. (2011), The value of ethics: Monitoring normative complicance in ethical consumption marklets, In: Beckert, J. and Aspers, P. eds., *The worth of goods: Valuation and pricing in the economy*, Princeton: Princeton University Press, pp. 86–105.

Grewal, David Singh (2014), The laws of capitalism, *Harvard Law Review*, 128(2): 626–668.

Griffin, John M. and Maturana, Gonzalo (2016), Who facilitated misreporting in securitized loans? *Review of Financial Studies*, 29(2): 384–419.

Gubler, Zachary J. (2014), Regulating in the shadows: Systemic moral hazard and the problem of the twenty-first century bank run, *Alabama Law Review*, 63: 221–273.

Guironnet, A., Attuyer, K., and Halbert, L. (2016), Building cities on financial assets: The financialisation of property markets and its implications for city governments in the Paris city-region, *Urban Studies*, 53(7): 1442–1464.

Gurran, Nicole and Phibbs, Peter (2017), When tourists move in: How should urban planners respond to Airbnb?, *Journal of the American Planning Association*, 83(1): 80–92.

Hacker, Jacob S., Rehm, Philipp, and Schlesinger, Mark (2013), The insecure American: Economic experiences, financial worries, and policy attitudes, *Perspectives on Politics*, 11(1): 23–49.

Hall, Peter A. and Thelen, Kathleen (2009), Institutional change in varieties of capitalism, *Socio-Economic Review*, 7: 7–34.

Hansson, Anna Granath (2017), Promoting planning for housing development: What can Sweden learn from Germany?, *Land Use Policy*, 64: 470–478.

Harding, David J. (2009), Violence, older peers, and the socialization of adolescent boys in disadvantaged neighborhoods, *American Sociological Review*, 74(3): 445–464.

Harty, C. (2008), Implementing innovation in construction: Contexts, relative boundedness and actor-network theory, *Construction Management and Economics*, 26: 1029–1041.

Hayward, M.L.A. and Boeker, W. (1998), Power and conflict of interest in professional firms: Evidence from investment banking, *Administrative Science Quarterly*, 43: 1–22.

Harvey, David (2005), Neo-liberalism as creative destruction, *Geografiska Annaler. Series B, Human Geography*, 88(2): 145–158.

Hedin, Karin, Clark, Eric, Lundholm, Emma, and Malmberg, Gunnar (2012), Neoliberalization of housing in Sweden: Gentrification, filtering and social polarization, *Annals of the Association of American Geographer*, 102(2): 1–21.

Henrekson, M. and Rosenberg, N. (2001), Designing efficient institutions for science-based entrepreneurship: Lessons from the US and Sweden, *Journal of Technology Transfer*, 26: 207–231.

Himick, Darlene (2016), Actuarialism as biopolitical and disciplinary technique, *Accounting, Organizations and Society*, 54: 22–44.

Hockett, Robert (2015), The macroprudential turn: From institutional 'safety and soundness' to systematic 'financial stability' in financial supervision, *Virginia Law & Business Review*, 9(2): 201–256.

Hockett, Robert C. and Omarova, Saule T. (2016), "Special," vestigal, or visionary: What bank regulation tell us about the corporation—and vice versa, *Seattle University Law Review*, 39(2): 453–500.

Hodgson, D.E. (2004), Project work: The legacy of bureaucratic control in the post-bureaucratic organization, *Organization*, 11(1): 81–100.

Hood, K. (2017), The science of value: Economic expertise and the valuation of human life in US federal regulatory agencies, *Social Studies of Science*, 47(4), 441–465.

Hsu, J.W., Matsa, D.A., and Melzer, B.T. (2018), Unemployment insurance as a housing market stabilizer, *American Economic Review*, 108(1): 49–81.

Huber, E., Huo, J., and Stephens, J.D. (2019), Power, policy, and top income shares, *Socio-Economic Review*, 17(2): 231–253.

Hui, E.C.-M., Ng, I., and Lau, O.M.-F. (2011), Speculative bubbles in mass and luxury properties: An investigation of the Hong Kong residential market, *Construction Management and Economics*, 29(8): 781–793.

Hurley, Mikella, and Adebayo, Julius (2016), Credit scoring in the era of big data, *Yale Journal of Law & Technology*, 18: 148–216.

Hwang, Jackelyn and Ding, Lei (2020), Unequal displacement: Gentrification, racial stratification, and residential destinations in Philadelphia, *American Journal of Sociology*, 126(2): 354–406.

Ivanova, Maria N. (2019), Inequality, financialization, and the US current account deficit, *Industrial and Corporate Change*, 28(4): 707–724.

Jacobides, Michael G. (2005), Industry change through vertical disintegration: How and why markets emerged in mortgage banking, *Academy of Management Journal*, 48(3): 465–498.

Jakobsen, Katerine, Jakobsen, Kristian, Kleven, Henrik, and Zucman, Gabriel (2020), Wealth taxation and wealth accumulation: Theory and evidence from Denmark, *Quarterly Journal of Economics*, 135(1): 329–388.

Jeon, J. (2020), Invisibilizing politics: Accepting and legitimating ignorance in environmental sciences, *Social Studies of Science*, 49(6): 839–862.

Johnston, A. and Kurzer, P. (2020), Bricks in the wall: The politics of housing in Europe, *West European Politics*, 43: 275–296.

Jones Paul R. (2006), The sociology of architecture and the politics of building: The discursive construction of ground zero, *Sociology*, 40: 549–565.

Jordà, Ò., Schularick, M., and Taylor, A.M. (2016), The great mortgaging: Housing finance, crises and business cycles, *Economic Policy*, 31(85): 107–152.

Jordà, O., Knoll, K., Kuvshinov, D., Schularick, M. and Taylor, A.M. (2019), The rate of return on everything, 1870–2015, *Quarterly Journal of Economics*, 134(3): 1225–1298.

Judge, Kathryn (2018), Investor-driven financial innovation, *Harvard Business Law Review*, 8(2): 291–348.

Judge, Kathryn (2020), The new mechanisms of market inefficiency, *Journal of Corporation Law*, 45(4): 915–930.

Justiniano, Alejandro, Primiceri, Giorgio E., and Tambalotti, Andrea (2019), Credit supply and the housing boom, *Journal of Political Economy*, 127(3): 1317–1350.

Kaplan, Greg, Mitman, Kurt, and Violante, Giovanni L. (2020), The housing boom and bust: Model meets evidence, *Journal of Political Economy*, 128(9): 3285–3345.

Kaplan, Roberta A. and Nadler, Michael L. (2017), Airbnb: A case study in occupancy regulation and taxation, *University of Chicago Law Review Dialogue*, 82: 103–115.

Karger, H. (2005), *Shortchanged: Life and debt in the fringe economy*, Oakland: Berrett-Koehler Publishers.

Karpik, L. (2010), *Valuing the unique: The economics of singularities*, Princeton: Princeton University Press.

Kear, M. (2017), Playing the credit score game: Algorithms, "positive" data and the personification of financial objects, *Economy and Society*, 46(3–4): 346–368,

Keys, B.J., Mukherjee, T, Seru A., and Vig, V. (2009), Did securitization lead to lax screening? Evidence from subprime loans, *Quarterly Journal of Economics*, 125: 307–362.

Kellogg, K.C. (2014), Brokerage professions and implementing reform in an age of experts, *American Sociological Review*, 79(5): 912–941.

Kerstenetzky, Celia Lessa and Guedes, Graciele Pereira (2021), Great Recession, great regression? The welfare state in the twenty-first century, *Cambridge Journal of Economics*, 45(1): 151–194.

Khatri, N. and Ng, H.A. (2000), The role of intuition in strategic decision making, *Human Relations*, 53(1): 57–86.

Kinderman, Daniel (2017), Challenging varieties of capitalism's account of business interests: Neoliberal think-tanks, discourse as a power resource and employers' quest for liberalization in Germany and Sweden, *Socio-Economic Review*, 15(3): 587–613.
King, Desmond and Le Galès, Patrick (2017), The three constituencies of the state: Why the state has lost unifying energy, *British Journal of Sociology*, 68 (S1): S11–S33.
Kingsley, Patrick (2021), After years of quiet, Israeli-Palestinian conflict exploded. Why now? *New York Times*, May 15, 2021, www.nytimes.com/2021/05/15/world/middleeast/israel-palestinian-gaza-war.html (Accessed June 14, 2021).
Kiviat, Barbara (2019), The moral limits of predictive practices: The case of credit-based insurance scores, *American Sociological Review*, 84(6): 1134–1158.
Knoll, K., Schularick, M., and Steger, T. (2017), No price like home: Global house prices, 1870–2012, *American Economic Review*, 107(2): 331–353.
Kohl, Sebastian (2019), The political economy of homeownership: A comparative analysis of homeownership ideology through party manifestos, *Socio-Economic Review*, 18(4): 913–940.
Kohl, Sebastian (2021), Too much mortgage debt? The effect of housing financialization on housing supply and residential capital formation, *Socio-Economic Review*, 9(2): 413–444.
Kornberger, M. (2017), The values of strategy: Valuation practices, rivalry and strategic agency, *Organization Studies*, 38(12), 1753–1773.
Korpi, Walter and Palme, Joakim (2003), New politics and class politics in the context of austerity and globalization: Welfare state regress in 18 Countries, 1975–95, *American Political Science Review*, 97(3): 425–446.
Korver-Glenn, Elizabeth (2018), Compounding inequalities: How racial stereotypes and discrimination accumulate across the stages of housing exchange, *American Sociological Review*, 83(4): 627–656.
Kosack, S. and Fung, A. (2014), Does transparency improve governance? *Annual Review of Political Science*, 17: 65–87.
Krippner, G.R. (2017), Democracy of credit: Ownership and the politics of credit access in late twentieth-century America, *American Journal of Sociology*, 123(1): 1–47.
Kroll, J.A., Huey, J., Barocas, S., Felten, E.W., Reidenberg, J.R., Robinson, D.G., and Yu, H. (2017), Accountable algorithms, *University of Pennsylvania Law Review*, 165(3): 633–705.
Kumhof, Michael, Rancière, Romain, and Winant, Pablo (2015), Inequality, leverage, and crises, *American Economic Review*, 105(3): 1217–1245.
Lakoff, Andrew (2006), *Pharmaceutical reason: Knowledge and value in global psychiatry*, Cambridge: Cambridge University Press.
Lamont, Michele (1987), How to become a dominant French philosopher: The case of Jacques Derrida, *American Journal of Sociology*, 584–622.
Lamont, Michèle and Molnár, Virág (2002), The study of boundaries in social sciences, *Annual Review of Sociology*, 28: 167–195.
Larson, Magali Sarafatti (1977), *The rise of professionalism: A sociological analysis*, Berkeley, Los Angeles, and London: University of California Press.
Lasswell, Harold ([1936] 1958), *Politics: Who gets what, when, how*, New York: Whittlesey House.
Lauer, J. (2017), *Creditworthy: A history of consumer surveillance and financial identity in America*, New York: Columbia University Press.
Lavinas, Lena (2018), The collateralization of social policy under financialized capitalism, *Development and Change*, 49(2): 502–517.
Lee, D. (2016), How Airbnb short-term rentals exacerbate Los Angeles's affordable housing crisis: Analysis and policy recommendations, *Harvard Law & Policy Review*, 10: 229–253.

Lefebvre, Henri (1991), *The production of space*, Oxford: Blackwell.

Lenfle, S. and Söderlund, J. (2019), Large-scale innovative projects as temporary trading zones: Toward an interlanguage theory, *Organization Studies*, 40(11): 1713–1739.

Levitin, Adam J. (2011), In defense of bailouts, *Georgetown University Law Review*, 99: 435–514.

Levitin, Adam J. (2014), The politics of financial regulation and the regulation of finacial politics: A review essay, *Harvard Law Review*, 127(7): 1991–2068.

Levitin, Adam and Wachter, Susan M. (2020), *The great American housing bubble: What went wrong and how we can protect ourselves in the future*, Cambridge: Harvard University Press.

Lifshitz-Assaf, H. (2018), Dismantling knowledge boundaries at NASA: The critical role of professional identity in open innovation, *Administrative Science Quarterly*, 63(4): 746–782.

Lindblom, C.E. (1959), The science of muddling through, *Public Administration Review*, 19(2): 79–88.

Linos, Katerina (2021), Organizational rights in times of crisis, *University of Chicago Law Review*, 88(3), 729–756.

Liscow, Zachary (2014), Reducing inequality on the cheap: When legal rule design should incorporate equity as well as efficiency, *Yale Law Journal*, 123: 2478–2511.

Livne, Roi (2015), Economies of dying: The moralization of economic scarcity in US hospice care, *American Sociological Review*, 79(5): 888–911.

Lupo-Pasini, Federico (2017), *The logic of financial nationalism: The challenges of cooperation and the role of international law*, New York: Oxford University Press.

Luther, Jeffrey (2020), Twenty-first century financial regulation: P2P lending, fintech, and the argument for a special purpose fintech charter approach, *University of Pennsylvania Law Review*, 168(4): 1013–1059.

Lysandrou, Photis and Stassinopoulos, Yorgos (2020) Resisting the gravitational pull of the dollar: The economic rationale behind a large Eurozone, *Economy and Society*, 49(3): 382–405.

Mackie, John L. (1978), Can there be a right-based moral theory? *Midwest Studies in Philosophy*, 3(1): 350–359.

Manzo, L.K.C., Druta, O., and Ronald, R. (2019), Supported home ownership and adult independence in Milan: The gilded cage of family housing gifts and transfers, *Sociology*, 53(3): 519–537.

Markides, Costas (2007), In search of ambidextrous professors, *Academy of Management Journal*, 50(4): 762–768.

Marshall, Wesley C. and Concha, Elizabeth (2012), Fannie Mae and Freddie Mac: A bailout for the people? *Journal of Economic Issues*, 46 (2): 557–564.

Marti, Emilio and Gond, Jean-Pascal (2018), When do theories become self-fulfilling? Exploring the boundary conditions of performativity, *Academy of Management Review*, 43(3): 487–508.

Marti, Emilio and Scherer, Andreas George (2015), Financial regulation and social welfare: The critical contribution of management theory. *Academy of Management Review*, 41(2): 298–323.

McConnell, Patrick (2013), Systemic operational risk: The LIBOR manipulation scandal, *The Journal of Operational Risk*, 8(3): 59.

McCoy, Patricia A., Pavlov, Andrey D., and Wachter, Susan M. (2009), Systemic risk through securitization: The result of deregulation and regulatory failure. *Connecticut Law Review*, 41(4): 1327–1375.

McGarvey, Darren (2017), *Poverty safari: Understanding the anger of Britain's underclass*, London: Picador.

McGoey, L. (2012), Strategic unknowns: Towards a sociology of ignorance, *Economy & Society*, 41: 1–16.

Mehrpouya, A. and Salles-Djelic, M.-L. (2019), Seeing like the market: Exploring the mutual rise of transparency and accounting in transnational economic and market governance, *Accounting, Organizations, and Society*, 76: 12–31.

Metcalf, G. (2018), Sand castles before the tide? Affordable housing in expensive cities, *Journal of Economic Perspectives*, 32(1): 59–80.

Mian, A. and Sufi, A. (2014), House of debt, Chicago and London: The University of Chicago Press.

Mian, A. and Sufi, A. (2018), Finance and business cycles: The credit-driven household demand channel, *Journal of Economic Perspectives*, 32(3): 31–58.

Mian, A., Sufi, A., and Trebbi, F. (2010), The political economy of the US mortgage default crisis, *The American Economic Review*, 100(5): 1967–1998.

Mian, Atif, Sufi, Amir, and Verner, Emil (2017), Household debt and business cycles worldwide, *The Quarterly Journal of Economics*, 132(4): 1755–1817.

Mijs, Jonathan (2019), The paradox of inequality: Income inequality and belief in meritocracy go hand in hand, *Socio-Economic Review*, 19(1): 7–35.

Miller, Geoffrey P. and Rosenfeld, Gerald G. (2010), Intellectual hazard: How conceptual biases in complex organizations contributed to the crisis of 2008, *Harvard Journal Law & Public Policy*, 33: 807–838.

Miller, P. (2001), Governing by numbers: Why calculative practices matter, *Social Research*, 68(2): 379–395.

Miltko, Caelin Moriarity (2020), "What shall I give my children?": Installment land contracts, homeownership, and the unexamined costs of the American dream, *University of Chicago Law Review*, 87: 2273–2319.

Min, David (2018), Housing finance reform and the shadow money supply, *Journal of Corporation Law*, 43(4): 899–937.

Moor, Liz and Friedman, Sam (2021), Justifying inherited wealth: Between "the bank of mum and dad" and the meritocratic ideal, *Economy and Society*, 50(4): 618–642.

North, Douglass C. (1991), Institutions, *Journal of Economic Perspectives*, 5(1): 97–112.

Oliver, Amalya L. and Montgomery, Kathleen (2000), Creating a hybrid organizational form from parental blueprints: The emergence and evolution of knowledge firms, *Human Relations*, 53(1): 33–56.

Olson, Mancur (1965), *The logic of collective action*, Cambridge: Harvard University Press.

Omri, Marian (2013), Are cryptocurrencies super tax havens? *Michigan Law Review First Impressions*, 112: 38–48.

Parkin, Jack (2019), The senatorial governance of Bitcoin: Making (de)centralized money, *Economy and Society*, 48(4): 463–487.

Paruchuri, Srikanth and Misangyi, Vilmos F. (2015), Investor perceptions of financial misconduct: The heterogeneous contamination of bystander firms, *Academy of Management Journal*, 58: 169–194.

Pasquale, Frank (2015), *The black box society: The secret algorithms that control money and information*. Cambridge: Harvard University Press.

Pattillo, Mary (2013), Housing: Commodity versus right, *Annual Review of Sociology*, 39: 509–531.

Peck, Jamie and Whiteside, Heather (2016), Financializing Detroit, *Economic Geography*, 92(3): 235–268.

Perry, Alexander R. (2020), The Federal Reserve's questionable legal basis for foreign bank liquidity swaps, *Columbia Law Review*, 120(3): 729–767.

Peterson, Eric David (2019), The urban development corporation's 'imaginative use of credit': Creating capital for affordable housing development, *Journal of Urban History*, 45(6): 1174–1192.

Pfeffer, Fabian T. and Waitkus, Nora (2021), The wealth inequality of nations, *American Sociological Review*, 86(4): 567–602.

Philips-Fein, Kim (2011), Conservatism: A state of the field, *Journal of American History*, 98(3): 723–743.

Pierce, Justin R. and Schott, Peter K. (2016), The surprisingly swift decline of US manufacturing employment, *American Economic Review*, 106(7): 1632–1662.

Pierson, Paul (1996), The new politics of the welfare state, *World Politics*, 48(02), 143–179.

Piskorski, Tomasz, Seru, Amit, and Vig, Vikrant (2010), Securitization and distressed loan renegotiation: Evidence from the subprime mortgage crisis. *Journal of Financial Economics*, 97(3): 369–397.

Pistor, Katharina (2009), Sovereign wealth funds, banks and governments in the global crisis: Towards a new governance of global finance? *European Business Organization Law Review*, 10(3): 333–352.

Pistor, Katharina (2019), The code of capital. How the law creates wealth and inequality, Princeton: Princeton University Press.

Pistor, Katharina (2020), The value of law, Theory and Society, 49(1): 165–186.

Polillo, S. (2011), Money, moral authority, and the politics of creditworthiness, *American Sociological Review*, 76(3): 437–464.

Poon, M. (2007), Scorecards as devices for consumer credit: The case of Fair, Isaac & Company Incorporated, *The Sociological Review*, 55(2): 284–306.

Power, Michael (1997), *The audit society: Rituals of verification*, Oxford and New York: Oxford University Press.

Power, Michael K. (2003), Auditing and the production of legitimacy, *Accounting, Organization and Society*, 28: 379–394.

Power, M. (2010), Fair value accounting, financial economics and the transformation of reliability, *Accounting and Business Research*, 40(3): 197–210.

Power, M. (2021), Modelling the micro-foundations of the audit society: Organizations and the logic of the audit trail, *Academy of Management Review*, 46(1): 6–32.

Pozen, D.E. (2018), Transparency's ideological drift, *Yale Law Journal*, 126(1): 100–165.

Prasad, M. (2012), *The land of too much: American abundance and the paradox of poverty*, Cambridge and London: Harvard University Press.

Pressman, Steven (2007), The decline of the middle class: An international perspective, *Journal of Economic Issues*, 41 (1): 181–200.

Punwani, A. (1997), A study of the growth-investment-financing nexus of the major UK construction groups, *Construction Management & Economics*, 15(4): 349–361.

Putnam, Hilary (2002), *The collapse of the fact/value dichotomy and other essays*, Cambridge: Harvard University Press.

Quine, Willard Van Orman ([1966] 1976), *The ways of paradox and other essays*, 2nd. ed. Cambridge: Harvard University Press.

Quinn, Sarah (2017), "The miracles of bookkeeping": How budget politics link fiscal policies and financial markets, *American Journal of Sociology*, 123(1): 48–85.

Rappaport, J. (2008), Consumption amenities and city population density, *Regional Science and Urban Economics*, 38(6): 533–552.

Richardson, Matthew P., Van Nieuwerburgh, Stijn, and White, Lawrence J. (2017), What to do about the GSEs? *Annual Review of Financial Economics*, 9: 21–41.

Ricks, Morgan (2018), Money as infrastructure, *Columbia Business Law*, 3: 757–851.

Riles, A. (2010), Collateral expertise, *Current Anthropology*, 51(6): 795–818.

Riles, A. (2011), *Collateral knowledge: Legal reasoning in the global financial markets*, Chicago: The University of Chicago Press.

Rivera, Lauren A. and Tilcsik, András (2019), Scaling down inequality: Rating scales, gender bias, and the architecture of evaluation, *American Sociological Review*, 84(2): 248–274.

Romano, R. (2005), The Sarbanes-Oxley act and the making of quack corporate governance, *Yale Law Journal*, 114: 1521–1611.

Rona-Tas, Akos and Hiss, Stefanie (2010), The role of ratings in the subprime mortgage crisis: The art of corporate and the science of consumer credit rating is, *Research in the Sociology of Organizations*, 30A: 115–155.

Rodriguez, Lorena (2020), All data is not credit data: Closing the gap between the fair housing act and algorithmic decisionmaking in the lending industry, *Columbia Law Review*, 120(7): 1843–1884.

Roe, Mark J. (2018), Stock market's short-termism's impact, *University of Pennsylvania Law Review*, 167(1): 71–121.

Rogoff, Kenneth (2017), Dealing with monetary paralysis at the zero bound, *Journal of Economic Perspectives*, 31(3): 47–66.

Rolnik, Raquel (2019), *Urban warfare: Housing under the empire of finance*, Trans. by Felipe Hirschhorn, London: Verso.

Rona-Tas, A. (2017), The off-label use of consumer credit ratings. *Historical Social Research*, 42(1): 52–76.

Rona-Tas, Akos and Guseva, Alya (2018), Consumer credit in comparative perspective, *Annual Review of Sociology*, 44: 55–75.

Rueda, David and Pontusson, Jonas (2000), Wage inequality and varieties of capitalism, *World Politics*, 52(3): 350–383.

Ruef, M. (2012), Constructing labor markets: The valuation of black labor in the US south, 1831 to 1967, *American Sociological Review*, 77(6): 970–998.

Santos, F. and Eisenhardt, K.M. (2005), Organization boundaries and theories of organizations, *Organization Science*, 16: 491–508.

SCB (2021), Hushåll i Sverige, www.scb.se/hitta-statistik/sverige-i-siffror/manniskorna-i-sverige/hushall-i-sverige/ (Accessed June 8, 2021).

Schaefer, S.M. (2019), Willful managerial ignorance, symbolic work and decoupling: A socio-phenomenological study of 'managing creativity', *Organization Studies*, 40(9): 1387–1407.

Schleicher, David (2017), Stuck!: The law and economics of residential stagnation, *Yale Law Journal*, 127(1): 78–155.

Schragger, Richard C. (2010), Rethinking the theory and practice of local economic development, *University of Chicago Law Review*, 77: 311–339.

Schwartz, Herman (2012), Housing, the welfare state, and the global financial crisis: What is the connection? *Politics & Society*, 40(1): 35–58.

Schwartz, Herman M. and Seabrooke, Leonard (2008), Varieties of residential capitalism in the international political economy: Old welfare states and the new politics of housing, *Comparative European Politics*, 6: 237–261.

Schwarzkopf, S. (2020), Sacred excess: Organizational ignorance in an age of toxic data, *Organization Studies*, 41(2): 197–217.

Schwert, Michael (2017), Municipal bond liquidity and default risk. *Journal of Finance*, 72(4): 1683–1722.

Searle, J.R. (1995), *The construction of social reality*, London: Penguin.

Setterfield, Mark and Kim, Yun K. (2020), Varieties of capitalism, increasing income inequality and the sustainability of long-run growth, *Cambridge Journal of Economics*, 44(3): 559–582.

Shamir, Ronen (2008), The age of responsibilization: On market embedded morality, *Economy and Society*, 37: 1–19.

Shapiro, S.P. (2005), Agency theory, *Annual Review of Sociology*, 31: 263–284.

Simon, H.A. (1987), Making management decisions: The role of intuition and emotion, *Academy of Management Executive*, 1(1): 57–64.

Simon, Jonathan (1988), The ideological effects of actuarial practices. *Law and Society Review*, 22: 771–800.

Simon, William E. (1978), *A time for truth*, New York: Reader's Digest Press.

Simsek, Alp (2021), The macroeconomics of financial speculation, *Annual Review of Economics*, 13: 335–369.

Skeel, David A. (2001), Shaming in corporate law, *University of Pennsylvania Law Review*, 149(6): 1811–1868.

Soener, Matthew and Nau, Michael (2019), Citadels of privilege: The rise of LLCs, LPs and the perpetuation of elite power in America, *Economy and Society*, 48(3): 399–425.

Soo, Cindy K. (2018), Quantifying sentiment with news media across local housing markets, *The Review of Financial Studies*, 31(10): 3689–3719.

Souleles, D. (2019), The distribution of ignorance on financial markets, *Economy and Society*, 48(4): 510–531.

Spears, Taylor (2019), Discounting collateral: Quants, derivatives and the reconstruction of the 'risk-free rate' after the financial crisis, *Economy and Society*, 48(3): 342–370.

Stake, R.E. (1996), *The art of case study research*, Thousand Oaks, London, and New Delhi: Sage.

Stein, Jeremy C. (2012), Monetary policy as financial stability regulation, *Quarterly Journal of Economics*, 127(1): 57–95.

Stein, Judith (2011a), Pivotal decade: How the United States *traded factories for finance in the seventies*, New Haven: Yale University Press.

Stein, Judith (2011b), *Pivotal decade: How the United States traded factories for finance in the seventies*, New Haven: Yale University Press.

Stein, S. (2019), *Capital city: Gentrification and the real estate state*, London: Verso.

Stets, Jan E. and Carter, Michael J. (2012), A theory of the self for the sociology of morality, *American Sociological Review*, 77(1): 120–140.

Strauss, A.L. and Corbin, J. (1998), *Basics of qualitative research*, 2nd ed., London, Thousand Oaks, and New Delhi: Sage.

Styhre, Alexander and Bergström, Ola (2019), The benefit of market-based governance devices: Reflections on the issue of growing economic inequality as a corporate concern, *European Management Journal*, 37: 413–420.

Suchman, Mark (1995), Managing legitimacy: Strategic and institutional approaches, *Academy of Management Review*, 20(3): 571–610.

Sullivan, Teresa A., Warren, Elizabeth, and Westbrook, Jay Lawrence (2006), Less stigma and more financial distress: An empirical analysis of the extraordinary increase in bankruptcy filings, *Stanford Law Review*, 59(1): 213–256.

Summers, Nicole (2020), The limits of good law: A study of outcomes in housing court, *The University of Chicago Law Review*, 87: 145–221.

Taylor, Keeanga-Yamahtta (2018), How real estate segregated America, *Dissent*, 65(4): 23–32.

Taylor, Keeanga-Yamahtta (2019), *Race for profit: How banks and the real estate industry undermined black homeownership*, Chapel Hill: University of North Carolina Press.

Terner Center for Housing Innovation (2017), *Housing in Sweden: An overview*, Berkeley: University of California Berkeley. [URL: http://ternercenter.berkeley.edu/uploads/Swedish_Housing_System_Memo.pdf. (Accessed March 6, 2020) Swedish_Housing_System_Memo

The Economist (2016), The problem with profits, *The Economist*, March 26, 2020, https://perma.cc/5JGR-HKVC (Accessed November 26, 2020).

The Economist (2020), The horrible housing blunder: Home ownership is the West's biggest economic-policy mistake, *The Economist*, Jan 16, 2020, www.economist.com/leaders/2020/01/16/home-ownership-is-the-wests-biggest-economic-policy-mistake (Accessed November 20, 2020).

Thörn, Catharina and Thörn, Håkan (2017), Swedish cities now belong to the most segregated in Europe, *Sociologisk Forskning*, 54(4): 293–296.

Törnqvist, Maria (2019), Living alone together: Individualized collectivism in Swedish communal housing, *Sociology*, 53(5): 900–915.

Travis, A. (2019), The organization of neglect: Limited liability companies and housing disinvestment, *American Sociological Review*, 84(1): 142–170.

Tsui, A.S., Enderle, G., and Jiang, K. (2018), Income inequality in the United States: Reflections on the role of corporations, *Academy of Management Review*, 43(1): 156–168.

Tushman, Michael L. and O'Reilly, Charles A. III. (1996), The ambidextrous organization: Managing evolutionary and revolutionary change, *California Management Review*, 38(4): 8–30.

Tyrväinen, L and Miettinen, A. (2000), Property prices and urban forest amenities, *Journal of Environmental Economics and Management*, 39(2): 205–223.

Van Bortel, G., Gruis, V., Nieuwenhuijzen, J., and Pluijmers, B., eds. (2019), *Affordable housing governance and finance: Innovations, partnerships and comparative perspectives*, Abingdon and New York: Routledge.

Van Staveren, Irene (2020), The misdirection of bankers' moral compass in the organizational field of banking, *Cambridge Journal of Economics*, 44(3): 507–526.

Van der Zwan, Natascha (2014), Making sense of financialization, *Socio-Economic Review*, 12(1): 99–129.

Vaughan, Liam and Finch, Gary (2017), Libor scandal: The bankers who fixed the world's most important number, *The Guardian*, January 18, 2017, www.theguardian.com/business/2017/jan/18/libor-scandal-the-bankers-who-fixed-the-worlds-most-important-number (Accessed January 25, 2017).

Voegtlin, Christian, Moritz Patzer, and Andreas Georg Scherer (2012), Responsible leadership in global business: A new approach to leadership and its multi-level outcomes, *Journal of Business Ethics*, 105(1): 1–16.

Wallace, Terry (1999), 'It's a man's world!': Restructuring gender imbalance in the Volvo Truck Company, *Gender, Work and Organization*, 6(1): 20–31.

Walter, Timo and Wansleben, Leon (2020), How central bankers learned to love financialization: The Fed, the bank, and the enlisting of unfettered markets in the conduct of monetary policy, *Socio-Economic Review*, 18(3): 625–653.

Wansleben, Leon (2020), Formal institution building in financialized capitalism: The case of repo markets, *Theory and Society*, 49(1): 187–213.

Weick, K.E. (1995), *Sensemaking in organizations*, Sage: London.

Westphal, J.D. and Bednar, M.K. (2005), Pluralistic ignorance in corporate boards and firms' strategic persistence in response to low firm performance, *Administrative Science Quarterly*, 50(2): 262–298.

Westphal, J. and Zajac, E. (2001), Decoupling policy from practice: The case of stock repurchase programs, *Administrative Science Quarterly*, 46(2): 202–228.

White Lawrence J. (2013), Credit rating agencies: An overview, *Annual Review in Financial Economics*, 5: 93–122.

Whyte, W.F. ([1943] 1993), *Street corner society*, 4th ed. Chicago: Chicago University Press.

Wiener, Anna (2020), *Uncanny valley: A memoir*, London: The 4th Estate.

Wijburg, G. and Aalbers, M. (2017), The alternative financialization of the German housing market, *Housing Studies*, 32(7): 301–320.

Wijburg, Gertjan, Aalbers, Manuel B. and Heeg, Susanne (2018), The financialisation of rental housing 2.0: Releasing housing into the privatised mainstream of capital accumulation. *Antipode*, 50(4): 1098–1119.

Wilmarth, Arthur E. (2013), Turning a blind eye: Why Washington keeps giving in to Wall Street, *University of Cincinnati Law Review*, 81(4): 1283–1445.

Wilmers, N. (2018), Wage stagnation and buyer power: How buyer-supplier relations affect US workers' wages, 1978 to 2014, *American Sociological Review*, 83(2): 213–242.

Wisman, Jon D. (2013), Wage stagnation, rising inequality and the financial crisis of 2008, *Cambridge Journal of Economics*, 37(4): 921–945.

Wirth, Louis (1938), Urbanism as a way of life, *American Journal of Sociology*, 44(1): 1–24.

Yakura, E.K. (2002), Charting time: Timelines as temporal boundary objects, *Academy of Management Journal*, 45(5): 956–970.

Zelizer, Viviana (1985), *Pricing the priceless child: The changing social value of children*, New York: Basic Books.

Zinman, Jonathan (2015), Household debt: Facts, puzzles, theories, and policies, *Annual Review of Economics*, 7: 251–276.

Zuckerman, E.W. (2012), Construction, concentration, and (dis)continuities in social valuations, *Annual Review of Sociology*, 38: 223–245.

Zukin, S. (2010), *Naked city: The death and life of authentic urban places*, New York: Oxford University Press.

Index